Visual Studio 2019 Tricks and Techniques

A developer's guide to writing better code and maximizing productivity

Paul Schroeder

Aaron Cure

BIRMINGHAM—MUMBAI

Visual Studio 2019 Tricks and Techniques

Group Product Manager: Aaron Lazar

Publishing Product Manager: Richa Tripathi

Senior Editor: Nitee Shetty

Content Development Editor: Ruvika Rao

Technical Editor: Gaurav Gala

Copy Editor: Safis Editing

Project Coordinator: Francy Puthiry

Proofreader: Safis Editing

Indexer: Manju Arasan

Production Designer: Vijay Kamble

First published: January 2021

Production reference: 1150121

Published by Packt Publishing Ltd.

Livery Place

35 Livery Street

Birmingham

B3 2PB, UK.

ISBN 978-1-80020-352-5

www.packt.com

To my mother, Karen, and to the memory of my father, Robert, for creating the company that set our family on this path decades ago. To the memory of my brother, Michael, whose son, Robert, now connects a third generation of Schroeders to that very company.

– Paul Schroeder

To my loving family, Sherry, Katy, Kenzie, and Tee, for all their support and patience in all the craziness that is our life. Also, to my parents, Charles and Karen, who raised us to believe that through hard work and dedication, anything is possible, and for moving us out of a place that thought that computers were "a passing fad."

– Aaron Cure

`Packt.com`

Subscribe to our online digital library for full access to over 7,000 books and videos, as well as industry leading tools to help you plan your personal development and advance your career. For more information, please visit our website.

Why subscribe?

- Spend less time learning and more time coding with practical eBooks and Videos from over 4,000 industry professionals

- Improve your learning with Skill Plans built especially for you

- Get a free eBook or video every month

- Fully searchable for easy access to vital information

- Copy and paste, print, and bookmark content

Did you know that Packt offers eBook versions of every book published, with PDF and ePub files available? You can upgrade to the eBook version at `packt.com` and as a print book customer, you are entitled to a discount on the eBook copy. Get in touch with us at `customercare@packtpub.com` for more details.

At `www.packt.com`, you can also read a collection of free technical articles, sign up for a range of free newsletters, and receive exclusive discounts and offers on Packt books and eBooks.

Foreword

By combining Visual Studio Code and **Visual Studio (VS)**, the brand is over two times more commonly used by developers than any other environment (Stack Overflow, 2019). What that means is that this topic is vital for 80% of all developers.

It also means that with this book, Paul Schroeder and Aaron Cure had the opportunity to provide something incredibly valuable and essential for developers, a vital reference for the global developer community.

I personally think there are two ways to learn in life: you can learn from your own failures and mistakes, or you can learn from someone else's failures and mistakes. I'll pick the second option, every time.

With this book, Paul and Aaron have cracked the code. Everything in here is a lesson learned. It's like you're getting all the advice that was learned from the mistakes and failures of thousands of developers... including (1) the developers who Paul and Aaron learned from (via books, articles, and advice), (2) the developers at Microsoft, who got feedback from customers and built the great features you'll find in VS (not to mention the customers who struggled and needed those features), (3) the developers in the community who helped create some of the amazing extensions covered in this book, and (4) the personal insights discovered directly by Paul and Aaron, through their combined experience of 40+ years in software development!

You now have a book (in your hands or on a screen) that not only teaches beginners how to use VS but is also useful for intermediate developers pursuing knowledge to become more effective. Simply put, this could very well be one of the greatest investments you make for your career. Even if you are a very experienced developer, you'll still gain a lot from this book... you'll learn a few new techniques and, more importantly, you'll have a cheat sheet to look back on as a reference.

New developers will rapidly learn about the different types of VS, the shortcuts, how to use the interface, how to use a repo, exploring data, and compiling/debugging. Meanwhile, experienced developers will pick up a few new tricks in those topics, and they will also learn (and have as a reference to come back to) how to better leverage code snippets, how to become a legend with templates, and how to take full advantage of extensions.

If you apply the snippets, templates, and extension practices found in this book, not only will you become a drastically more efficient and effective coder, but you'll also become your team's hero and thought leader!

What does all this mean? It means that if you're a developer, you owe it to yourself to learn from as many failures as you can. This book is born out of the mistakes and failures of thousands of developers who came before you. You would be wise to read it now and revisit it each year. If you do that, you'll get faster and better, every time.

Ed Price
Senior Program Manager (of Architectural Publishing)
Microsoft | Azure Architecture Center (http://aka.ms/Architecture)
Co-author of four books, including Hands-On Microservices with C# 8 *and* .NET Core 3 *(from Packt)*

Contributors

About the authors

Paul Schroeder is a versatile application developer, speaker, author, and managing director at MSC Technology Consulting (MSCTek.com). Along with a multi-decade professional IT career, Paul has a bachelor's degree in computer science and an MBA, and has earned an MCSD certification for web development.

Whether coding or not, Paul enjoys spending time with his marvelous and talented wife, Robin, herself a Xamarin developer/speaker who creates Bluetooth mesh mobile applications.

Drawn to code generation, Paul is the inspiration behind CodeGenHero™, an innovative Visual Studio extension, covered in *Chapter 14, Be Your Team's Hero with CodeGenHero*. You are encouraged to register for a free trial at CodeGenHero.com so that you, too, can save oodles of time on software projects. Follow Paul at @PaulBSchroeder.

Firstly, thank you to our technical reviewers, Robin Schroeder and Eric Mead, whose feedback and testing was invaluable. Likewise, to the whole team at Packt whose patience and persistence made this book possible.

Shoutout to James Wall, an MSC employee whose determined effort helped bring the concept of CodeGenHero™ to life. Likewise, thanks to Patrick Goode, an employee who brought fresh ideas to support the completion of that journey.

I'd like to express gratitude to Microsoft, for creating the tooling and products that empower me to help numerous organizations and make an excellent living.

Finally, thanks COVID-19, for making this such an awful year that I finally made time to write a book – good riddance, 2020!

Aaron Cure is a principal security consultant for Cypress Data Defense specializing in penetration testing, secure SDLC, static code review, and secure architectures. His certifications include CISSP, GPEN, GMOB, GWAPT, and GSSP-NET. As a global speaker and instructor, Aaron is passionate about helping developers understand and write safe and secure code.

Aaron transitioned to programming after a decade as a Russian linguist and a satellite repair technician in the Army. He was an early adopter of technologies such as Mono and NHibernate for cross-platform development. Besides .NET, he has programmed in PHP, Python, Perl, TCL/TK, and Java.

Currently, Aaron programs almost entirely in VS Code and .NET Core with projects transitioning to .NET 5.

I'd like to thank our reviewers, Robin Schroeder and Eric Mead, for reviewing all of our words and code and providing invaluable feedback.

I'd also like to thank my co-author, Paul Schroeder, for beginning this adventure with me, and like our last hike together, dragging me to the finish line.

About the reviewers

Robin Schroeder has been writing code professionally for over two decades. She is currently a cross-platform mobile Xamarin developer, software consultant, girls, coding club volunteer, and public speaker. She finds herself bouncing between all flavors of Visual Studio on a regular basis.

> *To my brilliant husband, Paul, who has loved elegant code generation since before we fell in love 18 years ago. I am so thankful to be able to rely on your support to reach my career goals, so humbled to see what a great father you are to our kiddos, and so proud to have been able to support this amazing project and your vision of CodeGenHero.*

Eric Mead has more than 15 years of experience in software development, primarily in the financial and agriculture industries. His primary focus is .NET Framework; however, he also has a considerable amount of experience in frontend frameworks such as Angular and React. As a co-founder of Puma Security, he is a software architect who writes static source code analysis rules and contributes to the open source version. Eric has held positions as a software consultant, business intelligence developer, and senior software developer. Eric holds a bachelor of science degree in computer engineering from Iowa State University, with an emphasis on software engineering and information security.

Packt is searching for authors like you

If you're interested in becoming an author for Packt, please visit authors. packtpub.com and apply today. We have worked with thousands of developers and tech professionals, just like you, to help them share their insight with the global tech community. You can make a general application, apply for a specific hot topic that we are recruiting an author for, or submit your own idea.

Table of Contents

3
IDE Tips and Tricks

4
Working with a Repository

5
Working with Snippets

6
Database Explorers

7
Compiling, Debugging, and Versioning

Section 2: Customizing Project Templates and Beyond

8
Introduction to Project and Item Templates

9
Creating Your Own Templates

10
Deploying Custom Templates

Section 3:
Leveraging Extensions for the Win

11
Overviewing Visual Studio 2019 Extensions

12
Overviewing VS Code Extensions

13
CodeMaid is Your Friend

14
™

Be Your Team's Hero with CodeGenHero

15

Secure Code with Puma Scan

Appendix
Other Popular Productivity Extensions

Other Books You May Enjoy

Index

Preface

Visual Studio 2019 for Windows, Visual Studio Code, and Visual Studio 2019 for Mac are full-featured **integrated development environments (IDEs)** for building and debugging modern web, mobile, desktop, and cloud applications. They can be used to write applications that target .NET 5.0 or .NET Core for Linux, macOS, and Windows. Likewise, they support containerized development with Docker, mobile apps with Xamarin, desktop using WPF or Windows Forms, and game development with Unity.

In this book, we cover numerous productivity tips, shortcuts, and snippets that you need to make the most of your coding time. For newer developers, the book includes content to help determine the right flavor of Visual Studio for your needs. Also, instructions on how to work with Git source control, databases, and debugging are included. For more advanced professionals, lesser-known capabilities such as how to create and deploy your own custom project and item templates are explained in detail. Everyone can appreciate the considerable coverage of extensions that extend and enhance the features and functionality available out of the box with Visual Studio.

Using several hands-on exercises, we go beyond the basics of working with Visual Studio 2019. Through these exercises and extensions, you will see how to clean code, how to generate code, and also how to secure code. The examples used in this book are simple and easy to understand. There are numerous images and clear step-by-step directions for guidance. Throughout this book, you will travel down a path that both enhances existing skills and helps you master a few new ones. By the end, you will have a deeper knowledge of the Visual Studio IDE and, hopefully, be ready to put these techniques into practice.

Who this book is for

This book is for any C# and .NET developer who wants to increase their productivity and write code fast by fully utilizing the power of the Visual Studio IDE. It helps take your understanding of Visual Studio 2019 to the next level. Those who want to delve deeper and peek under the hood to learn what Visual Studio does behind the scenes will be satisfied. Application architects will learn techniques that improve standardization across multiple projects and reduce ramp-up time. Additionally, coders who want to see how the development process can be reimagined using code generation and secure code scanning technology will be impressed.

Users of any IDE flavor will benefit from this book, including Visual Studio 2019 for Windows, Visual Studio Code, and Visual Studio 2019 for Mac. Several chapters include specific content for each version. A few chapters contain hands-on exercises that target only Visual Studio 2019 for Windows.

The material in the first and third sections of this book is appropriate for developers of any skill level (*Visual Studio IDE Productivity Essentials* and *Leveraging Extensions for the Win*). Those newer to developing with Visual Studio may find the content in the third section of the book interesting but a bit abstract (*Customizing Project Templates and Beyond*).

What this book covers

Chapter 1, Flavors of Visual Studio, is primarily for those new to programming or .NET development. This chapter describes the key factors to consider when deciding which version of Visual Studio is right for you.

Chapter 2, Keyboard Shortcuts, shows how most tasks can be performed directly from the keyboard, without a mouse. It pulls back the curtain on the magic of keyboard shortcuts in Visual Studio 2019 for Windows and teaches you how to customize the tool.

Chapter 3, IDE Tips and Tricks, demonstrates ways to organize code files and quickly navigate in the IDE/solution files. How to access preview features and use Live Sharing is covered, as well as tips for faster code insertion and editing.

Chapter 4, Working with a Repository, provides all the basic knowledge you need to know to work with Git source control via Visual Studio. It covers how to create/clone a repo as well as how to add files, get updates, and commit code. Branching, merging, and pull requests are also topics.

Chapter 5, Working with Snippets, explains how to use snippets that come pre-installed with Visual Studio, how to manage them with the Code Snippets Manager dialog, and even how to make and import your own custom creations.

Chapter 6, Database Explorers, teaches you how to manage databases in Visual Studio 2019 for Windows as well as Visual Studio Code, and how to create a database, table, and data rows. Then, you'll see how to select and export that data.

Chapter 7, Compiling, Debugging, and Version Control, explores conditional compilation symbols, breakpoints, and immediate and watch windows. How to install Docker is covered before remote debugging is performed in a hands-on exercise using a Docker container. An automated approach to versioning assemblies wraps up this chapter.

Chapter 8, Introduction to Project and Item Templates, is a primer for the chapters that follow. It includes information on when to use templates and how template tags work. The sample project that is used in subsequent chapters is introduced here.

Chapter 9, Creating Your Own Templates, demonstrates how to export and import custom project templates to/from Visual Studio. You will create a new project using a custom template, provided in the download accompanying this book, identify and fix issues with it, and then learn how to make your own project item template.

Chapter 10, Deploying Custom Templates, contains more advanced content leveraging knowledge gained in the two prior chapters. You are guided step by step through an exercise that examines VSIX deployment package creation for a sample client-server solution. By the end, a multi-project template, complete with an IWizard UI implementation, is ready to go. Simply add a new project, enter a database connection string, and out pops a working Web API server sending data down to a WPF client. Information on how to distribute your custom templates to the marketplace rounds out this chapter.

Chapter 11, Overviewing Visual Studio 2019 Extensions, eases in with an introduction to extensions and searching for them in Visual Studio Marketplace. Learn how to manage them and how to create them in both Windows and Mac. Finish with a tour of Roslyn analyzers and create one that analyzes code related to the extension created in the prior exercise.

Chapter 12, Overviewing VS Code Extensions, is dedicated to extensions in Visual Studio Code. How to create extensions is covered through a step-by-step exercise that is designed to put a licensing header at the top of code files. The chapter ends with how to create a VSIX installer file to share the extension or deploy it to the marketplace.

Chapter 13, CodeMaid Is Your Friend, extolls the benefits of organized code, along with a brief history of this popular extension, CodeMaid. Cleanup actions and features such as CodeMaid Spade are explored along with the many configurable options available.

Chapter 14, Be Your Team's Hero with CodeGenHero™, studies a unique perspective on code generation. You are guided through an example project where many classes are auto-generated, including the web API and client-side data access components. Key topics such as how to configure a metadata source, blueprints, choosing templates, configuring parameters, and merging output results are covered. Changing the database schema and regenerating the source code adds a finishing touch.

Chapter 15, Secure Code with Puma Scan, helps you understand common application security vulnerabilities such as SQLi, XSS, and security misconfiguration. It talks about how to find vulnerabilities for fun and profit before automating vulnerability detection using the Puma Scan extension. How to extend Puma Scan with custom sinks is discussed as well as how to incorporate it into a DevSecOps pipeline.

Chapter 16, Other Popular Productivity Extensions, is a great, light way to close out this book. This chapter provides an overview of great extensions for Visual Studio, favorite extensions for Visual Studio Code, and some useful extensions for Visual Studio for Mac. Whereas prior chapters on extensions went deep with exercises, this one goes wide. Information is provided on 15 different extensions that can improve your developer experience.

To get the most out of this book

You will need Microsoft Visual Studio 2019 or Visual Studio Code installed on your system. Choosing the right version of Visual Studio 2019 is covered in the first chapter. Some of the chapters cover all three major flavors of Visual Studio. A few chapters are more partial to Visual Studio for Windows and some exercises contain sample code that uses the full .NET Framework v4.7.2.

Software/Hardware covered in the book	OS Requirements
Visual Studio	Windows, Mac OS X, and Linux (any)
Docker	
CodeMaid, CodeGenHero™, Puma Scan	

Although not strictly required, installing the following workloads with Visual Studio for Windows will allow you to walk through all examples:

- ASP.NET and web development
- .NET desktop development
- .NET Core cross-platform development
- Visual Studio extension development

In chapters that require special setup or attention, specific instructions are provided at the outset. For example, the chapters on CodeGenHero™ and Puma Scan contain plenty of screenshots to communicate the material, but registration for free trial versions is necessary to walk through the step-by-step exercises.

If you are using the digital version of this book, we advise you to type the code yourself or access the code via the GitHub repository (link available in the next section). Doing so will help you avoid any potential errors related to the copying and pasting of code.

Download the example code files

You can download the example code files for this book from your account at www.packt.com. If you purchased this book elsewhere, you can visit www.packtpub.com/support and register to have the files emailed directly to you.

You can download the code files by following these steps:

1. Log in or register at www.packt.com.
2. Select the **Support** tab.
3. Click on **Code Downloads**.
4. Enter the name of the book in the **Search** box and follow the onscreen instructions.

Once the file is downloaded, please make sure that you unzip or extract the folder using the latest version of:

*   WinRAR/7-Zip for Windows
*   Zipeg/iZip/UnRarX for Mac
*   7-Zip/PeaZip for Linux

The code bundle for the book is also hosted on GitHub at https://github.com/PacktPublishing/Visual-Studio-2019-Tricks-and-Techniques. In case there's an update to the code, it will be updated on the existing GitHub repository.

We also have other code bundles from our rich catalog of books and videos available at https://github.com/PacktPublishing/. Check them out!

Code in Action

Please visit the following link to check the CiA videos: https://bit.ly/3oxE5QM.

Download the color images

We also provide a PDF file that has color images of the screenshots/diagrams used in this book. You can download it here: https://static.packt-cdn.com/downloads/9781800203525_ColorImages.pdf.

Conventions used

There are a number of text conventions used throughout this book.

`Code in text`: Indicates code words in text, database table names, folder names, filenames, file extensions, pathnames, dummy URLs, user input, and Twitter handles. Here is an example: "Mount the downloaded `WebStorm-10*.dmg` disk image file as another disk in your system."

A block of code is set as follows:

```
<Header>
    <Title>API Method Timer</Title>
    <Shortcut>apitimer</Shortcut>
    <Description>Leverages System.Diagnostics.Stopwatch to log
how long it took to execute a method.</Description>
</Header>
```

When we wish to draw your attention to a particular part of a code block, the relevant lines or items are set in bold:

```
<LanguageTag>C#</LanguageTag>
<PlatformTag>windows</PlatformTag>
<ProjectTypeTag>console</ProjectTypeTag>
<ProjectTypeTag>desktop</ProjectTypeTag>
<ProjectTypeTag>TipTrick</ProjectTypeTag>
```

Any command-line input or output is written as follows:

```
$ git config --global init.defaultBranch main
```

Bold: Indicates a new term, an important word, or words that you see onscreen. For example, words in menus or dialog boxes appear in the text like this. Here is an example: "To see the installed keyboard mapping schemes in Visual Studio 2019 for Windows, navigate to the **Tools Menu | Options | Environment | Keyboard** dialog."

> **Tips or important notes**
> Appear like this.

Get in touch

Feedback from our readers is always welcome.

General feedback: If you have questions about any aspect of this book, mention the book title in the subject of your message and email us at customercare@packtpub.com.

Errata: Although we have taken every care to ensure the accuracy of our content, mistakes do happen. If you have found a mistake in this book, we would be grateful if you would report this to us. Please visit www.packtpub.com/support/errata, selecting your book, clicking on the Errata Submission Form link, and entering the details.

Piracy: If you come across any illegal copies of our works in any form on the Internet, we would be grateful if you would provide us with the location address or website name. Please contact us at copyright@packt.com with a link to the material.

If you are interested in becoming an author: If there is a topic that you have expertise in and you are interested in either writing or contributing to a book, please visit authors.packtpub.com.

Reviews

Please leave a review. Once you have read and used this book, why not leave a review on the site that you purchased it from? Potential readers can then see and use your unbiased opinion to make purchase decisions, we at Packt can understand what you think about our products, and our authors can see your feedback on their book. Thank you!

For more information about Packt, please visit packt.com.

Section 1: Visual Studio IDE Productivity Essentials

This section provides the foundational knowledge all developers using Visual Studio should know in order to improve their productivity. Beyond the basics, some of the lesser-known features of the **integrated development environment (IDE)** are uncovered. Numerous hands-on exercises dive deep into how Visual Studio works behind the scenes.

This section has the following chapters:

- *Chapter 1, Flavors of Visual Studio*
- *Chapter 2, Keyboard Shortcuts*
- *Chapter 3, IDE Tips and Tricks*
- *Chapter 4, Working with a Repository*
- *Chapter 5, Working with Snippets*
- *Chapter 6, Database Explorers*
- *Chapter 7, Compiling, Debugging, and Version Control*

1
Flavors of Visual Studio

Microsoft Visual Studio is an **Integrated Development Environment** (IDE) from Microsoft. Over its more than twenty-year history, it has been used by developers to develop all kinds of computer programs, web applications, web APIs, and mobile apps. A 2019 survey by Stack Overflow found Visual Studio and its cousin, **Visual Studio Code (VS Code)**, to be two of the most popular development environments among all survey respondents (see `https://insights.stackoverflow.com/survey/2019`):

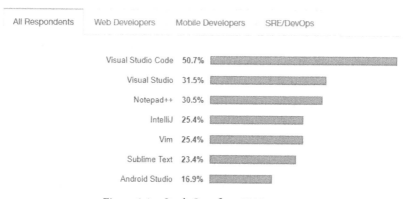

Figure 1.1 – Stack Overflow 2019 survey

> **Note on Stack Overflow 2020 survey results**
> Although Stack Overflow's 2020 survey results were available at the time of writing, they did not seem to include the same specific question on development environments.

Visual Studio provides robust coding and debugging capabilities as well as extensive integration for deployment and source control needs. You can use it to program anything from a desktop business application, to a web site, mobile application, or Unity game.

If you are new to programming or .NET development, it is important to understand that there are several options to consider before starting. This chapter's primary focus is to cover some key factors you should consider when deciding which product "flavor" of Visual Studio is right for you, including the following:

- Primary operating system (Windows, macOS, or Linux)
- Target framework (.NET full framework, .NET Core)
- Team size and budget
- Application type (Windows, web, mobile, server, or console)
- Cross-platform portability requirements
- Chosen programming language (such as C#, VB, Python, Ruby, or NodeJS)

The reason why we must examine the aforementioned points in detail is because Microsoft has combined what are actually multiple, separate, products under a single marketing umbrella. This can make choosing between these products confusing and so we will take a moment to clearly identify each version, differentiate their features, and provide some guidance on which version may be best for your purposes.

Technical requirements

The code for this book is available on GitHub at: https://github.com/PacktPublishing/Visual-Studio-2019-Tricks-and-Techniques/tree/main/.

Please check the following link for CiA videos: http://bit.ly/3oxE5QM.

Quick reference cheat sheet

With so many options, how does a developer know which version to use? The following is a list of simplified suggestions to help you choose a particular flavor:

- If you are using a PC and are brand new to software development, start with **VS 2019 Community**.

- If you are using a PC as an experienced developer, or have a well-funded company footing the bill, consider the **VS 2019 Professional** or **VS 2019 Enterprise** editions.

- If you're primarily a web developer planning to use NodeJS and TypeScript, try **VS Code**.

- If you're developing cross-platform iOS/Android mobile apps, consider using **VS for Mac**.

> **Have you already decided on which version to use?**
>
> If you have already figured out which version of Visual Studio is right for you, then feel free to skip this chapter's content. Alternatively, if you are an experienced developer, skim this material looking for new tidbits, such as GitHub Codespaces.

For those readers that need more information to decide, let's begin digging into the details of the most long-lived product flavor, Visual Studio for Windows.

Visual Studio 2019 (Windows)

Let's start with **Visual Studio 2019** (**VS 2019**), a Windows-based IDE (pronounced *AYE-dee-ee*). Some people will refer to this product as *the full version*. This version only runs on Windows (not cross-platform), but it does support both .NET "full framework" and .NET Core (cross-platform) project targets. Something all versions of Visual Studio do exceptionally well is work with diverse programming languages (including C, C++, Visual Basic. NET, C#, F#, JavaScript, TypeScript, Python, Ruby, and Node.js).

Different tiers of features are offered, depending on your needs and budget. Current versions of VS 2019 include a free **Community** edition as well as paid **Professional**, **Enterprise**, and **Test Professional** versions. The **Community** and **Professional** editions are nearly identical when it comes to operational features and, for most development tasks, *any* version of Visual Studio will work.

The Community version is depicted in the screenshot that follows and you will find virtually no difference between its appearance and that of the other versions:

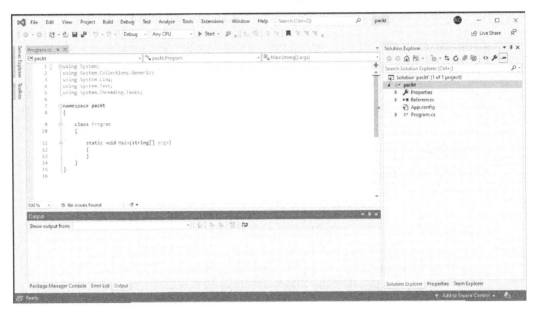

Figure 1.2 – VS 2019 Community – Windows

Even with multiple options, choosing a Visual Studio edition is much easier today than in the past. Previously, certain project types could only be loaded in one edition or another, and many add-ins would not run in certain editions. Complex licensing issues compounded these problems, making it more difficult to choose.

Today, even the free Community edition is a powerful environment with much to offer. Many of the popular features, such as peeking at definitions, multi-targeting of release targets, and refactoring are supported in all editions.

More succinctly, the major versions of VS 2019 are as follows:

- **Community** – Free for students, open source contributors, and individuals
- **Professional** – The best choice for small teams
- **Test Professional** – An option for dedicated **Quality Assurance (QA)** roles
- **Enterprise** – Offers extra features (mentioned later in this chapter) and works well for teams of any size

In the past, the **Community** version, originally labeled "Express," was a very limited version that allowed only basic application development but would not allow for particular target types (such as Visual Studio plugins), and would also not allow a number of plugins to run. While some of these limitations seemed minor, they were enough to create negative perceptions of the platform among some developers and sour development community sentiment on the **Community** version. In recent years, Microsoft has removed many of the original restrictions and enabled so much functionality in this version that the experience is now very similar to the **Professional** version.

Traditionally, the **Professional** version was the lowest tier version for "true" developers. Because of the limitations of other versions, this was the only way to do "actual" development. This version tier is (and always has been) a full-featured IDE with all the bells and whistles you would expect in a professional development tool.

A key difference is that **VS 2019 Community** is free, while the **Professional** version retails for about $1,199 for the first year's subscription and $799 annually for renewal thereafter. However, there are license restrictions that limit use of **Visual Studio Community** to teams of less than five developers. Also, it cannot be used by commercial organizations with over $1 million US dollars in annual revenue.

For those whose focus is purely QA, and not development, **Test Professional** is another option to consider. It provides an integrated testing toolset for QA teams, but does not include an IDE to build applications. Instead, this product flavor focuses on the creation and execution of tests and test suites. It also integrates nicely with **Visual Studio Team Foundation Server** (**VSTFS**) and **Azure DevOps** (**ADO**).

Finally, the **Enterprise** version of VS 2019 is available for organizations with more than 25 developers, or those seeking to take advantage of advanced features only available at this highest tier. This level includes advanced functionality such as memory profilers, Snapshot Debugger, Live Unit Testing, architectural layer diagrams, and architecture validation. An overview of some of these capabilities is provided next.

Features of VS 2019 Enterprise edition

The following provides a brief overview of a few features that are specific to the Enterprise version of VS 2019. These items may help you decide whether this is the right flavor of the IDE for your needs:

- **Performance profiling tools**: VS 2019 provides a dozen or more profiling tools that can help diagnose different kinds of performance issues. Common metrics you may want to analyze include CPU usage, memory usage, and database performance. Some of these tools require the Enterprise edition, and some do not. Use this link to investigate the specific tools that match your needs: `https://docs.microsoft.com/en-us/visualstudio/profiling/profiling-feature-tour?view=vs-2019`.

- **Live Unit Testing**: While you are coding, Live Unit Testing automatically runs unit tests in the background and shows your code coverage live in Visual Studio. It provides a line-by-line visual indicator of test coverage as well as the status of passing/failing tests. As you modify code, this feature dynamically executes tests and provides immediate notification when changes cause tests to fail.

- **Snapshot Debugger**: If you are using **Azure Application Insights**, the Snapshot Debugger can be used to capture the state of source code and variables from a live, running, application. This can be helpful for troubleshooting exceptions that occur in a production environment. If you do not have the Enterprise edition of Visual Studio, you can view debug snapshots in the online portal, but using the Enterprise edition provides a more robust debugging experience.

- **Live Dependency Validation**: Another feature, only available in the Enterprise edition, is Live Dependency Validation. This lets teams validate architectural dependencies to ensure that they respect defined architectural constraints. In complex multi-layer applications, this can help ensure code dependencies flow in the right direction, which is important for maintainability. This can be useful on project teams with junior developers who may not fully understand the design. Detailed coverage of the Live Dependency Validation feature is beyond the scope of this chapter, but this video link provides a basic overview: `https://channel9.msdn.com/Events/Visual-Studio/Visual-Studio-2017-Launch/T123`.

Visual Studio Installer

To use certain features, like Code Map and Live Dependency Validation components, you must run the **Visual Studio Installer**, select the **Individual components** tab, and scroll down to the **Code tools** section. From there, select the **Code Map** and **Live Dependency Validation** components, as shown in the following screenshot. When you are ready, click the **Modify** button:

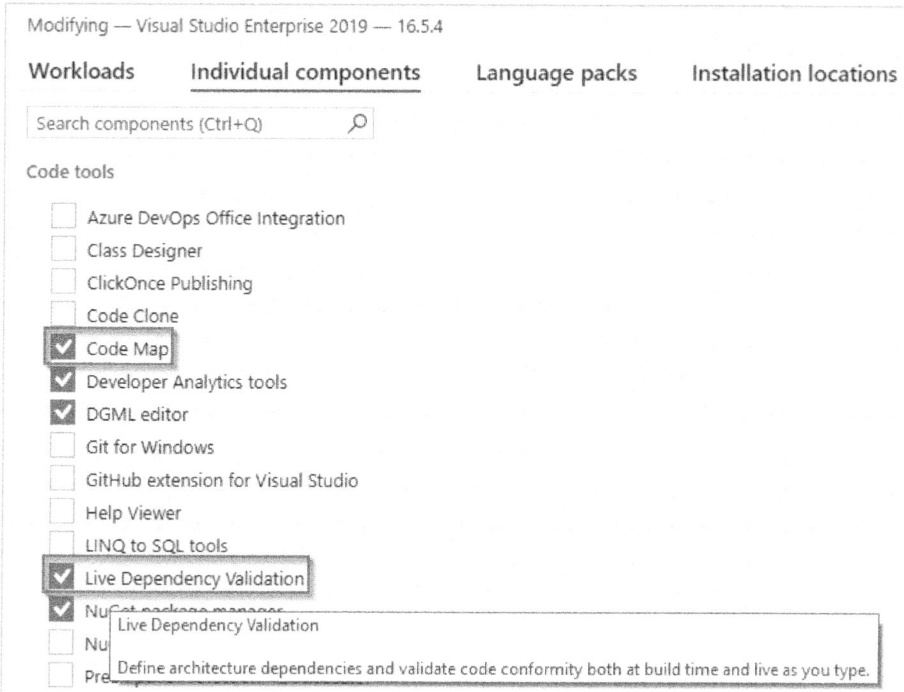

Modifying — Visual Studio Enterprise 2019 — 16.5.4

Workloads   Individual components   Language packs   Installation locations

Search components (Ctrl+Q)

Code tools

☐ Azure DevOps Office Integration
☐ Class Designer
☐ ClickOnce Publishing
☐ Code Clone
☑ Code Map
☑ Developer Analytics tools
☑ DGML editor
☐ Git for Windows
☐ GitHub extension for Visual Studio
☐ Help Viewer
☐ LINQ to SQL tools
☑ Live Dependency Validation
☑ Nu
☐ Nu
☐ Pre

Live Dependency Validation

Define architecture dependencies and validate code conformity both at build time and live as you type.

Figure 1.3 – Visual Studio Installer

> **Note**
> To be accurate, Visual Studio's Community and Professional editions do allow you to open diagrams that were generated using the Enterprise edition, albeit in read-only mode.

Despite their differences, from a functionality standpoint, the look and feel of all the editions are pretty much the same. Menus, tools, and functional controls are all implemented consistently, perform the same functions, and are mostly indistinguishable from one another.

Use the following link to review specific differences between versions: `https://visualstudio.microsoft.com/vs/compare/`.

In short, whichever version you choose, the experience should be nearly the same. For most development tasks, it makes no difference which version you are running: they all have the basic software development life cycle tools to create, debug, and run web, mobile, console, library, and just about any other project you can devise.

Visual Studio 2019 for Mac

If Windows isn't your primary operating system, Microsoft also offers **Visual Studio for Mac**, which unsurprisingly runs on Apple's macOS operating system. Historically, this product evolved from what was known as Xamarin Studio prior to Microsoft's acquisition of Xamarin in 2016.

Visual Studio 2019 for Mac supports development in C#, F#, Razor, HTML, CSS, JavaScript, TypeScript, XAML, and XML. It also supports ASP.NET Core and .NET Core development, Azure Functions, Azure Connected Services, and the ability to publish to Azure. Like its Windows parallel, the Mac version comes in **Community**, **Professional**, and **Enterprise** versions. It has support for using Docker containers, Unity game programming, and mobile app development using Xamarin and C#:

Figure 1.4 – Visual Studio 2019 – Mac

> **Note**
>
> One notable feature missing from VS 2019 for Mac, VS Code (discussed next), and .NET Core in general, is the ability to create cross-platform desktop applications (such as WPF, Windows Forms, and UWP). While there are several possible alternatives (Electron, Avalonia UI, Uno Platform, and so on), none truly stand out as a native interface like WPF on Windows with Visual Studio.

For convenience, the following figure shows a feature comparison between Visual Studio 2019 for Mac and VS 2019 (Windows). The few differences between these products lie in Mac's lack of support for some types of Windows desktop, Python, and Node.js development:

Supported Features	Visual Studio Community — Free download	Visual Studio Professional — Buy	Visual Studio Enterprise — Buy
Supported Usage Scenarios	●●●●	●●●●	●●●●
Individual Developers	●	●	●
Classroom Learning	●	●	●
Academic Research	●	●	●
Contributing to Open-Source Projects	●	●	●
Non-enterprise organizations ,1 for up to 5 users	●	●	●
Enterprise		●	●
Development Platform Support 2	●●●●	●●●●	●●●●
Integrated Development Environment	●●●●	●●●●	●●●●
Live Dependency Validation			●
Architectural Layer Diagrams			●
Architecture Validation			●
Code Clone			●
CodeLens	●	●	●
Peek Definition	●	●	●
Refactoring	●	●	●
One-Click Web Deployment	●	●	●
Model Resource Viewer	●	●	●
Visualize solutions with Dependency Graphs and Code Maps	●3	●3	●
Multi-Targeting	●	●	●
Advanced Debugging and Diagnostics	●●●●	●●●●	●●●●
IntelliTrace			●

Figure 1.5 – Visual Studio 2019 Comparison

Note

The full image is available in *Chapter 1, Flavors of Visual Studio* at `https://static.packt-cdn.com/downloads/9781800203525_ColorImages.pdf`

Alternatively, use this link to see a comparison between the two versions: `https://visualstudio.microsoft.com/vs/mac/#vs_mac_table`.

One of the most glaring shortcomings of Visual Studio for Mac is its lack of robust source control integration functionality. Developers often compensate for this using third-party tools such as Litracens, SourceTree, gmaster, and so on. That said, the Visual Studio for Mac experience improves with each release and includes more support for different application types. With the differences between the Mac and Windows versions shrinking, it is conceivable that within a few releases, the Mac and Windows experiences of Visual Studio will become nearly identical to VS Code.

Commonly referred to as **VS Code**, the **Visual Studio Code** product had humble beginnings as a text editor with support for optional plugins, similar to Atom or Sublime Text. Many developers consider it a lightweight tool specifically geared toward building and debugging modern web and cloud applications. However, it has grown into a full cross-platform (covering Linux, macOS, and Windows) editor that is free for both private and commercial use. It runs cross-platform, supports multiple programming languages, and has basic features such as syntax highlighting and code-completion aids (IntelliSense), as well as support for more advanced features such as debugging, refactoring, and code snippets, provided by plugins:

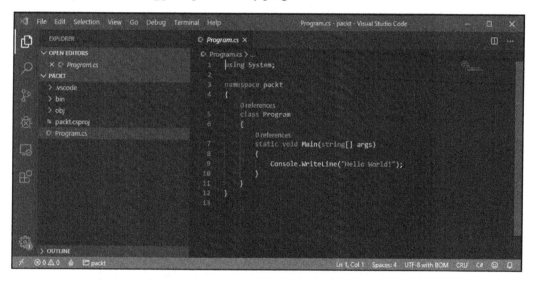

Figure 1.6 – VS Code – Windows

Both the popularity and the capabilities of VS Code have increased dramatically since Microsoft open-sourced this product back in late 2015. The integrated terminal is one thing many developers like about VS Code. This feature can be very convenient as you do not have to switch between applications to perform command-line tasks.

The ease of writing plug-ins, such as **OmniSharp** for debugging support, is credited with evolving this tool into (almost) a full-fledged IDE with support for many C# application types (including .NET Console, .NET Standard, and .NET MVC), as well as a number of other languages such as Java, Python, Ruby, and NodeJS. It supports common development operations including debugging, task running, and version control. It remains simplified to provide just what a developer needs for quick code-build-debug cycles.

The following screenshot depicts VS Code running on **Linux**, superimposed over a screenshot of VS Code running on **macOS**. Noteworthy is the striking similarity between the Windows, Mac, and Linux versions of VS Code. This makes for a consistent experience between platforms and makes shifting between them feel quite natural:

Figure 1.7 – VS Code on Mac (upper-left) and Linux (lower-right)

Microsoft has really made great strides to achieve a seamless experience here. The plugins are supported on each platform, the "look and feel" is seamless, and the capabilities are identical. With the cross-platform development and deployment features of .NET Core, and the IDE features and debugging of VS Code, many developers have made the switch to use this as their primary development environment. With the strength of the IDE, as well as the availability of strong plugins (see *Chapter 12, Overviewing VS Code Extensions*) the experience is pleasant, and the tool is very capable as a "daily driver."

Two is better than one

Lots of developers use *both* the full version of VS 2019 and install VS Code as well. The same code in most solutions can be opened and developed in either application. Some tasks, such as editing web files, may be done in VS Code, whereas the full version may be used for others, such as performing dependency validation.

Code examples in this book will alternate between the use of a "full version of VS 2019 and VS Code. The installation files for all versions described in this chapter can be downloaded from `https://visualstudio.microsoft.com/downloads/`.

GitHub Codespaces

A newcomer to the product flavors worth keeping an eye on is **GitHub Codespaces**, formerly called Visual Studio Codespaces, which provides cloudpowered development environments. In this case, an environment is considered the *backend compute* functions associated with software development, such as compiling and debugging. Working with this approach can be done using three possible clients: a browser-based editor, VS Code, or the Visual Studio IDE.

At the time of this writing, Codespaces is currently in beta and more information can be found at `https://code.visualstudio.com/docs/remote/codespaces`.

The bleeding edge

Like the public preview of GitHub Codespaces, VS 2019 and VS for Mac both have their own preview channels available. These allow developers to see and experiment with features that have not yet been released through the stable public channel. Similarly, VS Code has **Insider Edition**, a daily build that is essentially equivalent to the preview channels of the other flavors.

Summary

In this chapter, we overviewed the many flavors of Visual Studio that are available. We outlined the key differences between the various products Microsoft offers under the **Visual Studio** marketing umbrella to enable you to make an informed choice about which version will work best for you.

VS 2019 (Windows) is a very popular choice of IDE and has evolved considerably over its more than twenty-year existence. Simplified version differences and improved capabilities have made the **Community** version a usable tool for individuals and organizations that meet the licensing requirements. For those that don't, the **Professional** version is a relatively affordable version that is included in a number of **Microsoft Developer Network** (**MSDN**) subscriptions.

Visual Studio for Mac is a relatively new introduction but continues to improve with each release. The "look and feel" moves closer to the Windows version with each release, and the functionality continues to grow. For a full-featured IDE, it is becoming a very strong tool for non-Windows developers.

VS Code (Windows, Mac, and Linux versions) has grown into a very capable, useful IDE with support for multiple operating systems, multiple programming languages, and multiple workflows. From .NET to Python, NodeJS, Ruby, Java, and others, the support and strength of the plugins varies, but the core features of VS Code shine through and make the experience pleasant.

Regardless of your choice, operating system, or preferences, each tool comes with an excellent installation experience that makes it very easy for you to get up and running quickly. With Visual Studio now installed, you are ready to get started with keyboard shortcuts in the next chapter.

2
Keyboard Shortcuts

So much to code…so little time! reads the saying on one of my favorite programmer t-shirts. The focus of this chapter is how to save time and code more productively.

When developing, we form a mental construct of the program we are writing and break it down into components, APIs, methods, and logic/looping structures. Once we have imagined the next code bits, we need to transfer those thoughts into syntax on screen. The most common modalities for doing this are the keyboard and mouse. The assertion made in this chapter is that, for those of us with fewer than three hands, time is lost switching from keyboard to mouse and back again. Without getting into the details of scientific studies, our experience is that using keyboard shortcuts can save you boatloads of time. Now, I'm not sure how much time fits in a boat, but you get the point.

It is important to recognize that most tasks can be performed directly from the keyboard (without a mouse) in Visual Studio, **Visual Studio Code (VS Code)**, and Visual Studio for Mac. Whenever I present at a meeting or conference or do paired programming, I am often asked, "How did you do that?" The question is not directed at the code being written, but rather how I triggered a particular action so quickly. It is amusing to watch developers get sidetracked wanting to know a "trick" before they can re-focus on the presentation.

In this chapter, we are going to pull back the curtain on the magic of keyboard shortcuts in Visual Studio 2019 for Windows. We will also teach you how to customize the tool for your own personal preferences. What we will try to avoid is simply presenting page after page of keyboard shortcut lists for you to memorize in this book. There are plenty of online resources with these lists of key combinations to comb through at your leisure, if desired (see the *Further reading* section at the end of this chapter).

> **Shortcuts in Visual Studio for Mac**
>
> Visual Studio for Mac has very similar keyboard shortcuts to those presented in this chapter. However, on a Mac, the ⌘ key (the *Command* symbol) is used instead of *Ctrl*.
>
> For developers using a Mac with a PC keyboard, the Windows key equates to the Mac *Command* symbol by default. This can be very frustrating for developers who regularly switch between Mac and PC. Know that it can be customized in either environment to make one match the other.

This chapter will cover the following topics:

- Basic Windows and Visual Studio shortcuts
- Keyboard mapping schemes
- How to customize a keyboard mapping scheme
- Shortcuts every developer should know
- How to learn all the keyboard shortcuts

Through these topics, we want to teach you some of the more advanced concepts, such as how to do the following:

- Discover shortcuts for yourself
- Identify conflicts
- Create your own shortcuts and mapping schemes

We will conclude this chapter with a valuable exercise that you can use in your own environment to help identify and remember more shortcuts with less effort. Be sure to give this one a try.

> **Optional content**
>
> If you do not have the time or inclination to understand the sections on keyboard mapping schemes, feel free to skim over the *Customizing your own keyboard mapping schemes* and *Keyboard mapping scheme definitions* sections/exercises.

Technical requirements

The code examples in this chapter have been tested with Visual Studio 2019 and the full .NET Framework v4.7.2. Also, to follow along, make sure to clone the repository for this book. The code for this chapter is available on GitHub at `https://github.com/PacktPublishing/Visual-Studio-2019-Tricks-and-Techniques/tree/main/`.

Please visit the following link to check the CiA videos: `http://bit.ly/3oxE5QM`.

Warning: Please read the following if you receive an error while cloning the repository. Starting in Git 2.28, `git init` will look to the value of `init.defaultBranch` when creating the first branch in a new repository. If that value is unset, `init.defaultBranch` defaults to `master`. Because this repository uses `main` as its default branch, you may have to run the following code from Command Prompt or Git Bash to avoid the error:

```
$ git config --global init.defaultBranch main
```

Windows shortcuts

Whether you are using Windows, macOS, or Linux, knowing basic shortcuts is critical to efficient navigation. First, we are going to warm up with a few essential Windows shortcuts every developer should know:

- **Win + X**: This command opens the hidden Quick Link menu. Also known as the *Power User* menu, this provides shortcuts to common management, configuration, and other Windows tools. Forget app searches or hunting around Control Panel – jump straight into PowerShell or the Event Viewer using this feature:

Figure 2.1 – Win + X – Quick Link/Power User menu

- **Alt + F4**: This command closes the current/active application. It prompts the user to save any changes and then shuts down the application.

- **Alt + Tab**: This command allows you to toggle between open applications. This key combination switches between open applications; it is very useful for developers that tend to have many windows open simultaneously.

- **Win + D**: This command is used to show/hide the desktop. Press it once to minimize all open windows and repeat this combination a second time to restore open windows. This is a good command to know and use just before sharing your screen in virtual meetings!

- **Win + Q**: This is a useful command that opens a search window that can use Cortana and voice control. Alternatively, just type the first few letters of the program you want to open. The analogous command on Mac is ⌘ + spacebar. Both can save a ton of time hunting around.

> **Windows shortcuts = Visual Studio shortcuts**
>
> Note that many Windows shortcuts are standard across several applications. That means some of them are also available for use in the Visual Studio editor as well.

Shortcuts that work in both Windows and Visual Studio

Next, we are going to cover a few basic shortcuts that can be used in both Windows and Visual Studio:

- **F2** (rename file): Highlight a folder or file in Windows Explorer and then hit *F2* to give it a new name.

This avoids having to read down a list of literally almost 30 options in a context menu. This can also be used in programs such as SQL Server Management Studio or Microsoft Excel (edits the contents of the highlighted cell):

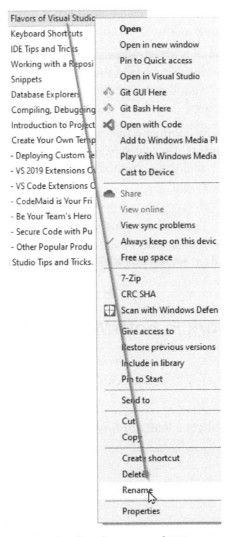

Figure 2.2 – F2 – Reading down around 30 items to rename

- **Ctrl + A** (select all): Highlight all the text in a document or select all the files in a folder. This avoids using *Shift* + click or drag-to-highlight operations with the mouse.

- **Ctrl + Z** (undo): Whoops, rollback that last action! If you just did something you did not mean to do, try this lifesaver first.

- **Alt + F4** (close app): Closes the running application.

- **Ctrl + W** (close tab): Closes the current window or tab. This is like a mini *Alt + F4* and saves having to mouse around with close buttons. Also used to close Explorer windows and browser tabs.

Intermediate-level shortcuts

We promised not to bore you with pages and pages of shortcuts, but here are a handful of productivity shortcuts that will prepare you to tackle the more advanced content of this chapter that follows:

> **Parity between Flavors**
>
> This chapter intentionally focuses on Visual Studio 2019 for Windows shortcuts and calls out equivalent VS Code shortcuts. However, know that VS Code and Visual Studio for Mac have similar, but different, functionality. For example, the *sync with active document* shortcut shown in the following list is the default behavior in VS Code, so no action is required. For simplicity and brevity, not every difference is called out. Just know that if you see something you like, chances are it's available in your flavor of Visual Studio, too.

- **Ctrl + -** (navigate backward) or **Ctrl + Shift + -** (navigate forward): Go to the last cursor location. In VS Code, use *Alt* + left and *Alt* + right, respectively.

- **Ctrl + Shift + backspace** (last code edit): Navigate to the last place where the code was edited. Experiment with this relative to the navigate backward shortcut to see the difference. In VS Code, the default key binding is *Ctrl + K, Ctrl + Q*.

- **Ctrl + [+ S** (sync with active document): It can be hard to find files in Solution Explorer when there are many files spread across many projects. Using this shortcut will trigger Solution Explorer to locate the current code file you are working on, scroll to it, and highlight it so that you can get your bearings. If you do not know this shortcut, please stop what you are doing, open a sample project, and give it a try:

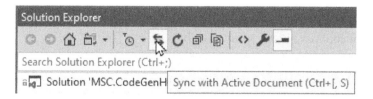

Figure 2.3 – Sync with Active Document

I had been coding for years in Visual Studio without knowing this very useful command. One day, during a paired programming session, my colleague used it and it has been one of my favorites ever since! There is even a **Track Active Item in Solution Explorer** configuration that you can enable in **Tools | Options** to do this automatically. In VS Code, Sync with Active Document is the default behavior, so no action is required.

- **Shift + Alt + arrow** (or **Alt + click + drag**): Use this in code to make a *vertical selection over multiple lines* down. Note that the same action is available in VS Code by using *Alt + Shift* + click + drag.

- **Ctrl + Shift + V** (clipboard history): Have you ever felt the sting of Windows' single-clipboard entry limitation? This happens when you copy something to the clipboard (*Ctrl + C*) move on, copy something else, then want to paste the thing you originally copied (*Ctrl + V*). Well, Visual Studio removes this limitation and tracks a list of clipboard items. Next time, instead of pressing the standard *Ctrl + V* to paste, try this shortcut instead:

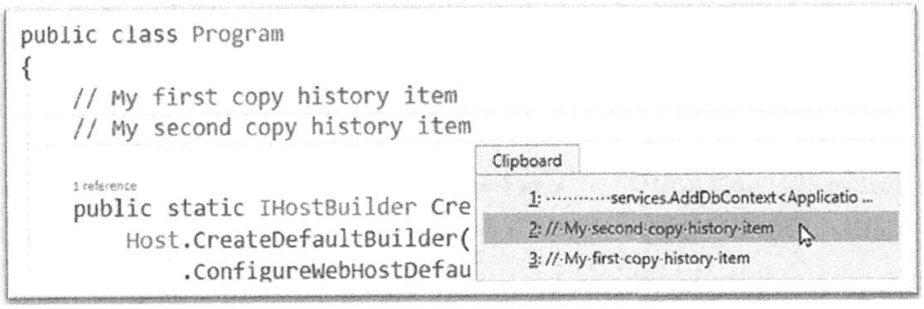

Figure 2.4 – Clipboard history

> **History of Windows' clipboard history**
>
> Many users of Windows are not aware that Microsoft added clipboard history capability to Windows 10 in late 2018. This feature supports text, HTML, and images under 4 MB in size. You can pin items in **Clipboard History** so that they persist across computer restarts. Note that this feature must be enabled either in **Settings** or by pressing *Windows + V*. Once you have enabled it, press *Windows + V*. to bring up a list of previously copied items.

In VS Code, there is a **Multiple clipboards for VSCode** extension that provides the equivalent clipboard history functionality.

- **Ctrl + G** (go to line): This one explains itself. Use this shortcut when you are in a large code file and you know the line number you want to see. For example, this is handy when researching an error that was logged. The same shortcut works in VS Code or, alternatively, you can open the go to the **File** menu with *Ctrl + P*, type :, then type the line number.

- **Ctrl + 1, Ctrl + R** (recent files): If you ever get tired of using *Alt + W, #* to access files you were working with recently, try this one. It is quite simply the fastest way to jump between a handful of files and it works in VS Code, too.

  Developers working with smaller screens can use this to avoid keeping three horizontal rows of file tabs open beneath the Visual Studio menus. This makes use of the search box feature, described next, and can also be accessed via *Ctrl + T, R*:

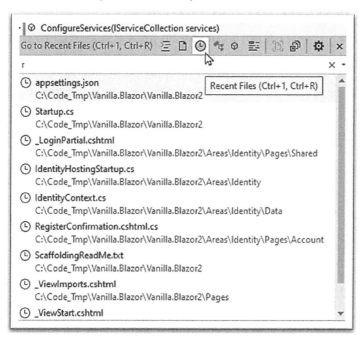

Figure 2.5 – Recent files

- **Ctrl + T** (open search box): Be sure to explore the different options available in the search box shown in *Figure 2.5*. In particular, note that you can use this to quickly perform searches of not only files but also types and members as well. This is useful if you have a good idea of the method name but cannot remember exactly which file contains it. In VS Code, type *Ctrl + P* (quick open) to quickly search and open a file by its name.

- **Shift + Ctrl + F** (find and replace or find all): Use this as an alternative to the search box and have the results displayed in one of the find output windows. Note that with this option, you can keep the results from past searches while you perform additional searches. The same shortcut works in VS Code; just click the down chevron when the search dialog appears to expose the replace textbox.

These are but a taste of what is available with keyboard shortcuts in Visual Studio. There are many online resources available listing shortcuts, and we could continue to simply feed you fish here. However, *you will get more out of the experience if we teach you how to fish*, instead. That is what we will begin to do with the next section on keyboard mapping schemes.

Keyboard mapping schemes

The next facet to understand is that Visual Studio supports more than one keyboard **mapping scheme**. This is just a fancy term that means a name is given to a set of key combinations used to trigger an action. A key combination that works in one keyboard mapping scheme might perform the same action when another keyboard scheme is set. However, it may instead perform a different action, or no action at all.

Visual Studio comes pre-installed with these keyboard mapping schemes by default:

- ReSharper (Visual Studio)
- Visual Basic 6
- Visual C# 2005
- Visual C++ 2
- Visual C++ 6
- Visual Studio 6
- VS Code

To see the installed keyboard mapping schemes in Visual Studio 2019 for Windows, navigate to the **Tools** menu | **Options** | **Environment** | **Keyboard**. If you are using Visual Studio for Mac, the equivalent is found under **Preferences** | **Environment** | **Key Bindings**, where you can choose from the following default mapping schemes: **Visual Studio for Mac**, **Visual Studio (Windows)**, **Visual Studio Code**, or **Xcode**:

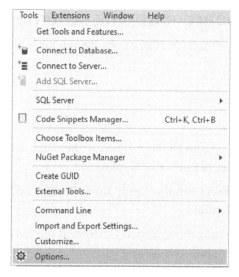

Figure 2.6 – Navigate to keyboard mapping schemes in Visual Studio

It will become more apparent in the following sections why there are multiple keyboard mapping schemes and what might make you choose one over another. The short answer is that people come from different developer backgrounds, used different tools in the past, and have personal preferences.

In general, I tend to start with the Visual C# 2005 scheme on a fresh install and eventually upgrade to a customized version of that scheme for Visual Studio 2019, which we will explore in an exercise later in this chapter.

> **Boredom warning**
>
> Some developers will be thrilled to learn the "behind-the-scenes" mechanisms of keyboard mapping schemes, while others may find the next couple of sections too low level. If you find yourself getting bored or pressed for time, it is fine to skip to the *Learning keyboard shortcuts* section toward the end of this chapter.   p 36

One thing we do not cover in depth in this chapter but is important to understand is the "context" of keyboard shortcuts. This subtle but important point means that the same keypress combinations can perform completely different actions depending on where you are in Visual Studio.

For example, consider the *F2* (rename) shortcut introduced earlier. In places like Solution Explorer or Team Explorer, it invokes the `File.Rename` command. However, if you are editing project settings using Settings Designer, then it will invoke the `Edit.EditCell` command instead.

Choosing a keyboard mapping scheme

In this exercise, we will set Visual C# 2005 as our default keyboard mapping scheme:

1. Open Visual Studio.

2. Click the **Tools** menu.

3. Select the **Options** sub-menu.

4. Either type keyboard into the search box at the upper left or scroll down and expand **Environment**, then choose **Keyboard**.

5. Choose **Visual C# 2005** from the **Apply the following additional keyboard mapping scheme** dropdown.

6. Click the **OK** button to confirm Visual C# 2005 as our active keyboard mapping scheme. This change is effective immediately:

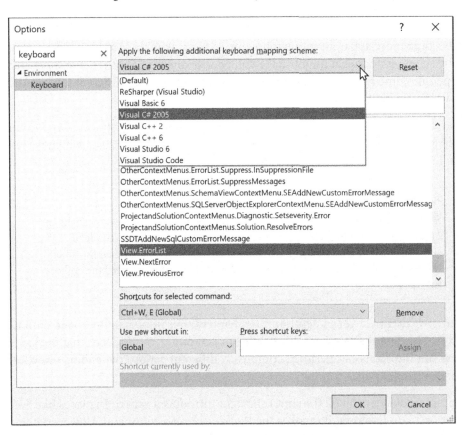

Figure 2.7 – Default keyboard mapping schemes

> **Only one keyboard mapping scheme can be active**
>
> Note that only one keyboard mapping scheme can be in use at a time and selecting another scheme will disable all others.

Customizing your own keyboard mapping schemes

You are not limited to the handful of default keyboard mapping schemes provided out of the box with Visual Studio. There are a few ways to create your own shortcuts:

- Individually.
- Create your own keyboard mapping scheme.
- Import sets created by others.

We will start by learning how to create your own individual shortcut.

Creating an individual shortcut

In this exercise, we will assign a keyboard shortcut to a Visual Studio automation command that does not have a current mapping:

1. Navigate to the **Keyboard** dialog (the **Tools** menu | **Options** | **Environment** | **Keyboard**).

2. Search for or scroll down to the `Help.About` command.

3. Use the mouse to select the **Press shortcut keys** textbox and then press the *Ctrl + H* key combination:

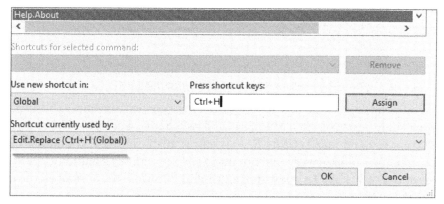

Figure 2.8 – Creating a shortcut for Help.About

4.   Notice that Visual Studio provides a warning that *Ctrl + H* is currently used by the `Edit.Replace` command. We could overwrite that setting, but press *A* instead. This should have the effect of making your full shortcut key combination *Ctrl + H, A*.

5.   Click the **Assign** button and then the **OK** button to close the dialog.

6.   Press *Ctrl + H, A* and you should see Visual Studio's **About** dialog appear.

Viewing existing shortcuts

The `Edit.InsertSnippet` command is selected in *Figure 2.9* and we can see this command is mapped to the *Ctrl + K, X* keyboard shortcut at the global level:

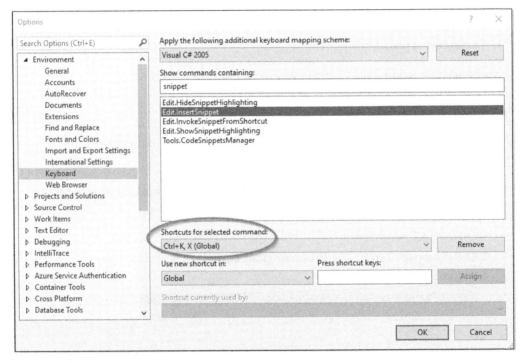

Figure 2.9 – Shortcut for Edit.InsertSnippet

This is a good point to reiterate that some shortcuts are context-sensitive. This means that they may only be active when a certain window is active. For example, the `Edit.ToggleBookmark` command (*Ctrl + B, T*) is only available in the Text Editor scope. Obviously, creating a bookmark would not make any sense if, say, Solution Explorer was the active window. Click the **Use new shortcut in** dropdown to see a list of all the different scopes available.

Importing an entire keyboard mapping scheme

In this section, we are going to unmask the magic behind keyboard shortcut mappings. You will see learn how Visual Studio loads available options and even how to create your own.

The whole point of keyboard mapping schemes is to facilitate developer productivity. Also, letting developers use shortcuts they already know can be a great way to assist those migrating to Visual Studio from different IDEs!

We will perform an exercise in which we will review a sample XML keyboard mapping scheme for *Sublime Text*, import it into Visual Studio, and make it available for selection:

> **Advanced material note**
>
> This is something of an advanced topic, so feel free to skim this content or skip this exercise.

1. Open the `Sublime with C# Partial.vssettings` file found in the `Chapter02/Keyboard Mappings` folder using Visual Studio.

2. Notice that this `.vssettings` is just a straightforward XML file. In the following screenshot, we can see that the `Edit.GoToFile` command is mapped to *Ctrl + P*. As a side note, the default open print dialog action will be overridden when this scheme is active:

```
<UserSettings>
  <ApplicationIdentity version="8.0.40218.0" name="Microsoft Development Environment" />
  <Category name="Environment_Group" RegisteredName="Environment_Group">
    <Category name="Environment_KeyBindings" Category="{F09035F1-80D2-4312-8EC4-4D354A4BCB4C}"
      <KeyboardShortcuts Version="8.0">
        <ScopeDefinitions>...</ScopeDefinitions>
        <ShortcutsSchemeDef Name="Sublime with C#">
          <!-- Sublime Text shortcuts -->
          <Shortcut Command="Edit.GoToFile" Scope="Global">Ctrl+P</Shortcut>
          <Shortcut Command="View.CommandWindow" Scope="Global">Ctrl+Shift+P</Shortcut>
          <!--Should be Command Palete-->
          <Shortcut Command="File.OpenFile" Scope="Global">Ctrl+O</Shortcut>
          <Shortcut Command="Window.CloseDocumentWindow" Scope="Global">Ctrl+W</Shortcut>
          <Shortcut Command="Edit.IncreaseLineIndent" Scope="Text Editor">Ctrl+]</Shortcut>
          <Shortcut Command="Edit.DecreaseLineIndent" Scope="Text Editor">Ctrl+[</Shortcut>
          <Shortcut Command="Edit.LineDelete" Scope="Text Editor">Ctrl+Shift+K</Shortcut>
```

Figure 2.10 – Sample Sublime Text keyboard shortcut schema XML definition file

3. Open the **Import and Export Settings Wizard** dialog by choosing **Import and Export Settings...** from Visual Studio's **Tools** menu.

4. Choose the **Import selected environment settings** radio button and click the **Next** button.

5. It is not necessary to do so, but save the current settings in this step if you want to keep them, and then click the **Next** button.

> **Note**
>
> It will become apparent in a few steps that we are not actually changing anything with this import and, besides, there is a reset button in the **Keyboard** dialog that can undo any changes.

6. Click the **Browse** button when prompted to choose a collection of settings to import. Navigate to the `Chapter02/Keyboard Mappings` sample code folder and select the `Sublime with C# Partial.vssettings` file. Click the **Next** button.

7. The only options you should see to import are for **Environment | Keyboard**. Click the **Finish** button.

> **Innocuous import warnings**
>
> If you are using the **Professional** or **Community** versions of Visual Studio, expect to see a few warnings. You can safely ignore messages that read something like **Keyboard: The command 'Debug.IntelliTraceCalls' does not exist. The keyboard shortcut bound to this command has been ignored.** You are receiving these warnings because you can use IntelliTrace in Visual Studio Enterprise edition, but not the Professional or Community editions.

8. At this point, all we have really done is told Visual Studio to import our keyboard mappings file. What it does behind the scenes is compile it into a binary file with a `.vsk` extension:

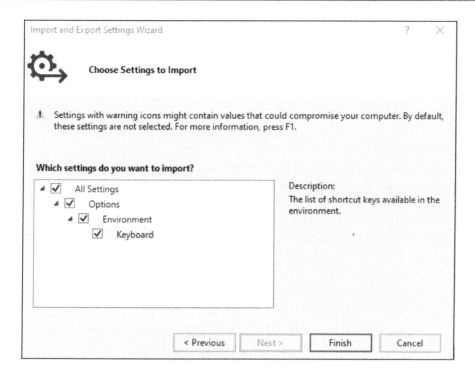

Figure 2.11 – Import schema XML definition file

9. In order to use our imported shortcuts, we must first copy the binary .vsk file that was generated in the prior step to a location where the IDE knows to look for it. To do this, use Windows Explorer and navigate to the hidden AppData directory that is specific to your user. In my case, the desired Sublime with C#.vsk file is here:

    ```
    %appdata%\Microsoft\VisualStudio\16.0_3656df8c
    ```

    Or, more specifically, the file can be found in your *Roaming* AppData folder:

    ```
    C:\Users\<username>\AppData\Roaming\Microsoft\
    VisualStudio\16.0_3656df8c
    ```

    Note that your file path may differ slightly, depending on the installed version of Visual Studio.

10. Copy the `Sublime with C#.vsk` file from the `Roaming` directory to the `Common7\IDE` directory on your machine. In my case, the target directory is as follows:

```
C:\Program Files (x86)\Microsoft Visual Studio\2019\
Enterprise\Common7\IDE
```

> **Administrator permission required**
>
> Note that in order to get the keyboard mapping scheme to appear in our options menu, we must put a binary VSK file into Visual Studio's `Common7\IDE` directory. Doing so will likely require administrator access due to its location underneath the `Program Files (x86)` directory at the root.

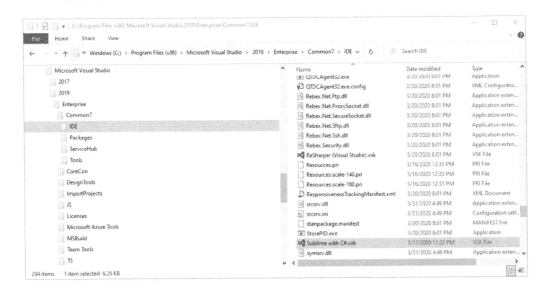

Figure 2.12 – Copying the VSK file from the user roaming profile to the IDE directory

11. Finally, once the VSK file has been copied into the IDE directory, return to Visual Studio and you should see **Sublime with C#** as an option in the keyboard mapping scheme dropdown. Choose this option and click the **OK** button:

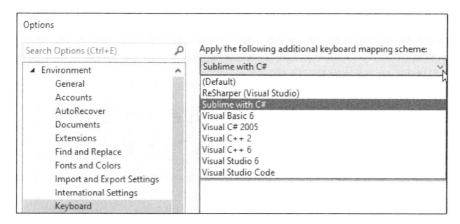

Figure 2.13 – Sublime keyboard mapping scheme dropdown item

12. Back in the Visual Studio editor, try pressing the *Ctrl + P* keyboard shortcut. The **Go to Files** dialog appears at the upper right of your window. In the following screenshot, typing `pro` brought up a couple of options:

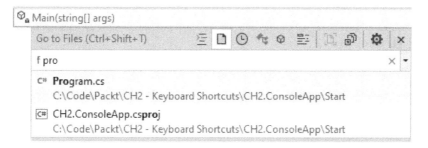

Figure 2.14 – Using Ctrl + P to trigger the Go to Files shortcut

As a final note on keyboard mapping scheme definitions, know that there are several existing definitions out there already for popular editors. Be sure to check the Internet first before creating your own from scratch.

Learning keyboard shortcuts

So far, I have kept my promise not to bore you with unending lists of keyboard shortcuts that you will have no chance of memorizing and putting to good use. Instead, for the last topic in this chapter, I would like to show you a neat Visual Studio extension that can help you memorize shortcuts for all your favorite actions.

Note that a future chapter does a deep dive into Visual Studio extensions and so we will not go into detail on them at this time.

Installing the Learn the Shortcut extension

In this exercise, we will install a Visual Studio extension written by Mads Kristensen. This extension monitors your actions and displays the keyboard shortcut for any command that you execute. In this way, it helps you learn the shortcuts that you need the most:

1. **Access the Extensions | Manage Extensions** menu item in Visual Studio.

2. Then, search for `Learn the Shortcut` and, once found, click the **Download** button.

3. Next, close all instances of Visual Studio and the VSIX installer will begin installing the extension. Finally, reopen Visual Studio once the installation successfully completes.

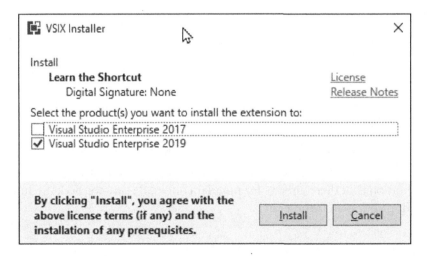

Figure 2.15 – Learn the Shortcut VSIX installer

4. Open a sample project and use the mouse to access some menu commands. *Figure 2.16* shows that I just clicked on the **Edit.ToggleOutliningExpansion** menu command, and that I could have used *Ctrl + M, Ctrl + M* instead. There is also a custom output window, **Learn the Shortcut**. This keeps a running list of all the commands you have run in a session. Review this output from time to time and see what shortcuts you could be using!

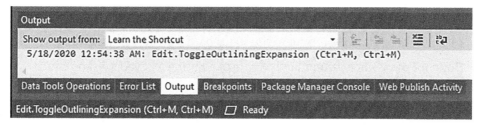

Figure 2.16 – Learn the Shortcut output window

Innocuous load error message

Note that this extension can cause an error message to be displayed when Visual Studio 2019 is first opened. This is a known issue related to the display of the start page and does not really affect anything (see the following screenshot).

If you see the error message shown in *Figure 2.17*, there are a few options. First, you can simply click **No** to stop seeing the message. Another option is to configure Visual Studio not to display the start page (which triggers the error) when it first opens. This option has the same effect as clicking **Continue without code** on the start page. To do this, navigate to the **Tools** menu | **Options** | **Startup**. Finally, since this extension is open source, consider forking the repo, fixing the bug, and making a pull request!

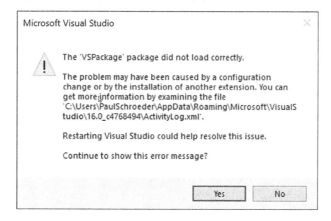

Figure 2.17 – Learn the Shortcut load error

Also, there have been reports that, in some cases, this extension may log errors to the **Learn the Shortcut** output window when developing .NET Core projects. Although it works for most, if this happens to you, simply experiment with a .NET full framework project instead.

Default Learn the Shortcut behavior

The following are the default behaviors of this extension:

- Displays the keyboard shortcut in the status bar for 5 seconds by default
- Does not show when a command was invoked using a keyboard shortcut
- Logs missed opportunities for shortcuts in a separate output window pane

Note that you can customize the behavior of this extension using **Tools | Options | Environment | Keyboard | Shortcuts**.

Justification for investing time

Why do we feel it is worth investing your time to learn keyboard shortcuts? Visual Studio aside, think about what you do when you are browsing the web and you want to open a new tab in your browser. Do you remove your hand from the keyboard, place it on the mouse, reposition the cursor over the + button to the right of other open tabs, click, and then switch your hand back to the keyboard? If so, you just lost precious seconds of your life that cannot be recovered. Many people are familiar with using the *Ctrl + T* shortcut (*Command + T* for Mac) and prefer doing so versus the fine motor coordination it takes to navigate and click the mouse.

Chances are you do not think much about the time lost by using a mouse more than is necessary. Personally, I'm reminded of it every time I start typing garbage and realize my fingers did not return perfectly to their home row position on the keyboard.

For the sake of making a point, pretend a scientific study was conducted that concluded it takes 3.5 seconds to perform the preceding "new tab" action using a combination of the keyboard and mouse. Further imagine that the same study concluded it takes only a half-second (0.5 seconds) to open that new browser tab by pressing the *Ctrl + T* key combination. Try the two approaches yourself, without racing, and see whether you notice a difference.

Individually, we may not care about that 3-second difference. However, it is quite likely that a similar opportunity for using keyboard shortcuts presents itself each and every minute we spend actively coding in Visual Studio, on average.

Let's do the math, assuming an 8-hour workday and 261 working days per year:

*3 seconds * 60 minutes per hour * 8 hours per day * 261 working days per year = 375,840 seconds*

In this example, we are suggesting it is possible to save 6,264 cumulative minutes over the course of a year. That translates into more than 100 hours, or **over 2 and a half weeks of your life each year**, conserved simply by using keyboard shortcuts!

Now, we programmers are a very logical bunch and I know half of you are bursting to tell me that very few people code in Visual Studio 8 hours per day each working day of the year. That may be true, but let's not miss the point that a significant time saving is possible. On the flip side, what if there is the opportunity to use a keyboard shortcut twice per minute instead of once?

Summary

In this chapter, we made the case for more efficient coding practices using keyboard shortcuts. We introduced a handful of everyday shortcuts as a primer for understanding Visual Studio's keyboard mapping schemes. You saw how to search for existing shortcuts and how to assign your own. Next, we pulled back the curtain on precisely how to import and create custom keyboard mapping schemes. Finally, we kept our promise to not bore you with lists of shortcuts to memorize, but rather showed you a handy Visual Studio extension to install that will have you learning those shortcuts in no time.

Your mileage may vary but memorizing some shortcuts could literally save weeks of your life every year. In the next chapter, we are going to broaden our perspective and discuss more general tips and tricks that are useful for developers to know.

Further reading

- This page lists the default command shortcuts for the general profile: `https://docs.microsoft.com/en-us/visualstudio/ide/default-keyboard-shortcuts-in-visual-studio?view=vs-2019`

- VS Code shortcuts: `https://code.visualstudio.com/shortcuts/keyboard-shortcuts-windows.pdf`

- Hot Keys – Keyboard Shortcuts: Provides alternative keyboard mapping schemes:

  `https://marketplace.visualstudio.com/items?itemName=JustinClareburtMSFT.HotKeys`

3
IDE Tips and Tricks

Knowing your IDE makes your life easier, helps you develop faster, and even trains you to write better code. In this chapter, we are going to cover IDE features such as refactoring that can save you time by automatically extracting code into methods, variables, parameters, and so on. Other features, such as column editing and multi-caret editing, help you make changes in multiple places without having to edit each one individually. There are also a number of command-line switches that you can pass to the IDE to control behavior and configuration, so when it starts you are up and ready to work! The terminal inside the IDE can help you perform functions and quickly test commands before you put them in your application. Overall, there are a number of things that you can do to make your experience better, faster, and more enjoyable.

In this chapter, we will specifically cover the following topics:

- Different ways to organize code files for easy access
- Techniques to quickly move between active windows and files
- Items to investigate, such as Preview Features and Live Sharing
- Tricks for faster code insertion and editing
- Easy methods to format and clean code

Technical requirements

The code examples in this chapter have been tested with Visual Studio 2019 and the full
.NET Framework v4.7.2. Also, to follow along, make sure to clone the repository for this
book. The code for this chapter is available on GitHub at `https://github.com/`
`PacktPublishing/Visual-Studio-2019-Tricks-and-Techniques/tree/`
`main/Chapter03`.

Please visit the following link to check the CiA videos: `http://bit.ly/3oxE5QM`.

> **Warning**
>
> Please read the following if you receive an error while cloning the repository.
> Starting in Git 2.28, `git init` will look to the value of `init.`
> `defaultBranch` when creating the first branch in a new repository. If that
> value is unset, `init.defaultBranch` defaults to `master`. Because this
> repository uses `main` as its default branch, you may have to run the following
> code from Command Prompt or Git Bash to avoid the error:
>
> **$ git config --global init.defaultBranch main**

Having fun with the file tabs

Almost any application of substance consists of dozens, hundreds, or even thousands of
separate code files. In this section, we will cover a few tricks that can make managing large
numbers of open files a breeze. This will give us the opportunity to demonstrate several
Visual Studio features along the way. We can start by launching Visual Studio 2019 for
Windows and then opening the provided `WritingExample.sln` solution file.

Pinning documents

Pinning documents is an easy way to keep the files you are currently interested in front
and center. In order to do that, take the following steps:

1. Start by opening the `WritingExample.sln` solution found in this
    chapter's sample code folder. Then, open *all four* of the code files in the
    `WritingInstruments` folder of the `WritingExample` project.

2. Move your mouse to hover over the **Marker.cs** file tab along the top until you see the **Toggle pin status** icon:

Figure 3.1 – Toggle pin status (before)

3. Click the pin icon and notice how the **Marker.cs** file tab is now positioned to the far left with a vertical pin icon, instead of a horizontal pin icon:

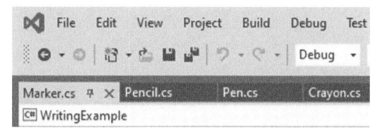

Figure 3.2 – Toggle pin status (after)

This file tab will now remain displayed in this spot, regardless of how many other documents you open. This functionality is also available in Visual Studio for Mac and Visual Studio Code. To pin tabs in Visual Studio Code, use either the context menu or the `workbench.action.pinEditor` command, which has a shortcut of *Ctrl + K, Shift + Enter*.

Next, let's consider an alternative to displaying our open documents horizontally.

Vertical documents

Every developer has their own preferences and hardware setup. Personally, I have very wide monitors and so my horizontal display real estate is often less precious relative to vertical. Because I tend to have numerous files open at once, I sometimes use the **Place Tabs** feature so that all my open file tabs do not wrap across multiple vertical lines. To try this out, use the following steps:

1. Right-click on any header of any file tab that is already open. Be sure to right-click on the filenames in the top tabs, not somewhere in the content of an open item.

2. Scroll to the bottom and choose **Set Tab Layout | Place Tabs on the Left**:

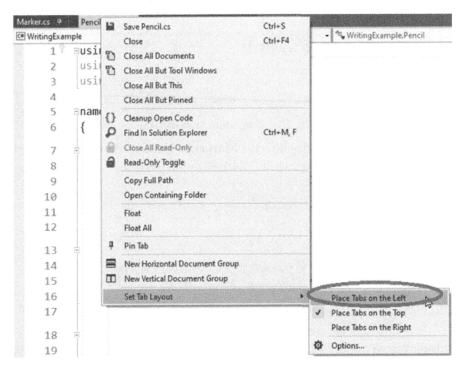

Figure 3.3 – Place Tabs on the Left menu item

3. Notice that your pinned documents now show at the top of the **Tabs** window. As depicted in the following screenshot, the **Pencil.cs** document that is currently being edited displays as highlighted. Also, the mouse pointer changes to double-arrows, allowing you to resize the window width to your liking:

Figure 3.4 –Tabs window

4. Click the **Settings** icon next to the **Tabs** header to open a popup with quick access
    to even more options, such as sorting and grouping. Alternatively, these settings can
    also be accessed via the **Tools** menu | **Options** | **Environment** | **Tabs and Windows**:

Figure 3.5 – Tabs options

While we are on the topic of document display, Visual Studio's horizontal and vertical
groups functionality is also quite useful for developers with large or multiple displays.

Horizontal and vertical groups

This next feature is useful if you ever find yourself simultaneously trying to
reference sections of two different documents or even two different areas within the
same document.

Right-click on the tab of an open document (top header displaying the filename) and
select either the **New Horizontal Group** or **New Vertical Group** option to *create
a split-screen view of the same or different files* at the same time.

This can be useful if you want to view different sections of the same file or see sections
in different files simultaneously. By comparison, in **Visual Studio for Mac**, equivalent
functionality can be activated via the **View** menu | **Editor Columns** | **Two Columns**.
Now that we have several files open, let's see how we can efficiently jump between them.
Alternately, you can also click and drag a file tab out of the IDE's main window and dock
it to a second screen.

Split editor in Visual Studio Code

In **Visual Studio Code**, many editors can be opened side by side, vertically, and horizontally. The following screenshot is all from a single screen with one file opened in three different editor windows and a second file opened in two more:

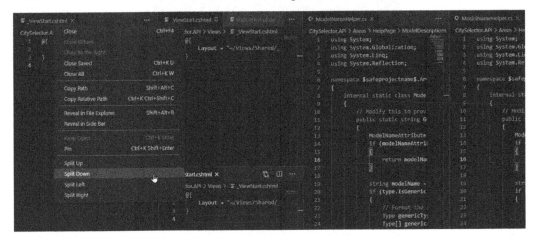

Figure 3.6 – Visual Studio Code split editor

There are numerous ways to open files in a new editor window that shares space with existing ones. Simply find the one that works best for you:

- *Alt + click* on a file in the explorer.
- The *Ctrl + * shortcut is the same as clicking the Split Editor Right icon at the upper right of each tab. This will create a new side-by-side window.
- Highlight a file in Visual Studio Explorer, then use *Ctrl + Enter*.
- Drag and drop a file to any side of the editor region.
- From inside the **Quick Open** (*Ctrl + P*) dialog, use the *Ctrl + Enter* shortcut (*Cmd + Enter* for Mac) when the file lists.

Now that we have options for viewing and organizing files of interest once they are open, let's explore some ways to find those files in the first place.

Traversing your solution

As the size and complexity of your code base grow, knowing strategies for getting to the code or tool window you need becomes essential. Extra time and energy spent simply finding the file or method that needs attention can detract from your overall effectiveness. In this section, we will cover a few of the lesser-known quick access tricks.

Navigating through active windows or tabs

In the last chapter, we showed how the search box (*Ctrl + T*) can be used to quickly locate files of interest. Another handy approach to quickly jump around is to cycle through the list of open windows and/or files. In this exercise, we will use more keyboard shortcuts to navigate through the active windows and open file tabs:

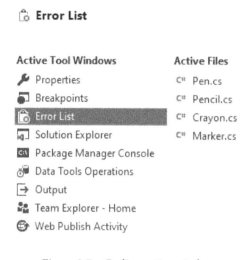

Figure 3.7 – Cycling active windows

To cycle through active windows in Visual Studio 2019 for Windows, use the following steps:

1. Press *Alt + F7* to bring up a navigation window (keep *Alt* pressed):

Figure 3.8 – Cycling active files

2. While holding *Alt*, repeatedly use the *F7* key to highlight the next item. Use *Shift + Alt + F7* to navigate backward instead of forward.

To cycle through open files, use the following steps:

1. Press *Ctrl + Tab* to bring up a navigation window (keep *Ctrl* pressed). Now you can quickly move between open files rather than tool windows.

2. Use *Shift + Ctrl + Tab* to select files in reverse order.

3. Repeat the same procedure but try using arrow keys to move the selection up and down.

> **Visual Studio for Mac tip**
> You can use the *Cmd* (⌘) key and numbered keys (*1, 2, 3, …*) to cycle through the number of documents you have open, numbered in the order they were opened.

Using Quick Launch

If you liked the search box accessed using *Ctrl + T* in the previous chapter, then you will also appreciate Visual Studio's **Quick Launch** feature. Use the *Ctrl + Q* keyboard shortcut to access the Quick Launch search, which provides a means to quickly query and execute actions or locate code within files. After activating the dialog, simply type your search string in the box and choose from the results.

For example, if I cannot remember the shortcut key for **Toggle Outlining Expansion** in the code editor, then I can simply press *Ctrl + Q* and type `toggle`. From the results, I can either click the desired item or instead use the shortcut that is displayed (*Ctrl + M*):

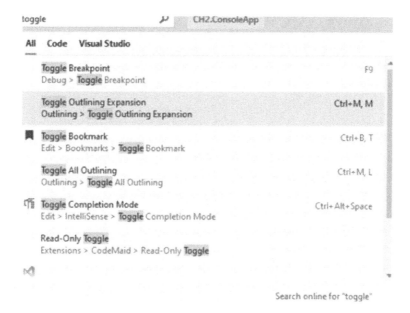

Figure 3.9 – Quick Launch (feature)

Quick Launch Filters

Shortcuts are available to limit your search to specific categories. Examples include the following:

- `@mru` for the *most recently used* filter

- `@menu` to limit the search to menu items

- `@opt` for searching only the settings in the **Options** dialog box

- `@doc` for documents

Now, let's take a look at an example where we will search for instances of a word in code:

1. Start by press *Ctrl + Q* to bring up the Quick Launch window.

2. Click in the **Code** header.

3. Type `Write`.

4. Use the arrow keys and press *Enter* or click on one of the search results to navigate to that location within the given file:

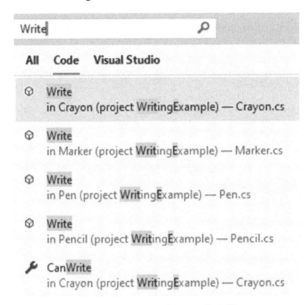

Figure 3.10 – Quick Launch (all)

Track Active Item

In the last chapter, you used the *Ctrl + [+ S* keyboard shortcut to invoke the **Sync Active Document** command. That works well enough, but it is kind of an awkward combination and you might be like me, too lazy to re-map it. Fortunately, as alluded to in the previous chapter, there is a better way that we will try now.

In this example, we will configure Solution Explorer so that its display constantly tracks the current file being edited. This avoids the need to find it manually or constantly use the cumbersome sync shortcut:

1. Press *Ctrl + Q* to bring up the Quick Launch window we just covered in the previous topic.

2. Type `track active` in the search box.

3. Click on the **Turn Track Active Item on or off** search result:

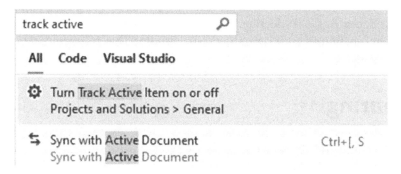

Figure 3.11 – Track Active Item

4. Make sure the **Track Active Item in Solution Explorer** menu item is checked and click **OK**:

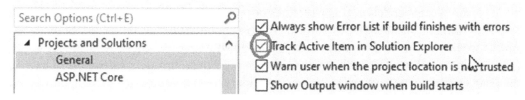

Figure 3.12 – Track Active Item checkbox

Now that we have configured the **Track Active Item in Solution Explorer** option, you will notice that the highlighted file in the Solution Explorer window remains synchronized with any open file tab you select. Note that this feature can also be accessed using the **Tools** menu | **Options** | **Projects and Solutions** | **General**.

> **Visual Studio Mac users, say what?**
>
> Visual Studio for Mac users are accustomed to this tracking behavior being the default behavior. Some developers may not realize that the same behavior is even an option in Visual Studio for Windows.

These are but a few of the lesser-known techniques available to you. If you are not already familiar with things such as **Go To Definition** or *Ctrl* + - to navigate backward and **Find All References**, be sure to spend a little time learning those as well.

Another useful item to know about is how to allow others to see exactly what you are seeing in real time as you code. Of course, there are virtual meeting applications such as MS Teams, Zoom, or GoToMeeting, but did you know that you have similar viewing, audio, and chat capabilities built right into Visual Studio? That is covered in our next topic, **Live Sharing**.

Live sharing

Have you ever emailed or instant messaged someone with what you thought was a quick coding question, only to have it end up as a very lengthy back-and-forth exchange? Virtual meetings can work well in these situations, but we recommend you consider Visual Studio's Live Share feature as well.

Visual Studio Live Share is like remote paired programming. It enables you to work together with a peer to edit and debug the same code base as though you were editing an online document (like in Google Docs or a Word doc). Each person gets their own cursor and can work independently, and there is audio and chat capability. This also works well if the person you are collaborating with does not want to stop what they are doing in their own environment, stash/shelve their local changes, clone/sync your repository branch, and so on. Instead, you can simply share your code with up to 30 guests who have read/write access in real time and collaborators do not need to go through the trouble of having the exact environment configured, as it is more like screen sharing with shared control, that is, *collaborative co-editing*.

This capability is surprisingly simple to use and you are encouraged to at least give it a try by following one of the links provided here:

- **How-to: Collaborate using Visual Studio**: https://docs.microsoft.com/en-us/visualstudio/liveshare/use/vs
- **Live Share Extension Pack for Visual Studio Code**: https://marketplace.visualstudio.com/items?itemName=MS-vsliveshare.vsliveshare-pack

Now let's look at the next topic, which is **Preview Features**.

Preview Features

One little-known item in the Visual Studio IDE is the ability to enable and disable Preview Features. These are typically IDE enhancements that are still considered under development but ready to try out. Note that it is possible to disable any of the features you enable if it causes problems. The exact list of items available tends to vary depending on the version of the IDE you currently have installed. In other words, each Visual Studio release has different items added and removed, so you must check the release notes for details. To see what is available to you, navigate through this menu structure, **Options | Environment | Preview Features**:

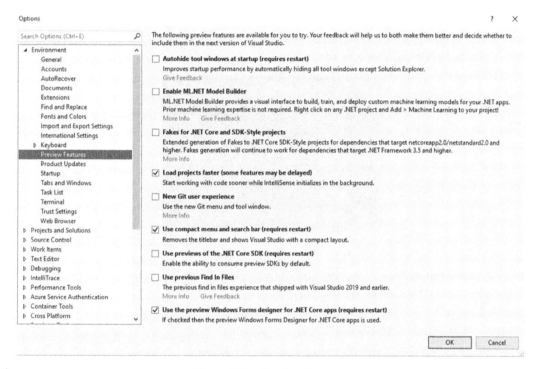

Figure 3.13 – Preview Features

Cool as they are, chances are you are not going to find anything critical to your project's completion in the Preview Features. Visual Studio, as a software product, has been around for a very long time. That means there has been ample opportunity to incorporate some sophisticated editor techniques. In the next section, we are going to go over a few practices that can make everyday code slinging easier.

Faster editing

If you have ever needed to alter multiple lines of code with the same change, there are a couple of tricks that can save you from having to repeat that change for each line. First, we will show how to edit when the change needs to be applied to lines that are stacked together, and then how to do it when they are not next to one another.

Column Mode

If you're like me, you might often end up having multiple lines of text that you need to edit with similar changes (that is, creating multiple variables with similar names, such as test1, test2, and so on). By using the **Column Mode** feature, you can edit all the items at the same time. This useful capability was briefly mentioned in the chapter on shortcuts and is reiterated here, in case you missed it:

Figure 3.14 – Column Mode selection

You can make this feature even more useful by pairing it with a plugin such as **Increment Selection** in Visual Studio Code, and turn var pencil into var pencil1, var pencil2, and so on. There is much more to learn about plugins/extensions, which are covered extensively in later chapters.

To activate this feature, use *Shift + Alt* + mouse click (or *Shift + Option* + mouse select on macOS) or *Shift + Alt* + arrow keys. Visual Studio for Mac uses *Option* + mouse click or *Option* + arrow keys.

Multi-caret selects

Now, if you need to edit code that is not on consecutive lines, then try multi-caret editing. Using the *Ctrl + Alt* + mouse click combination in Windows (*Ctrl + Option* + mouse click in macOS), you can select multiple blocks of non-contiguous text. When you do this, you should see multiple cursors flashing, as shown in the following screenshot. This indicates that whatever you type will affect all the selected text simultaneously:

Figure 3.15 – Multi-caret selection and editing

Making edits like this can certainly speed things up. The next timesaving feature we will describe is often used by developers who make presentations or do training. It can avoid dull periods of time spent waiting for chunks of code to be manually typed.

Toolbox

View / Toolbox

If you want to park a piece of code temporarily or find yourself typing the same code snippet over and over, the toolbox in Visual Studio 2019 for Windows might be just what you are looking for. Select a block of text, open the **Toolbox** tab, and drag the code into the **General** tab. Then, when you want to use it, either double-click on it to insert it at the cursor or drag and drop it where you want it. You can even rename the snippet by right-clicking and selecting **Rename Item**:

Figure 3.16 – Toolbox code snippet

The same functionality exists in Visual Studio 2019 for macOS, but it's not quite as easy to add snippets. You have to go into the **Visual Studio | Preferences | Text Editor | Code Snippets** menu item and then add new snippets there. Placing them in your code is very similar to the Windows sequence.

Cleaner code

Developers, in their attempts at slinging code, do not always take the time to consistently space lines of code. Nor do developers always go back and remove unused declarations and variables. Code that is riddled with spelling errors, inconsistent indentations, or unusual placement of curly braces leaves the impression of sloppiness. Thankfully, our tooling provides a few features that help us keep things clean and maintain a professional image.

Code Formatting

Code Formatting and **Code Cleanup** are a couple of Visual Studio features you should use frequently. While the implementation differs slightly across the various flavors of the Visual Studio IDEs, all offerings have some form of these features that are useful to know and very simple to use.

The following figure depicts a very simple before and after picture of code that demonstrates how Visual Studio Code fixes some indentations and curly brace placement:

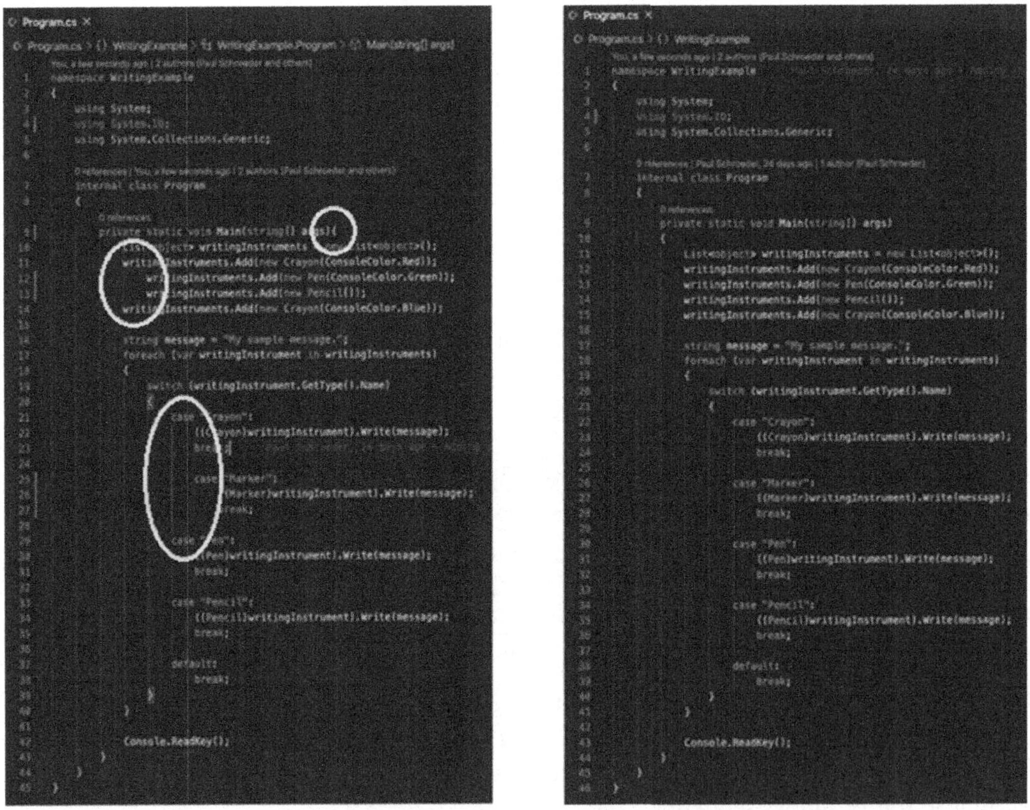

Figure 3.17 – Visual Studio Code format document – before and after

Notice that the improper indents (*line 12* and *line 13*) have been corrected and the curly brace at the end of *line 9* has been moved to the next line.

Formatting in Visual Studio Code can be accessed either from the **Context** menu or by using a keyboard combination. In Windows, *Shift + Alt + F* will invoke formatting, while *Shift + Option + F* executes it on macOS, and *Ctrl + Shift + I* is used on Linux.

This functionality can be accessed in Visual Studio 2019 for Windows using the *Ctrl + K*, *Ctrl + D* combination. Formatting in Visual Studio 2019 for macOS is controlled with *Ctrl + I* or by navigating through **Edit | Format | Format Document item**.

Code Cleanup

The Visual Studio 2019 for Windows offering is probably the strongest of any of the applications in the **formatting/cleanup** space. The Windows IDE has an additional feature called **Code Cleanup** that provides on-demand formatting and cleanup, and applies code style preferences.

There are several preferences you can control using the **Configure Code Cleanup** settings window, which you can reach by pressing the broom icon and selecting **Configure Code Cleanup**:

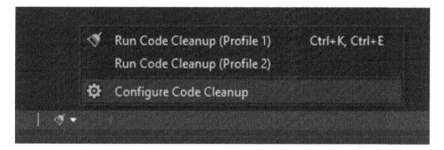

Figure 3.18 – Configure Code Cleanup

Multiple profiles can be configured for various projects, situations, and so on. This is especially helpful as you can switch between customers, teams, projects, or whatever and have the correct styling applied each time:

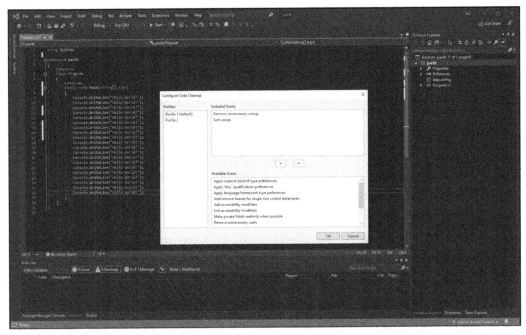

Figure 3.19 – Code cleanup settings

There are two ways to access the actual cleanup functionality: either by pressing the broom icon at the bottom of the text editor window, or by pressing the *Ctrl + K, Ctrl + E* key combination:

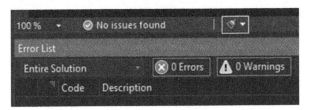

Figure 3.20 – Code cleanup "broom" button

So, I'm sure what you're thinking is *what's the difference between Code Cleanup and Code Formatting?* Well, the short answer is that Code Cleanup will not only format the code but also apply your coding style preferences. Such preferences are beyond the scope of this chapter, but one common example is the removal of unused using statements. Note that Code Cleanup can also be run across an entire project or solution.

Summary

This chapter outlined a number of IDE enhancements and features many developers do not know about that can greatly enhance your coding experience. You now know that file tabs can be organized either vertically or horizontally according to preference. Likewise, you can view two separate documents, or different sections of the same document, in a solution at the same time using horizontal and vertical groups. We covered a few navigation tricks that make it easier to move around your code, compare files, or quickly locate the files you need using features such as **Quick Launch**. You checked the **Track Active Item** option, which enables **Solution Explorer** to automatically stay in sync with the document being edited. The **Live Sharing** content described how to work with others using synchronous editing and we touched on how to investigate Preview Features. A few tips for quick multi-selection editing, such as **Column** and **multi-caret modes**, were given. Then, the **Toolbox** feature was shown as a way to help you type less code by reusing common code fragments. Finally, the **Code Cleanup** and **Code Formatting** exercises made the sample code more readable and maintainable for other developers.

Any way you look at it, these tips should help you leverage Visual Studio to write code better, faster, and easier than ever before.

Of course, as you write more code, being able to revert to prior versions and keep backups of your source files becomes more important. We are going to tackle how to do this in the next chapter, which introduces the concept of storing source code for your software applications in a centralized.

4
Working with a Repository

If you're like me, then you've had that moment when the day your code is due, you accidentally botch some code changes at 3 a.m. or accidentally delete a critical file. At first, there is panic and a frantic search for a backup or some copy of the code somewhere! Then, a wave of calmness washes over you when you realize a recent copy of that code is stored in source control and all you have to do is retrieve it. If you're using Git, for example, this may be as simple as issuing a `git reset` command. Likewise, if using Visual Studio's UI for Git, the **Undo Changes** functionality will have you covered.

Starting with version control should become deeply ingrained in your development processes. Think about it as performing on a high wire without a net. Even the best high-wire artists still use a net because it protects them, just like your code repository protects you.

When we talk about **version control systems** (**VCS**), we are talking about a repository where various versions of our artifacts (code, images, configuration files, and so on) are stored. They have various names (such as **Source Control Management** (**SCM**), version control, source control), but they all provide the same function—saving versions of our artifacts. There are a number of these systems available, such as Git, Azure Repos, Mercurial, Subversion, and so on.

In this chapter, we will talk about the following:

- Creating a repository
- Cloning a repository
- Getting updates (Fetch and Pull)
- Adding a file/project
- Stashing and undoing changes
- Creating a `.gitignore` file
- Creating a commit
- Creating a branch
- Working with a pull request

By the end of this chapter, you should have the skills necessary to perform the preceding functions using the Visual Studio IDE of your choice. This chapter is organized in a way that individually introduces each command and then provides contextual screenshots for Visual Studio 2019 for Windows, VS Code, and VS for Mac, respectively. If you are primarily using just one of those flavors of Visual Studio, then you can safely save reading time by ignoring the subsections under each command that are for the IDE(s) you are not using. Regardless of your IDE flavor, it is important to understand that all the IDE is really doing is automating command-line commands. This aspect is covered after a note on technical requirements.

Technical requirements

In this chapter, you are not necessarily required to use the code examples from this book. However, if you have not already, it would be a good idea to clone the repository for this book. The code for this chapter is available on GitHub at `https://github.com/PacktPublishing/Visual-Studio-2019-Tricks-and-Techniques/tree/main/`.

Please visit the following link to check the CiA videos: `http://bit.ly/3oxE5QM`.

> **Warning**
>
> Please read the following if you receive an error while cloning the repository. Starting in Git 2.28, `git init` will look to the value of `init.defaultBranch` when creating the first branch in a new repository. If that value is unset, `init.defaultBranch` defaults to `master`. Because this repository uses `main` as its default branch, you may have to run the following code from a command prompt or Git Bash to avoid the error:
>
> **$ git config --global init.defaultBranch main**

The preceding note is predicated on whether you have installed a more recent version of Git or not. Newer versions of Git acknowledge the charged nature of using a master branch. As such, Git's Setup application now allows developers to override the default branch name for new repositories. The authors of this book have chosen to use main as the default branch, as shown here:

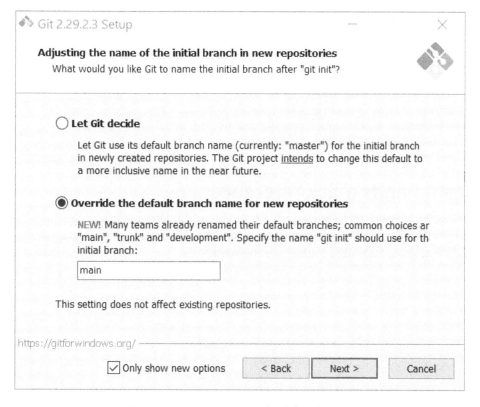

Figure 4.1 – Using main as the default branch

So, if you are wondering why we include that warning in the technical requirements of each chapter, now you know! With that understanding, let's now move on to the main content of this chapter (bad pun intended).

Automating Git commands

As mentioned in the introduction, there are numerous version control systems available and this chapter is going to focus on one of the more popular ones, Git. We will be using Git in this chapter since it is very commonly used in the development community. Also, it is supported by Microsoft in Azure as well as GitHub, which Microsoft acquired in 2018. Most of the other SCM providers behave very similarly, and the techniques we'll discuss can be applied to them as well.

We are about to show you how to do in each flavor of Visual Studio can also be done via the command line. In fact, many developers prefer to use the command line for source control tasks, particularly advanced scenarios. However, common needs are handled by Visual Studio just fine and that is going to be the focus of this chapter's content.

> **Alternative GUIs**
>
> In addition to Visual Studio, lots of developers install tools that are more geared towards a visual experience, such as GitKraken, gmaster, Sourcetree, Git Fork, and so on. Do not feel confined to limiting yourself to a single solution here as there are a number of great options available.

Git commands quick reference

For your convenience, the following table provides a summary list of the equivalent Git commands that Visual Studio automates through its GUI. To fully appreciate this chapter, you should at least be familiar with these commands.

Command root	Description / use
`git init`	Start a new repository; can create local-only repos
`git clone`	Download an existing repository using a URL (that is, from GitHub)
`git add`	Add a file to the staging area
`git commit`	Permanently record changes in the version history
`git status`	List all the files that have to be committed
`git rm`	Delete the file from your working directory and stage the deletion
`git tag`	Add a tag to the specified commit
`git branch`	List branches, create a new branch, delete a branch, depending upon command-line parameters
`git checkout`	Switch from one branch to another; also used to discard local changes (permanently) to a file, depending upon command-line parameters
`git merge`	Merge the specified branch's history into the current branch
`git remote`	Connect a local repository to the remote server
`git push`	Send local committed changes to the remote repository
`git pull`	Fetch changes from the remote server and merge them into your local working directory
`git stash`	Temporarily store all the modified files that are tracked
`git reset`	Discard all local changes to all files permanently; also used to unstage an individual file but preserve file contents, depending upon parameters
`git diff`	Show file differences for items that are not staged

> **Git is not GitHub**
>
> Sometimes people new to development using version control conflate Git with GitHub. The two are distinct and, put simply, Git is a version control system. It allows you to manage and track source code history. GitHub, by contrast, is a cloud-based hosting service designed to help you manage Git repositories.

Next, as we proceed through each operation using Visual Studio, try to think back to this list of commands. What arguments do you think the UI is passing to each command to perform a particular task?

Working with source control

When working with source control in Visual Studio 2019 for Windows, all of our source code actions take place in the **Git Changes** window. However, if you have a version that has not been updated since November 2020, then you will use the **Team Explorer** window, as shown in the following screenshot.

> **Visual Studio changes in version 16.8**
>
> One of the joys of writing a book is that things are always changing while content is being created, edited, and reviewed. This is exactly what happened with respect to Git source control and Visual Studio 2019 for Windows.
>
> In mid-November of 2020, developers who installed or upgraded Visual Studio found a new **Git Changes** window for handling source control, replacing functionality that was previously contained in the **Team Explorer** window. To aid readers with older versions, we will try to show versions of both the new **Git Changes** and previous **Team Explorer** windows:

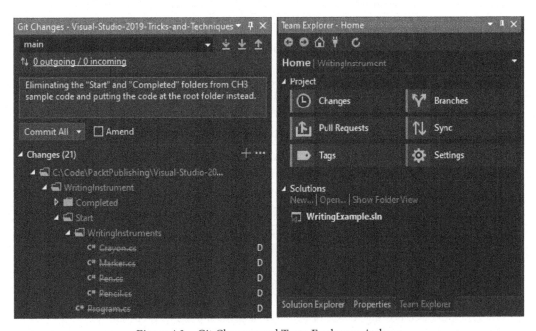

Figure 4.2 – Git Changes and Team Explorer windows

In VS Code, it's in the **SOURCECONTROL** view:

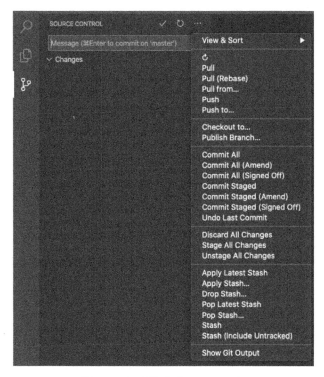

Figure 4.3 – VS Code commands

In Visual Studio 2019 for Mac, most things live in the **Version Control** menu, or in a right-click context on the solution:

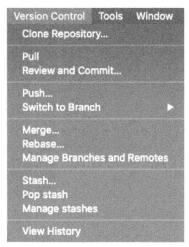

Figure 4.4 – Version control options – Mac

So, now that we know where to look in the IDE, let's now consider the initial steps required to get started. Generally, development will begin in one of two ways:

- Creating a new project and then creating a repository
- Cloning an existing repository and making changes

These methods, along with steps for each approach, are covered next. Just to reiterate, we will show how to accomplish each using multiple flavors of Visual Studio 2019, including Windows and Mac versions as well as VS Code. Feel free to skim or skip the screenshots and content that do not apply to the version you are using.

Creating a repository

Most of the time when I begin a new project, I also instantiate a new repository. I create a base project, then make changes such as configuring **Entity Framework** (**EF**) and creating a data layer project. Before making any consequential changes, I make a Git commit. This provides a baseline snapshot to revert back to in case things go sideways. Of course, I may already have those initial baseline changes captured in one of my custom project templates. You will see more on how quick this process can be in *Chapter 8, Introduction to Project and Item Templates.*

Once I create the project, it's time to create the repository and check it in. This functionality is the equivalent of the `git init` command.

In Visual Studio 2019 for Windows, Click the **Create Git Repository...** button or click the **New** chevron, depending on your version. Next, select or enter the path to your new repository, and click the **Create** button, as shown in the following screenshot:

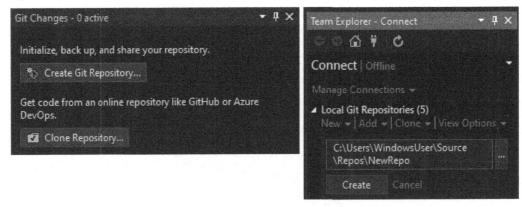

Figure 4.5 – Create a local repository

A local Git repository will be created and initialized with a `.gitignore` and `.gitattributes` file, ready for you to add your code.

Local repository tip

For individual projects, sometimes a fair amount of development can take place using a local, disconnected repo. This has all the benefits of tracking changes. If you later decide you want to synchronize everything with a remote repo, it's just a matter of connecting the provider with the local repo. Alternatively, this approach can be used to start a remote repository with a "clean" history. Once your local solution is settled, simply create the remote repo, clone it, and then copy/paste the local code into the cloned folder. It should be obvious that solely using a local repository takes away the benefit of having a backup copy of code on a remote server.

Now let's see how to create a repository in Visual Studio 2019 for Windows and Mac as well as VS Code.

For Windows

In Visual Studio 2019 for Windows, adding a project to source control and creating a repository is a really straightforward process:

1. *Newer versions*: After clicking the **Create Git Repository…** button, decide whether you want to push to a new remote repository on GitHub, connect to an existing remote repository, or simply create a local repository. The following screenshot depicts the options for creating a remote repository on GitHub:

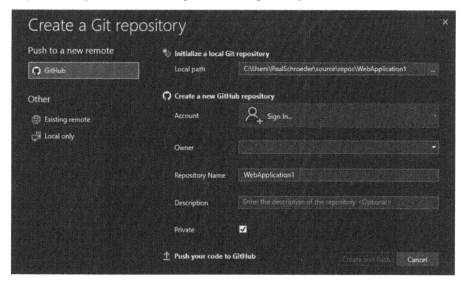

Figure 4.6 – The Create a Git repository dialog (Git Changes)

Older versions: In the bottom-right corner, there is a button labeled **Add to Source Control**. Click the button, select the correct source control provider, and you're in business:

Figure 4.7 – Add to Source Control (Team Explorer)

2. The next step will ask you where you want to store the repository. Some common locations are GitHub, Azure DevOps, BitBucket, AWS CodeCommit, or a private repository you control such as GitLab.

Credentials

Once you select a destination, the provider might prompt you for credentials before you can continue.

---

3. Next, you will need to provide the details for the repository. In the case of GitHub, just selecting the user account and providing a repository name is enough:

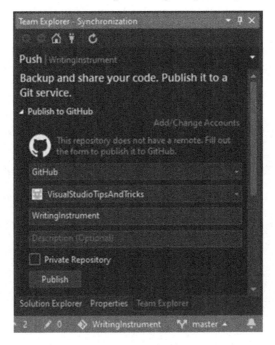

Figure 4.8 – Publish

One thing to note here: you can select **Private Repository** to make the repository private right away. Click the **Publish** button and you're in business!

For VS Code

In VS Code, we can control all of our repository actions from the **Source Control View** in the **Activity Bar**. We can initialize a local repository and later connect it to a provider (GitHub, Azure, and so on), or we can just publish it directly to GitHub:

1. Clicking the **Publish to GitHub** button gets us started. VS Code might prompt for credentials at this point – just enter your GitHub credentials and move on:

Figure 4.9 – VS Code repository actions

2. Next, VS Code will prompt you for a name for the repository. You can also choose to make the repository private by selecting the **Publish to GitHub private repository** button:

Figure 4.10 – VS Code name repository

3.   Next, you will be prompted to select the files you want in the repo. Remove and items such and the `bin` and `obj` folders, the `.VSCode` folder, and so on. When you remove these items, VS Code will automatically create a `.gitignore` file for you (explained later in this chapter). Click **OK** and VS Code will create your repository and commit your code!

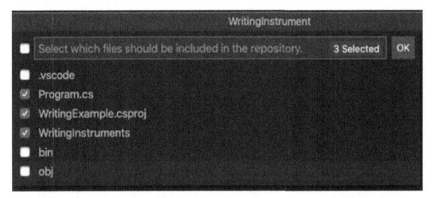

Figure 4.11 – VS Code select files

For Mac

It's just as simple using Visual Studio 2019 for Mac. Select the **Version Control** menu and then click **Publish in Version Control...**:

Figure 4.12 – Publish in Version Control

Visual Studio now shows the **Clone Repository** window. This is the window we use to define the connections to our repository. To add a new repository, all we have to do is click **Add** and fill in the details. Selecting **https** for **Protocol** and filling in **Path** is all we need to do to create our new repo:

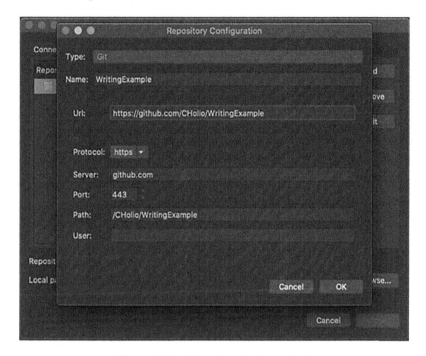

Figure 4.13 – Select from Registered tab

About the path

To create a project in GitHub, we need to enter the full path for the repository. This includes the username (in this case, CHolio) as well as the name for the new repository (WritingExample).

If you need to provide a user for this repository (that is, if you have multiple GitHub accounts), you can put the username in the **User** field.

Click **OK** and Visual Studio will add the repository definition to the list of repositories:

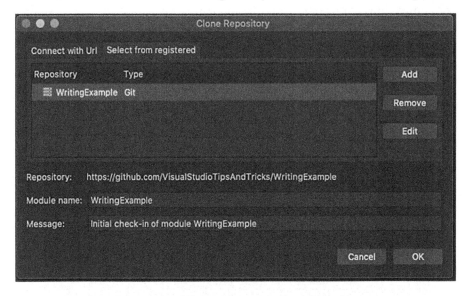

Figure 4.14 – Select new repository configuration

Select the new repository definition and click **OK**, and Visual Studio will create the repository for you.

> **Credentials**
>
> The repository provider may prompt you for credentials at this point. Enter the credentials for the provider and the creation will continue.
>
> Another way to authenticate to the repository is to use a **Personal Access Token (PAT)**. With Azure DevOps and GitHub, this is very useful so you don't have to give your account password out to third-party providers, and so on. You use the PAT, which is an alternate password, and if it becomes compromised or you want to revoke it, you can do so without impacting any of your other processes.

Cloning a repository

When you need to work with an existing repo, cloning is the way to go. You tell Visual Studio to clone a repository (or make a local copy and sync with the server) and it will copy all of the files from the source control server to your local machine. *This functionality is the equivalent of the* `git clone` *command.*

For Windows

Shown in the following screenshots, in post-16.8 versions of VS for Windows, the **Clone a repository** dialog replaces the **Connections** window in the **Team Explorer** tab of pre-16.8 versions. This can be accessed by hitting the green **Manage Connections** button at the top of the window. Click **Clone** and Visual Studio will prompt for the repository URL and a local location for saving the repository. Click the **Clone** button and Visual Studio will do all the work and we're ready to start coding!

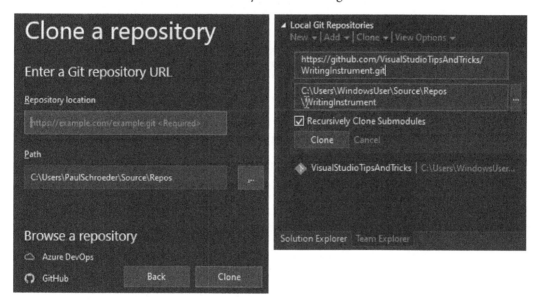

Figure 4.15 – Assign a location and clone the repo

For VS Code

It's just as easy in VS Code:

1. In the **SOURCE CONTROL** view, click the **Clone Repository** button:

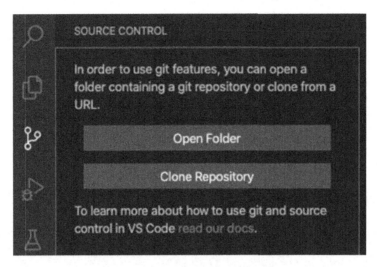

Figure 4.16 – Clone existing repository

2. This will bring up a selector window at the top, and we can either put in a URL to the repository or just hit **Clone from GitHub**:

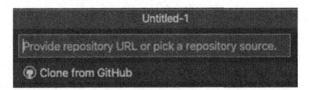

Figure 4.17 – Clone from GitHub

3. If we choose **Clone from GitHub**, we can search for the project name in GitHub by typing it in the box. VS Code will list the matching projects and we can just select the one we want:

Figure 4.18 – Search for a GitHub project name

4. Once the repository is cloned, VS Code will show a notification asking if we would like to open the cloned repository. We can either click on **Open** or **Open in New Window**, or just close and ignore the notification:

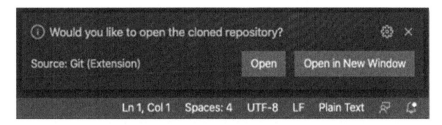

Figure 4.19 – Opening the cloned repository

For Mac

In Mac, it's a very similar process to creating a repo:

1. From the **Version Control** menu, select **Clone Repository…**:

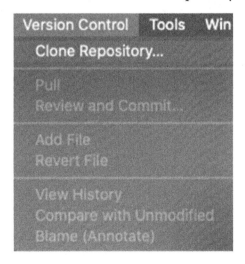

Figure 4.20 – Clone Repository – Mac

2. Visual Studio now shows the **Clone Repository** window. Just like when we created our repository, we can either select an existing connection or add a new one.

3. Select the appropriate **Repository** connection, set **Local path**, and hit the **Clone** button:

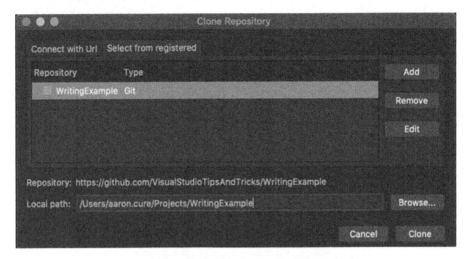

Figure 4.21 – Select repository and configure path

Getting updates (Fetch and Pull)

To get updates from a Git server, we need to pull updates. The fetch updates command works similarly and allows you to preview changes before merging them into the current branch of your local repo. These are very common actions and each is readily accessible from all of the Visual Studio products. *This functionality is the equivalent of the* git fetch *and* git pull *commands.*

For Windows

Shown in the following screenshots, in post-16.8 versions of VS for Windows, the pull icon in the **Git Changes** dialog replaces the **Sync | Pull** item in the **Team Explorer** home tab of pre-16.8 versions:

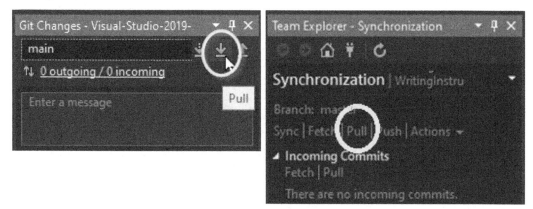

Figure 4.22 – Pulling changes

For VS Code

In Visual Studio Code, we can use the **Source Control** view. Click the **…** (ellipsis), and select **Pull**:

Figure 4.23 – VS Code Pull

For Mac

In Visual Studio 2019 for Mac, there is a context menu on the solution. Right-click on the solution, and then select **Version Control** and then **Pull**:

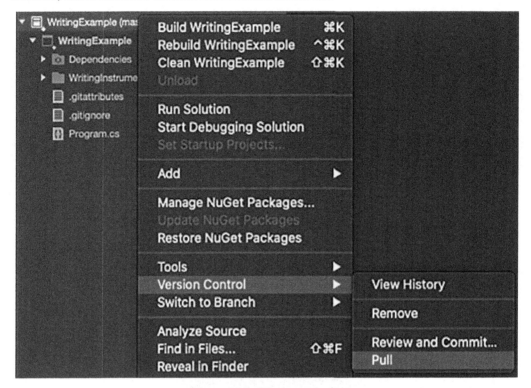

Figure 4.24 – Mac commands

We can also use the good old **Version Control** menu and select **Pull**:

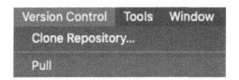

Figure 4.25 – Version Control | Pull – Mac

Adding files

Adding (staging) files to a Git repository is pretty straightforward. We just add the changes to the repository and then commit them. We'll split this into two separate actions since they often happen at different times. *This functionality is the equivalent of the* git add *command.*

> **Staging changes**
>
> We will not cover Git's staging area in detail, but it is useful for developers to know it is one of the *three trees* of Git (along with the working directory and commit history). It's roughly equivalent to TFS shelvesets, but can be a bit puzzling for developers who come from other version control products that do not have such a concept. In short, it can help to think of the staging area as a buffer between the working directory and the project history.
>
> One development technique is to make lots of changes to unrelated files but to be sure to break up those changes into stages prior to a permanent commit. By splitting related changes into smaller logical commits and making piece-by-piece commits, you help to create more atomic commits. This, in turn, makes it easier to track down bugs and revert changes, when necessary.

For Windows

If you are using the post-16.8 version of VS for Windows, newly added files should appear as shown in the following screenshot. Note the **A** character displayed in the lower-right corner, next to the Added Class.cs file. This indicates a commit will add the file to the repo, as opposed to **modified (M)** or **deleted (D)**.

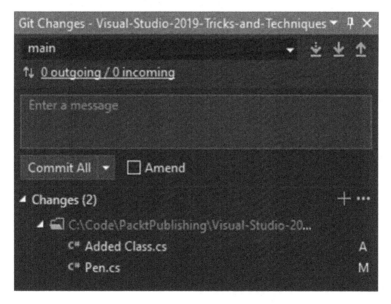

Figure 4.26 – Add file (Git Changes)

In pre-16.8 versions, equivalent functionality is accessible by selecting the **Changes** button in the **Team Explorer** home window. This will show a list of all of the changes we have made so far.

As mentioned, it is also possible to stage changes. Visual Studio does not require this intermediate step, however. If you make a commit when there are changes, but nothing has been staged, then Visual Studio assumes you want to commit all changes. The following screenshot depicts a changed file being staged. Here, you can right-click on a changed file and select **Stage**, or simply click on the + next to each of the changed files that you would like to stage. Clicking + next to the **Changes** header item will stage all changes. Using *Shift + click* or *Ctrl + click* to perform multi-select operations is also supported:

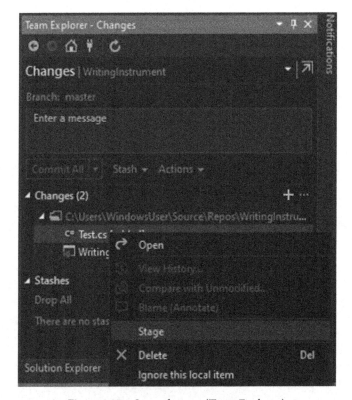

Figure 4.27 – Stage changes (Team Explorer)

For VS Code

In Visual Studio Code, we use the **Source Control** view. It will show files that have been **modified** (**M**), and new or **unstaged** (**U**) files as well as **deleted** (**D**). Hit + (plus) next to each of the items we want to stage to add them to the repository:

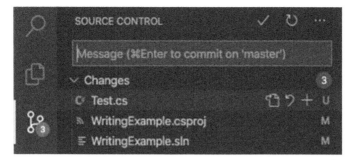

Figure 4.28 – Add to repository – VS Code

For Mac

In Mac, we can just right-click on the file and select **Version Control** and then **Add**:

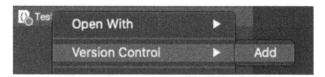

Figure 4.29 – Add to version control – Mac

Creating a .gitignore file

If you've used a Git repository before, you've probably seen a .gitignore file in there. This file is used to tell Git which files to ignore (you mean it's not just a clever name?) when it commits or suggests files that are untracked, changed, and so on:

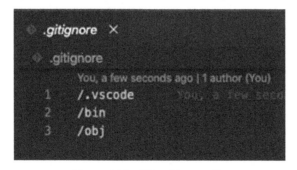

Figure 4.30 – The .gitignore file

You can also use this file to exclude files from the repository that contain sensitive information, or local files that should not be shared with others or placed in the repository. It's just a text file, and each line represents something to ignore. It can be either a file or a directory.

Committing (and pushing) your code

To add files to our repository so they are tracked, we need to create a **commit**. All committed changes are only kept in our disconnected local repository until we synchronize the changes with a remote repository using a `git push` command. Lucky for us, these are again very common actions, easily accessible from inside Visual Studio. *This functionality is the equivalent of the `git init` and `git push` commands.*

For Windows

Both pre- and post-16.8 versions of Visual Studio for Windows have similar steps for making a commit. Once items are staged, simply add a comment in the textbox near the top and hit the **Commit Staged** button:

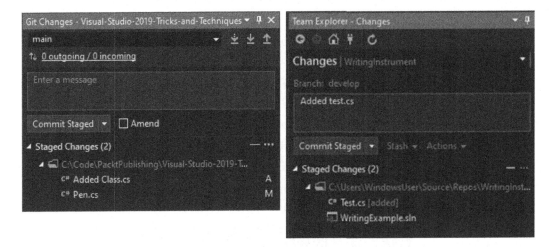

Figure 4.31 – Commit Staged

Next, we just go to the **Synchronization** window and select **Push** to send our commit to the server.

For VS Code

It's a very similar process for Visual Studio Code. We go to the **SOURCE CONTROL** view, and in the **Message** box, we add our commit message.

Next, we either press *Command + Enter* (*Ctrl + Enter*), or hit the check mark at the top to commit our changes:

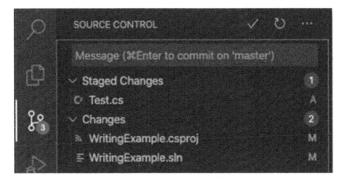

Figure 4.32 – Commit – VS Code

To push the changes to the server, we click the **…** (ellipsis) and select **Push**.

For Mac

In Mac, we can use our context menu to commit. Right-click on a solution item and select **Version Control** and then **Review and Commit…**:

Figure 4.33 – Version Control Review and Commit

There are times when we do not want to make a permanent commit in the repository. This is where a process known as **stash** is a good capability to know about.

Stashing (and applying) your code

There are a few scenarios where it makes sense to make a temporary, local copy of your changes. Sometimes you are in the middle of working on a feature and the following happens:

- Another priority comes up, requiring you to shift gears and quickly fix a bug.

- You have to review a pull request (covered near the end of this chapter) and need to check out a different branch.

- The code is working, but not quite the way you want it to and you want to do potentially risky refactoring.

In these scenarios, the stash function (`git stash`) can be a good option to use. This allows you to save the state of the code you are working on for now and look at the original branch, or switch to another branch, without any pending changes.

In the following screenshot, from Visual Studio 2019 for Windows, an optional message is entered to describe the stash and then either **Stash All** or **Stash All and Keep Staged** is clicked instead of **Commit Staged**:

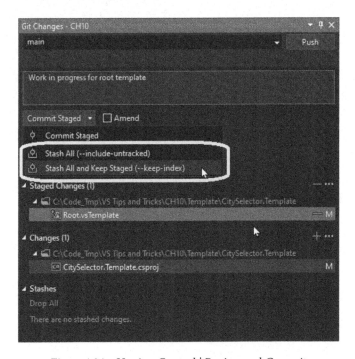

Figure 4.34 – Version Control | Review and Commit

The **Stash All** option creates a stash that contains all the uncommitted changes (like a local copy). This option also performs an undo of these changes in your local branch. This provides a clean slate if you want to work on something completely different. If, however, you want to continue working with those changes, then select the **Stash All and Keep Staged** option, instead. In the preceding example, this would maintain changes for the Root.vsTemplate file but not the CitySelector.Template.csproj file. Both, however, would be available in the new stash. Once you have made a stash, it will appear under the corresponding section in the **Git Changes** window:

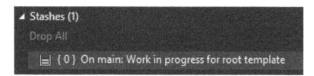

Figure 4.35 – Available stashes

The details of the stash can be seen by double-clicking on the stash to open the **Stash Details** view:

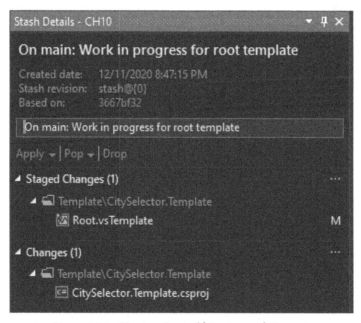

Figure 4.36 – Version Control | Review and Commit

Once you are ready to continue this unfinished work, use the **Apply** or **Pop** button to restore (merge) the files into your current branch. The difference between the two is that **Pop** will also **Drop** (delete) the stash unless there is a merge conflict. **Apply** will never drop the stash, even if there are no merge conflicts. Put another way, **Pop** is like doing both **Apply** and **Drop** in a single command.

Now that we've covered how to make permanent commits and temporary stashes of code, let's now explore some of the complexity that makes these concepts so important – branching.

Understanding branch and merge

There are multiple approaches development teams use to keep everyone contributing code to the source control repository synchronized. Some common approaches include **Feature Branching** (Branch and Merge), **Feature Flags** (Trunk development), and **GitFlow** (Release branching). Regardless of choice, each approach involves the basic premise that there must be a way to isolate sets of changes from one another. This is done by creating Git branches.

Branches are a construct used to keep changes out of the primary code base until they have been tested and are ready for production. If you are unfamiliar with branches, this resource may be helpful: `https://www.atlassian.com/git/tutorials/using-branches`.

So, when we make changes to the code, we **branch** the code (`git branch`) and make our changes. Our branch is like a copy of the main code base with our changes. We can update, add new features, or fix bugs on this branch, and then commit it to the repository server. Our changes are safe and versioned, but they are separate from the main code base. That said, if we push (`git push`) our changes to the remote server, other developers can also get a copy of the code in our branch (`git checkout`).

Once satisfied that changes in a given branch are complete, a developer can request to have that code merged and integrated into a more central, or root, branch by using a **pull request (PR)**. A PR is a formal request for review and to have our changes integrated with the main code base. Typically, another team member, such as a senior developer or release manager, will review the changes. If there are no merge conflicts and the functionality works as intended, the PR gets accepted by the reviewer. Once the PR is accepted and merged (`git merge`), the release branch will contain all of our changes and any other developers can pull (`git pull`) our changes. After review and integration, that feature branch can generally be deleted from the repository to keep the number of outstanding branches manageable.

Of course, this is a book about Visual Studio, so let's see how it manages the branch function.

Creating a branch

The process of creating a branch simply involves deciding upon a branch name and telling the tool to create a branch. Under the covers, some files are created to track the changes and register your branch with the server, but the developer does not need to be concerned with the technical happenings. If, however, you do want a more technical explanation, this link may be useful: https://git-scm.com/book/en/v2/Git-Branching-Branches-in-a-Nutshell.

For Windows

From the **Team Explorer** tab, selecting the **Branches** button takes us to the **Branches** tab. This tab allows us to view existing branches (including branches on the server created by other developers), as well as creating new branches of our own.

To create a new branch, select the **New Branch** button, give it a name, and Visual Studio will do the rest:

Figure 4.37 – Branches tab

For VS Code

To create a branch in Visual Studio Code, we use the Command Palette (*Ctrl + Shift + P* or *Command + Shift + P* on Mac):

1. Type git create branch and press *Enter*:

Figure 4.38 – Create branch

2. Type a name for the new branch and press *Enter*:

Figure 4.39 – Name branch

3. We can also create a branch (or check one out) from the **Source Control** view. All we have to do is hit the **...** (ellipsis) at the top and select the **Checkout to...** item:

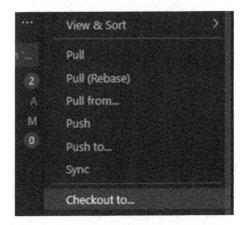

Figure 4.40 – Checkout to

4. A new command window will show up at the top, and we can create a new branch, or check out an existing one from the server:

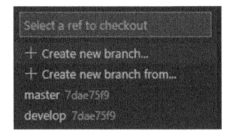

Figure 4.41 – Select branch

For Mac

In Visual Studio 2019 for Mac, we will use the **Git Repository Configuration** window. We can show this window by selecting **Manage Branches and Remotes** from the **Version Control** menu:

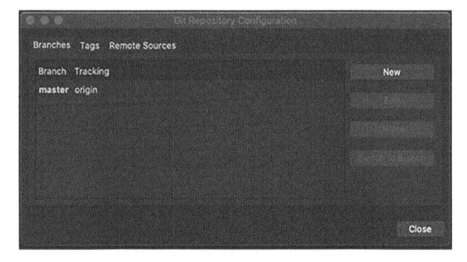

Figure 4.42 – Manage branches

You can select an existing branch from the list or click the **New** button and create a new branch. Once code is safely committed to a branch, it needs to be merged together with the main code using a pull request.

Working with pull requests

As mentioned earlier, pull requests, sometimes referred to as PRs or merge requests, are a formal request for someone to merge a set of changes (one or more commits) into a branch. Creating pull requests involves selecting a source and target branch to have code merged together in the target branch. Generally, this occurs from a feature branch in the main (or dev) branch, but the request can technically be between any two branches.

Pull requests provide a gating process that allows one or more different team members to put a fresh set of eyes on incoming code changes. Likewise, pull requests can be used to separate the roles of the developer from the release manager. Since outside processes such as continuous integration/continuous deployment are often tied to key branches, controlling who can commit code to them can be important.

In fact, many organizations remove commit rights to the main branch and only allow an admin or release manager to commit to them via a PR. Another common practice for enterprise teams is to require two people (other than the original developer) to approve each pull request. Typically, the two roles would comprise a senior developer and a member of the testing team.

Someone tasked with reviewing a PR examines the changes and adds comments. As shown in the following screenshot, a reviewer may even check out the branch to get a local copy. This makes it easier to ensure new code compiles, runs, and works as expected.

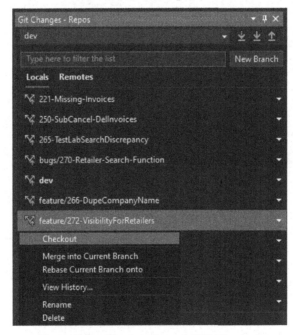

Figure 4.43 – Checkout branch (Git Changes)

Note that the development process workflow in some shops is simple enough that pull requests are not used. In these cases, users may simply use the **Merge into Current Branch** functionality, listed below the highlighted **Checkout** item in the preceding figure.

The reviewer may hold off on approving a PR until their comments receive satisfactory responses or associated code is refactored per the reviewer's findings. A reviewer also has the option of declining a pull request, which leaves code in the target branch unaffected. Once a PR has been approved, code from the source branch is merged into the target branch and it permanently becomes part of the target branch's code base.

> **Want to contribute to open source software projects?**
>
> Following the pull request process is how you can contribute to open source software projects. Contributing to open source projects can be a rewarding way to learn and gain experience. Every year, Microsoft and numerous other entities/developers maintain a myriad of code bases that accept countless community-driven pull requests.

Unfortunately, individual mechanisms to create pull requests can vary, depending on your remote repository provider and your flavor of Visual Studio. Also, the **Team Explorer** window in the pre-16.8 version of Visual Studio supports pull requests, whereas, as of this writing, the current version of the post-16.8 **Git Changes** window does not. Also, there are a number of Visual Studio extensions that support pull requests. For these reasons, and the already lengthy chapter content, we will conclude both this topic and the chapter!

Summary

In this chapter, we explained how the Visual Studio UI automates or simulates Git commands. A list of common commands was given that correspond to actions invoked through the Visual Studio UI. Two ways to start working with repositories, creating a new repository and cloning existing one, were discussed. Updating local code with remote commits using the pull operation was covered, as well as how to add new files to our local repository. Next, we saw how to create a list of files to ignore using a `.gitignore` file, and how to commit changes to the repository. Branching strategies were discussed, and how to create new branches was demonstrated. The chapter concluded with information about pull requests.

Whichever is your preferred flavor of Visual Studio, we hope you have gained a solid understanding of how to use the UI to perform necessary version control tasks for Git-based repositories. In the next chapter, we will discuss IntelliSense code snippets (or snippets for short) and how you can speed up your development by typing less code!

5
Working with Snippets

IntelliSense code snippets, or simply **snippets** for short, provide a way for developers to quickly insert customizable fragments of text (that is, code or comments) into project files. The use of snippets accelerates the creation of boilerplate code for things such as property creation, try/catch blocks, switch statements, and looping structures. Although snippets are usually designed for small needs such as adding a single property or method, they can also be used to insert entire classes.

In this chapter, we'll look at out-of-the-box snippets and then dissect a custom snippet. Once we demystify them, you will see how easy it is to make and import your own creations. We hope this chapter inspires you to think beyond the basics provided by default in Visual Studio.

In this chapter, you will learn how to do the following:

- Use the code snippets available out of the box
- Customize an existing code snippet to create a Web API method
- Leverage code snippet functions
- Create a surround-with code snippet that times code execution

> **Already familiar with snippets?**
>
> If you are not very familiar with snippets, then you will appreciate them as a new technique that you can immediately put to use. If, however, you already use snippets and have no desire to create your own custom snippets, then you may find this chapter boring. In that case, feel free to skim or skip this chapter.

Technical requirements

In this chapter, you are not necessarily required to use the code examples from this book. However, if you have not already, it would be a good idea to clone the repository for this book. The code for this chapter is available on GitHub at `https://github.com/PacktPublishing/Visual-Studio-2019-Tricks-and-Techniques/tree/main/`.

Please visit the following link to check the CiA videos: `http://bit.ly/3oxE5QM`.

> **Warning (P-callout style)**
>
> Please read the following if you receive an error while cloning the repository. Starting in Git 2.28, `git init` will look to the value of `init.defaultBranch` when creating the first branch in a new repository. If that value is unset, `init.defaultBranch` defaults to master. Because this repository uses main as its default branch, you may have to run the following code from a command prompt or Git Bash to avoid the error: `$ git config --global init.defaultBranch main`

Note, the reason for the preceding warning is detailed near the beginning of the next chapter.

> **VS Code and VS for Mac users**
>
> The content and exercises in this chapter use Visual Studio 2019 for Windows. VS Code and VS for Mac both provide functionality that is similar to what is covered here. Where there are differences, you are provided with convenient links that document the variance.

Snippet basics

At a basic level, snippets can be thought of as small blocks of reusable code. Typically, blocks of snippet code are inserted simply by typing an associated shortcut name such as `prop`, `foreach`, or `ctor` and then pressing *Tab* twice. Snippets are also accessible via a context menu command, but that approach is much slower and more cumbersome. To give this approach a try, simply right-click while editing a file:

Figure 5.1 – Accessing snippets from the context menu

Similarly, it is possible to use the *Ctrl + K + X* or *Ctrl + K + S* shortcuts to access available snippets. When you trigger this feature, an **Insert Snippet** or **Surround With** selection menu appears. Following this approach is also a good way to explore the list of snippets available for use:

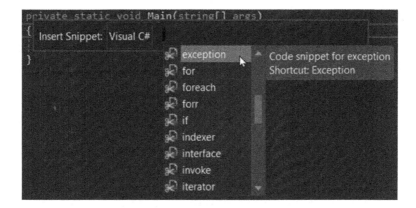

Figure 5.2 – List of available snippets

Both Visual Studio Code and Visual Studio for Mac also have snippet pickers as well as tabcompletion capability. Simply type a snippet prefix and available snippets will appear in IntelliSense as suggestions. Then, press *Tab* to insert the highlighted snippet in either of those IDEs.

Code snippets are designed to target a particular language, such as C#, Visual Basic, HTML, and so on. Visual Studio does its best to be context-sensitive and present only the snippets that are relevant based upon the type of file that is open and active (has the focus).

> **Separate your code**
>
> Certain files, such as **Razor Pages** allow developers to mix code blocks together with HTML. **Blazor app** templates do this by default for new projects using `@code` blocks. This practice of having variable declarations and methods embedded into what is essentially an HTML file tends to throw off the snippet options presented by IntelliSense. The separation of C# code into separate files (that is, files with `.cs` extensions) and the use of the `@inherits` directive fixes this issue.

Inserting snippets

In this section, we will look at an example where we will use Visual Studio 2019 to test a couple of common snippets. To follow along, locate and open the starting solution named `VSTT.Snippets.Cnsl.sln` found in the `\Start` folder for `Chapter 5`.

> **Moving forward**
>
> The sample project used in this chapter is kept rudimentary to make it easy to digest the concepts. This is priming you for *Section 2, Customizing Project Templates and Beyond*, which deals with larger project and item template concerns. Then, in *Section 3, Leveraging Extensions for the Win*, we kick it up a notch and incorporate custom code generation techniques. It is important to understand these fundamentals before graduating to those more complex topics.

It is recommended that you start with the Visual C# 2005 keyboard mapping scheme applied (**Tools | Options | Environment | Keyboard**), just to ensure the shortcuts described work properly:

1. Open the existing `ScratchPad.cs` class file if you are using the sample solution.

2. Make a new line after the `// Insert snippets here` comment inside the `ScratchPad` class and place your cursor there.

3. Press *Ctrl + K + X* in succession. If done properly, you should see a small **Insert Snippet** dialog appear.

4. Choose **Visual C#** from the options and then scroll down and select the **ctor** item:

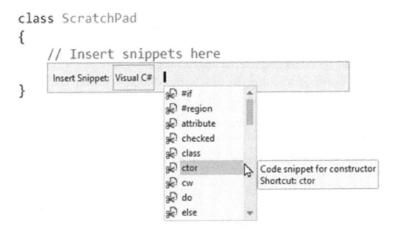

Figure 5.3 – Insert the ctor snippet

The code for a public constructor definition is now inserted.

5. With your cursor placed on a blank line within the constructor, simply type `fore` and press *Tab* twice. A `foreach` code block should be inserted:

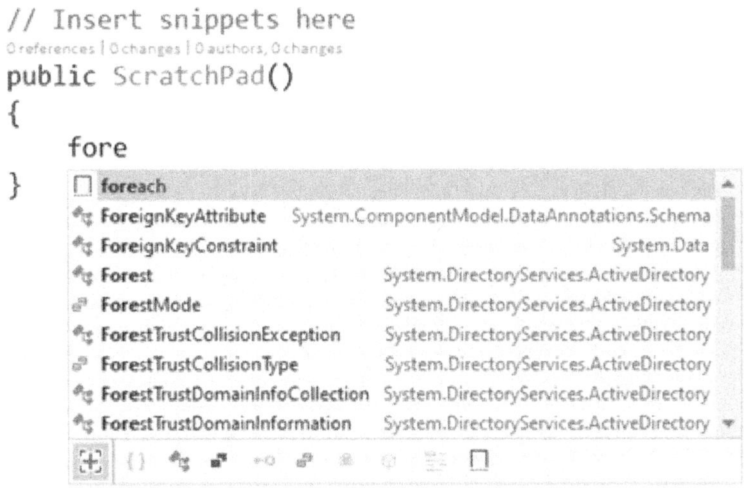

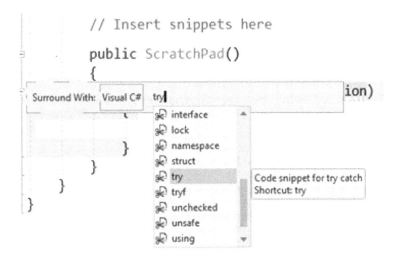

Figure 5.4 – Insert the foreach snippet

6. Highlight the entire `foreach` block (four lines of code) that gets inserted and press *Ctrl + K + S* in succession. The **Surround With** dialog should appear:

Figure 5.5 – Surround With try snippet

7. If necessary, again choose **Visual C#** from the options and then scroll down and select the **try** item. If you prefer look-ahead searches to scrolling, type `try` once you have selected Visual C# in the **Surround With** dialog to perform a lookup.

8. The `ScratchPad.cs` file content should now match the code shown in the following screenshot:

```
internal class ScratchPad
{
    // Insert snippets here
    public ScratchPad()
    {
        try
        {
            foreach (var item in collection)
            {

            }
        }
        catch (System.Exception)
        {
            throw;
        }
    }
}
```

Figure 5.6 – ScratchPad.cs completed

Congratulations – that is all it takes to use snippets! Often, you can just start typing and IntelliSense will present you with matching snippets. In other words, you do not even have to bother with pressing *Ctrl + K + X* (insert) or *Ctrl + K + S* (surround-with). By the way, did you notice the difference between the two? *Surround-with snippets are designed to take whatever code you have highlighted and include it somewhere in the middle of the snippet.*

To see a list of more snippets to experiment with, go to `https://docs.` `microsoft.com/en-us/visualstudio/ide/visual-csharp-code-` `snippets?view=vs-2019`.

A few frequently used snippets are the following:

- `prop`: This snippet creates an auto-implemented property declaration.
- `propfull`: This snippet creates a property declaration with `get` and `set` accessors.
- `enum`: This snippet creates an `enum` declaration.
- `switch`: This snippet creates a `switch` block.

Personally, I tend to use enumerated values as frequently as possible relative to constants or *magic strings*. That means I often find myself writing `switch` statements as well.

If you are feeling adventurous and using the sample solution, try this experiment, which uses the `EmployeeType` enumeration:

1. Place the cursor on a new line within the `foreach` loop created in the prior step. Start typing `swi` and press *Tab* twice to invoke the `switch` snippet.

2. Before doing anything else, replace the `switch_on` text with `EmployeeType`; the name of the enumeration we want to switch on. Then, press *Enter* to see how `case` statements are automatically generated for each value in the enumeration. I like to use this little time-saving trick at each opportunity.

3. Alternatively, you can accomplish the same thing by replacing the `switch_on` text with a variable of the enumeration type instead of the type itself. This is more aligned with the actual use of parameters and variables, as shown in the following screenshot:

```
var myEnum = EmployeeType.Contractor;
switch (myEnum)
{
    case EmployeeType.Volunteer:
        break;
    case EmployeeType.Unpaid_Intern:
        break;
    case EmployeeType.Hourly:
        break;
    case EmployeeType.Salaried:
        break;
    case EmployeeType.Contractor:
        break;
    default:
        break;
}
```

Figure 5.7 – Combined use of switch and enum snippets

At this point, you have seen enough to get the gist of how snippets can be used to quickly insert boilerplate code. In the next section, we introduce a tool used to identify available snippets, assign shortcuts to existing snippets, and even add or import new ones that you or other developers create.

Code Snippets Manager dialog

The **Code Snippets Manager** dialog is another way to view and manage the snippets that are available to you. To open the **Code Snippets Manager** window and browse through the available snippets, use the *Ctrl + K + Ctrl + B* shortcut or navigate through **Tools | Code Snippets Manager**. Choose a language from the drop-down menu at the top. I'm selecting CSharp in the screenshot shown here and expanding the Visual C# folder:

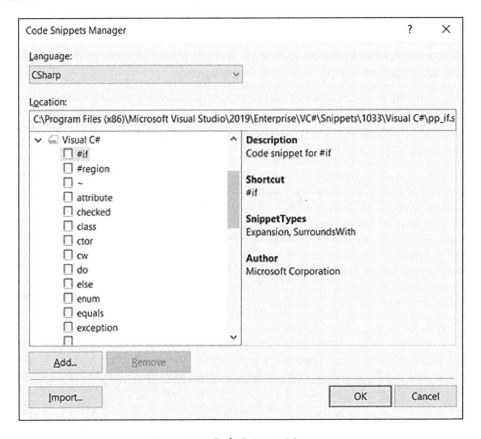

Figure 5.8 – Code Snippets Manager

Highlight a snippet to see its properties. In the preceding screenshot, an `#if` preprocessor directive is selected. Its properties tell us that this snippet can be invoked using the shortcut `#if`. It is also a `SurroundsWith` snippet, meaning the user can highlight existing code and the snippet definition includes content to insert both before and after the highlighted selection. In this case, an `#if` would be inserted before and an `#endif` inserted after.

> **What are preprocessor directives?**
>
> The above **#if** example is one of many available snippets. So, do not fret if you are not familiar with preprocessor directives as they are somewhat of a specialized construct. Conditional compilation symbols such as the `DEBUG` and `TRACE` constants may be more familiar and function similarly. Directives such as the `#if`, `#else`, `#endif`, and `#define` directives instruct the compiler to include or exclude code based on the existence of defined symbols. This can be useful to isolate code that should only run in a debug or only run in a production build. They can also be used to create build packages for very specific configurations.

What we are about to show is that you are in no way limited to only the available code snippets that come pre-packaged with Visual Studio. In fact, **IntelliSense code snippets** are just XML files that adhere to the IntelliSense Code Snippets XML schema. This means we can create our own either by copying and modifying an existing one or by making one from scratch. Looking back at the previous screenshot, notice that the location of the snippet definition file is displayed towards the top of the **Code Snippets Manager** dialog. If you ever want to know how a snippet works, use this to locate and open its definition file for examination. Instead of creating snippet definitions from scratch, you can customize an existing one, save it with a new name, and then import it as a different snippet if you like.

The **Code Snippets Manager** dialog allows an entire folder of snippets to be added all at once or snippet files to be imported individually. In more advanced scenarios, you can even download or create VSIX packages that install one or more snippets without even using this dialog.

Of course, before you can create snippets, you need to understand what they are made of, which is covered next.

Examining a custom snippet's XML definition

One thing that I like to do when creating new service methods is to understand how long they take to execute. There is a pattern I like to follow when doing this that involves the use of the `Stopwatch` class in the `System.Diagnostics` namespace. I do not want to have to remember implementation details and so we are going to capture them in a reusable snippet.

> **Note**
> If you are using a Web API, know that there are filters that allow code to run before or after each action method executes. That is not quite the same as the generic snippet that we will use for time-specific methods of interest on an ad hoc or as-needed basis.

In this example, we'll examine a snippet that makes use of several features, including the following:

- Variable substitution
- Using a function to obtain the class name
- Automatically adding `using` statements for required namespaces
- Placing the cursor after selected code in a `surrounds-with` snippet

Let's get started:

1. Open the `apitimer.snippet` file located at the root of this chapter's sample code using your favorite text editor. Note that this is not a file referenced by the `VSTT.Snippets.Cnsl` solution/project.

   Visual Studio Code works nicely for editing XML files, Visual Studio 2019 is also fine, and even Notepad would work. We are going to examine this file one XML element at a time.

2. To start, we have some boilerplate lines that define the XML document and open the `<CodeSnippets>` element with the appropriate XML namespace. This text is common across all snippets:

```
<?xml version="1.0" encoding="utf-8" ?>
<CodeSnippets xmlns="http://schemas.microsoft.com/
VisualStudio/2005/CodeSnippet">
    <CodeSnippet Format="1.0.0">
```

3. Next, the `<Header>` element includes child elements for `title`, `shortcut`, `description`, and `author`. Technically, only `title` is required, but it is recommended that you provide the others for completeness. As previously mentioned, the `<Shortcut>` element is particularly important for ease of use. The keyword you place here is what developers can type to have IntelliSense find the snippet:

```
<Header>
        <Title>API Method Timer</Title>
        <Shortcut>apitimer</Shortcut>
        <Description>Leverages System.Diagnostics.
            Stopwatch to log how long it took to execute a
            method.
        </Description>
        <Author>Paul Schroeder</Author>
        <SnippetTypes>
                <SnippetType>Expansion</SnippetType>
                <SnippetType>SurroundsWith</SnippetType>
        </SnippetTypes>
</Header>
```

> **Tip: Always define shortcuts**
>
> Although technically not required, you should always define a shortcut for your custom snippets. Snippets without defined shortcuts can be inserted by right-clicking in code to access the **Snippet** menu. However, doing so is clunky and thwarts our aims of speed and convenience.

Typically, the API method timer snippet we are looking at should be used in scenarios where the developer highlights a section of code to surround. This is because it contains content to insert both before and after user code. However, I see no reason to limit its use. Thus, both the `Expansion` (insert) and `SurroundsWith` snippet type elements are included in the definition.

> **Snippet types**
>
> There are two basic types of snippets:

- `SurroundsWith`: Here, the code snippet is placed around a selected piece of code.

- `Expansion`: Here, the code snippet gets inserted at the cursor.

4. `<Snippet>` is the next element to review, and here, we define variables that can be substituted into the code snippet. Let's take a moment to describe snippet variables, also known as tokens.

    Recall the `foreach` snippet used in a prior exercise. Its definition includes three declarations (that is, variables or tokens) that manifest into tokens the developer can freely replace when inserting the snippet into code. Such tokens might appear multiple times in the CDATA section, which will be described shortly. If a developer changes the value of one token, all other tokens matching that name are also updated with the new value. For example, the `$type$` token in the `foreach` snippet definition defaults to `var` and the developer is free to change it to something else, such as `int` when looping over a collection of integers. The same applies to the `$identifier$` and `$collection$` tokens shown in the following screenshot:

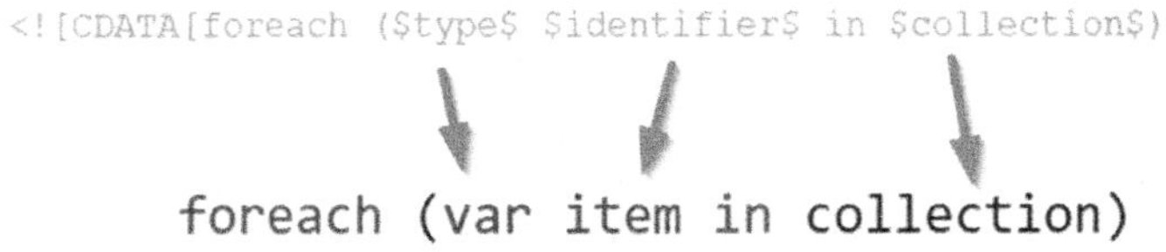

    Image 5.9 – Code result of foreach snippet declaration literals

5. Our `apitimer` example XML makes use of two variables, `sw` and `classname`. As you will soon see in the `<Code>` element, a snippet variable can be used to substitute a value into the text being inserted, one or many times. The `<ID>` value can be whatever makes sense for you to use as a replacement token and `<Default>` is the initial value presented to the developer for possible change. The following example will default the `sw` token to `stopwatch` and the developer using this snippet may choose to leave this variable name matching the default value or change it to something else such as, say, `myLittleTimer`:

```
<Snippet>
  <Declarations>
   <Literal>
   <ID>sw</ID>
   <Default>stopwatch</Default>
   <ToolTip>Variable name for the stopwatch object.
</ToolTip>
   </Literal>
   <Literal default="true" Editable="false">
   <ID>classname</ID>
   <ToolTip>Class name</ToolTip>
```

```
<Function>ClassName()</Function>
<Default>ClassNamePlaceholder</Default>
</Literal>
</Declarations>
```

The classname declaration in the preceding snippet is special because it makes use of one of a handful of functions available to snippet creators. As you will see in the <Code> element in the following snippet, this function is used to substitute the current class name into a logging statement.

Infrequently used <Object> declaration

Although snippets typically only use the <Literal> declaration element, it is worth mentioning that there is also an <Object> element that, according to the documentation *is used to identify an item that is required by the code snippet but is likely to be defined outside of the snippet itself.*

---

6. At last, the <Code> element we have been waiting to see! Whatever code we want to be inserted when our snippet gets evaluated gets placed in the CDATA section. The term **CDATA** means **Character Data**. In practical terms, this means the text gets read verbatim and will not be parsed by the XML parser. Do not worry about formatting or preserving spaces here. When Visual Studio inserts the character data, it will use the current developer settings to format the code. If the developer is using tabs, the snippet will be inserted with tabs. Likewise, if the developer is using spaces to format code, Visual Studio will insert the snippet using spaces.

7. There are a couple of special reserved keywords to discuss here. First, the $selected$ reserved token is used to indicate where existing code that the user has highlighted should be preserved. Recall in a prior exercise that we selected the foreach loop code prior to invoking the try snippet. You may have observed that the foreach code was preserved in the middle of the try block that we inserted. Second, notice the end reserved token is used in our sample. This is used to mark the location where Visual Studio will place the cursor after the code snippet is inserted:

```
<Code Language="csharp">
    <![CDATA[var $sw$ = Stopwatch.StartNew();
$selected$
$end$
$sw$.Stop();
```

```
    Log.LogInformation($$"Executed {nameof($classname$)}.
    {MethodBase.GetCurrentMethod().Name} in {($sw$.Elapsed.
    TotalMilliseconds)} Milliseconds");
        ]]>
    </Code>
```

8. Finally, we can wrap up this snippet XML definition with the <Imports> element. This optional element is used to ensure that any namespaces required by the snippet are available as using statements at the top of the file. In our example, we need to have using statements for System.Diagnostics to get access to the Stopwatch class. We need System.Reflection for the call to MethodBase. GetCurrentMethod(). Lastly, we are using Microsoft.Extensions. Logging to gain access to the LogInformation extension method:

```
<Imports>
    <Import>
        <Namespace>System.Diagnostics</Namespace>
    </Import>
    <Import>
        <Namespace>System.Reflection</Namespace>
    </Import>
    <Import>
        <Namespace>Microsoft.Extensions.Logging</Namespace>
    </Import>
</Imports>
```

Whew, that was a lot to digest, but now you understand all the key sections that comprise snippet definition files! The mystery has been unraveled; it really is straightforward, and you should feel comfortable crafting your own custom snippets.

> **More information for other IDE flavors**
>
> For more information on creating custom snippets for VS Code, start with this link: https://code.visualstudio.com/docs/editor/userdefinedsnippets.
>
> Likewise, to learn more about crafting VS Mac snippets, start with this link: https://docs.microsoft.com/en-us/visualstudio/mac/snippets?view=vsmac-2019.

Next, let's see how we can incorporate our custom snippet for use in everyday development.

Deploying snippets

In this section, you will learn how to deploy and use the snippet we examined in the previous example. As previously mentioned, one option is to import code snippets using the Code Snippets Manager. A non-standard approach is to simply copy one or more snippet files directly into a subfolder of your `Documents\Visual Studio 2019\Code Snippets` directory. If you have a lot of great snippets to share broadly, it is also possible to bundle snippet files into a Visual Studio extension (VSIX file) for easy distribution and installation. That is a bit beyond the scope of this chapter, but instructions on how to do so can be found at `https://docs.microsoft.com/en-us/visualstudio/ide/how-to-distribute-code-snippets?view=vs-2019`.

Importing a custom snippet

In this example, we are going to import the snippet we examined in the previous example. You will then be able to easily use it in other projects to time how long it takes to execute code within a method. Let's begin:

1. Open the **Code Snippets Manager** dialog using the *Ctrl + K, Ctrl + B* shortcut or using **Tools | Code Snippets Manager**:

2. Click the **Import** button, navigate to the `apitimer.snippet` file located at the root of this chapter's sample code, and select it:

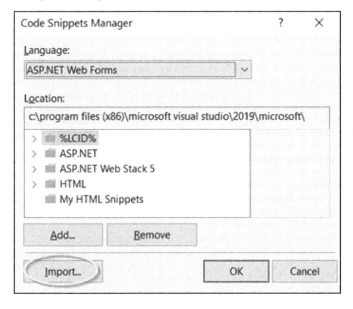

Figure 5.10 – Importing a snippet

3. Choose an import folder location – typically, the `My Code Snippets` folder works nicely.

4. Click the **Finish** button and then **OK** to close the dialog.

5. Return to the Highlight the `ScratchPad.cs` file used previously. Select/highlight the entire `foreach` loop code used in earlier examples, including the `switch` statement if you added it. Press *Ctrl + K + S* in succession to open the **Surround With** dialog.

6. Select **My Snippets | API Method Timer** or simply type `api` after selecting **My Snippets** and press *Enter*.

7. Notice that the variable name `stopwatch` is selected. You can choose to change the name or leave it as is. Press *Enter* a second time and notice that our cursor moves to the line just above the `stopwatch.Stop();` code. This is because we placed our `$end$` reserved keyword token here in the snippet's XML definition.

Although we named our example snippet `apitimer`, it can really be used in any method where we want to record execution times. At this point, you may choose to go back and customize this snippet for your own use. Besides the name and shortcut, another possible modification might be to adjust the use of the `Log` property, which currently will not compile in our `ScratchPad.cs` file.

The project won't compile

It is intentional that our end solution does not compile as it is purely a teaching sample. If this bothers you, alter the snippet to use `System.Console.WriteLine` in place of `Log.Information` and then that line will compile. To get the project itself to compile, you may also have to define a collection of something to iterate over in the `foreach` loop and ensure a variable is used in the `switch` statement, such as `var myEnum = EmployeeType.Contractor; switch (myEnum)`....

That covers what you need to know about snippets, a useful feature that has been around a long time.

Summary

In this chapter, you learned how to use snippets that come pre-installed with Visual Studio and how to manage them with the **Code Snippets Manager** dialog. We also detailed the special keywords and different XML elements and that make up a snippet file's definition. Finally, you were able to import a custom snippet and put it to use in a sample project.

Sharing and using snippets is one technique developer teams can use to make it easier to standardize common internal practices. Moreover, code snippets simply make you a more efficient developer; knowing how they work makes you more proficient, and knowing how to craft your own is even better!

In the next chapter, we are going to add another tool to your utility belt when we examine database explorers. This handy bit of functionality is available right within the Visual Studio IDE without the need to use separate tools, unless you prefer that approach, of course.

Further reading

- If you want to check out snippets other people have created that you can import, here is a link to get you started on Visual Studio 2019 for Windows: `https://marketplace.visualstudio.com/search?term=snippet&target=VS`

- For VS Code: `https://marketplace.visualstudio.com/search?term=snippet&target=VSCode`

- VS for Mac as well as the others: `https://www.benday.com/2019/06/20/code-snippets-for-visual-studio-visual-studio-code-and-visual-studio-for-mac/`

6
Database Explorers

As developers, we frequently connect to backend databases to store values and data from the application. Being able to inspect the database, view data, and make changes to it directly in Visual Studio is very helpful and a huge timesaver over opening a client, connecting to the database, and so on.

In this chapter, we will discuss database explorers for **Visual Studio 2019 for Windows** and **Visual Studio Code (VS Code)**.

> **What about Mac?**
>
> Currently, there is no database explorer solution for Visual Studio 2019 for Mac. Hopefully, there will be something in an upcoming release, but for now, Microsoft recommends using the *Azure Data Studio* client on macOS.

In this chapter, we will discuss the following topics:

- Managing databases in Visual Studio 2019 for Windows
- Interacting with databases in VS Code

By the end of this chapter, you will be able to create a database, add tables and columns, and even add data to those tables!

Technical requirements

To run the VS Code exercises in this chapter on Linux or macOS, you will need to install Docker on your machine to host SQL Server. Docker can be downloaded for free from `https://www.docker.com`. If you have not done so already, it would be a good idea to clone the repository for this book. The code for this chapter is available on GitHub at: `https://github.com/PacktPublishing/Visual-Studio-2019-Tricks-and-Techniques/tree/main/`

Please visit the following link to check the CiA videos: `http://bit.ly/3oxE5QM`.

Managing databases in Visual Studio 2019 for Windows

The Windows offering is by far the most impressive out-of-the-box, as it includes **SQL Server Data Tools (SSDT)**. This is a pretty full-featured database explorer for SQL Server, with many of the features that a typical development task requires. There are also options for other databases, such as SQLite and MySQL, provided by third-party add-ins.

SSDT has a number of things that can be useful to us, such as Azure SQL Database and Azure SQL Data Warehouse database management. Let's talk about one of the most commonly used tools, SQL Server Object Explorer.

Working with SQL Server Object Explorer

SQL Server Object Explorer is the primary interface to the database from within Visual Studio 2019 for Windows. From this window, we can create, manage, drop, or alter the database. We can manage table creation and deletion and even add data. Let's take a look at some of the capabilities.

If the **SQL Server Object Explorer** window isn't visible, you can show it by selecting **View | SQL Server Object Explorer**.

From the **SQL Server Object Explorer** window, we can add and drop databases; add, modify, and delete tables; and query and modify data. It's a full-featured database tool:

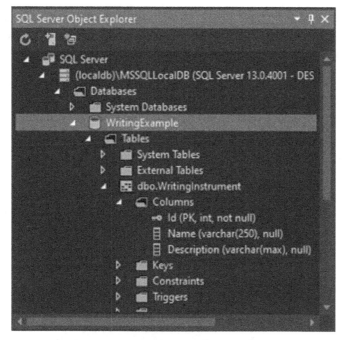

Figure 6.1 – SQL Server Object Explorer

Let's get started with our `WritingExample` project from earlier, and add a database to store some writing instruments:

1. Open the `WritingExample` project from the Chapter06 folder from the GitHub repository.

2. To create a new database, open `localdb` (or any other server connection) and right-click on **Databases**, and then select **Add New Database**:

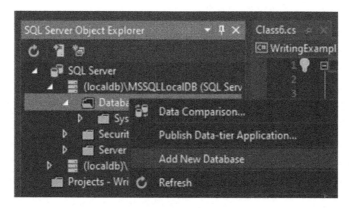

Figure 6.2 – Add New Database

3. Enter a name (`WritingExample`) for the database and click **OK**. That's it, we've successfully created a database! I will admit that it's not a really useful database at the moment, so we should add some more functionality to it.

4. We should add a table to contain our writing instruments. We will create fields in the database to hold **Name** and **Description**, as well as a primary key named `Id`. Expand the new database we created so that you can see the details, such as **Tables** and **Views**.

5. To add a new table, right-click on the **Tables** folder and select **Add New Table…**:

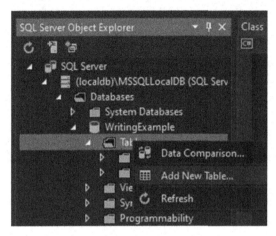

Figure 6.3 – Add New Table…

6. This will bring up the **Table Design** window, where we can add fields, constraints, foreign keys, triggers, and so on:

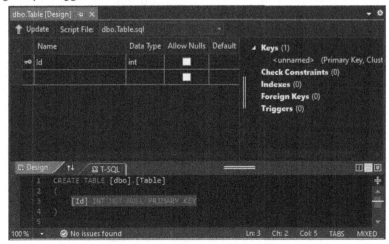

Figure 6.4 – Table Design window

7. Now, we can create the fields in our table, and give it a name. In the **T-SQL** window, add the following SQL (it's also in the dbo.WritingInstrument.sql file in the repository):

```
CREATE TABLE [dbo].[WritingInstrument] (
    [Id]          INT           NOT NULL IDENTITY,
    [Name]        VARCHAR (250) NOT NULL,
    [Description] VARCHAR (MAX) NULL,
    PRIMARY KEY CLUSTERED ([Id] ASC)
);
```

8. You can also create all of the fields in the **Design** window, so use whichever method you prefer.

    To set the [Id] field as an **identity** (automatically generated) column, right-click on it and select **Properties**. This will bring up the **Properties** window and you can select **Identity Specification** and set it to **True** as seen in the following screenshot:.

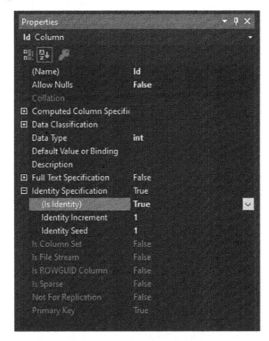

Figure 6.5 – Identity property

Once you are done adding fields, indexes, and so on, it's time to update the database. Click **Update** at the upper left of the **Table Design** window, then the **Update Database** button, and your table will be created.

9. Next, we will add some data to the table. In **SQL Server Object Explorer**, right-click on the writing instrument table and select **View Data** to show the **Data Visualizer** window. We can add our rows to the table by filling in any required fields (in this case, **Name**). Add rows for each of our classes: **Crayon**, **Pencil**, **Marker**, and **Pen**:

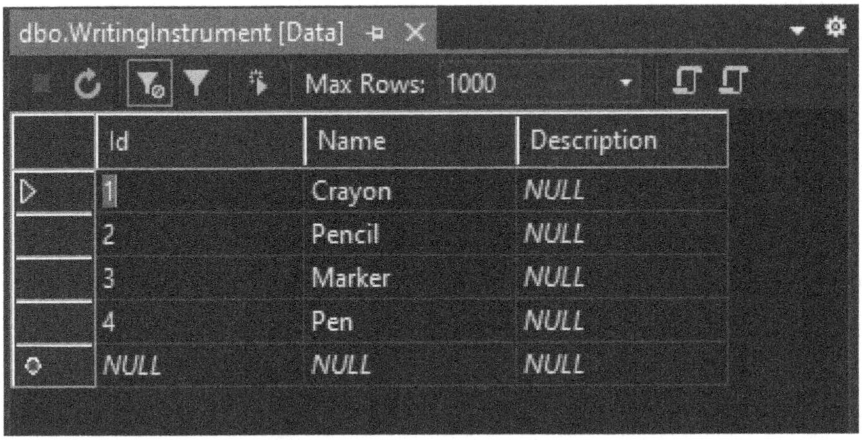

Figure 6.6 – View data

This exercise shows the power and ease of working with databases in Visual Studio 2019 for Windows. Using just the built-in tools, we can quickly define databases, tables, and columns, and even add data to those tables. Next, let's discuss managing databases in VS Code.

Interacting with databases in VS Code

While there is no built-in database manager for VS Code like there is in Visual Studio 2019 for Windows, Microsoft has published a very nice extension called SQL Server (`mssql`). For more information on installing this extension, refer to *Chapter 12, Overviewing VS Code Extensions*. The following screenshot shows the extension after it's installed:

Figure 6.7 – SQL Server (mssql) extension

Can you run SQL Server on Linux and Mac?

In a word, yes. You can run SQL Server on Linux or Mac in a Docker container. Once you have Docker running on your machine, run the following commands from the terminal:

```
sudo docker pull mcr.microsoft.com/mssql/
server:2019-latest
```

```
sudo docker run -d --name vstt -e 'ACCEPT_EULA=Y'
-e 'SA_PASSWORD=!mySuper_Secure_Password787' -p
1433:1433 mcr.microsoft.com/mssql/server:2019-
latest
```

Make sure you change the `--name` and `SA_PASSWORD` values to reasonable values according to your preferences.

If you would like SQL Server to automatically restart after reboots and restarts, add `--restart always` to your command string before the image name:

```
docker run -d --name vstt -e 'ACCEPT_EULA=Y' -e
'SA_PASSWORD=!mySuper_Secure_Password787' -p
1433:1433 --restart always mcr.microsoft.com/
mssql/server:2019-latest
```

Once you have the extension installed, you will get a new icon on the left side for **SQL SERVER**. Click on this icon and you will see a **CONNECTIONS** label with **+ Add Connection** below it, like the one in the following screenshot:

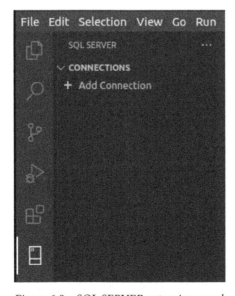

Figure 6.8 – SQL SERVER extension panel

> **Difference from Visual Studio 2019 for Windows**
>
> One thing you will notice right away if you have used Visual Studio 2019 for Windows' **SQL Server Object Explorer** is that there are no fun graphical windows to type things into. The VS Code experience is similar to the **Azure Data Studio** tool experience, if you have used that.

Let's use the newly installed extension to create a new database and add some data to it. But first, we need to create a connection to the database server.

Getting connected

Before we can do anything useful with the extension, we will need to create a connection to SQL Server. If you are running VS Code in Windows, you can connect to LocalDB. If you are running on Mac or Linux, you can connect to the Docker database server we created earlier:

1. To get started, we need to click the **+ Add Connection** button. This will bring up the **Server name or ADO.NET connection string** window shown in the following screenshot:

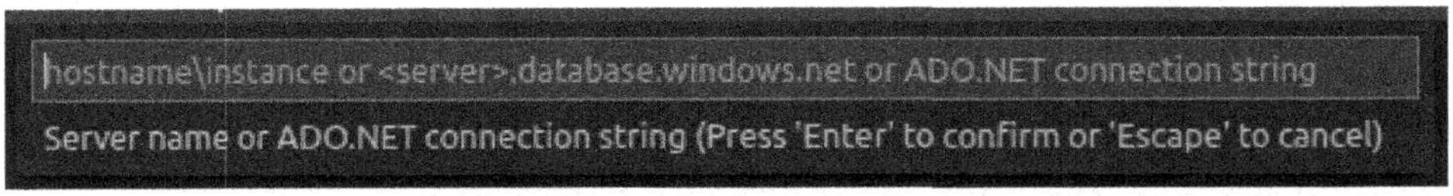

Figure 6.9 – Server name or ADO.NET connection string

2. Enter the server name to connect to your local database server. To connect to **LocalDB** on Windows, use `(localdb)\MSSQLLocalDB`. To connect to a local instance of SQL Server, or SQL Server on Docker, use `(local)`.

3. When it prompts you for a database name, leave it blank and hit *Enter* as we want to see all the databases on the server.

4. VS Code will next ask for an authentication type. We have three options here: **SQL Login**, **Integrated** (Windows Authentication), and **Azure Active Directory**. If you are on Windows and using LocalDB or a local SQL Server, the **Integrated** auth is the simplest to use. If you are hitting a Docker instance, use **SQL Login**:

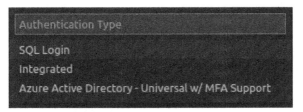

Figure 6.10 – Authentication types

5. If you selected **SQL Login**, you will need to now enter the username and password. If you are connecting to Docker, this will be `sa` and the `SA_PASSWORD` value you created when you launched the instance (`!mySuper_Secure_Password787`):

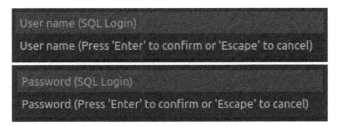

Figure 6.11 – SQL Login username and password

You will also be prompted to save the password. From a security standpoint, this is generally a bad idea, but you will have to make the decision for your individual situation:

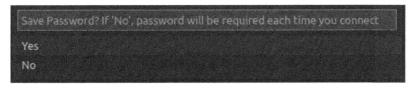

Figure 6.12 – SQL login save password

6. Finally, you will be prompted for a **profile name**. This is the name that will be displayed under the **CONNECTIONS** label in the extension panel. I generally enter something like `Local` or `LocalDB`:

Figure 6.13 – SQL profile name

7. You should now have a new connection under the **CONNECTIONS** label, and it should have a green light in the lower-right corner showing that it is connected:

Figure 6.14 – New connection

If it is not connected, expand it using the arrow on the left and click **Connect**:

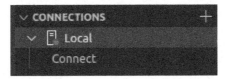

Figure 6.15 – Connect

Now that we have a database connection, we can create our database.

Creating our database

Let's start with our `WritingExample` project from earlier, and add a database to store some writing instruments:

1. Open the `WritingExample` project from the `Chapter06` folder from the GitHub repository.

2. To create a new database, we will have to create it using SQL. Right-click on the connection we created earlier (or any other server connection), and select **New Query**:

Figure 6.16 – New Query

3. VS Code will open a new window on the right with the title Untitled-1. The difference between this and any other window that we open is the addition of the **Execute Query** and **Cancel Query** buttons in the top-right corner. Enter the following SQL in the window and press the **Execute Query** button:

```
CREATE DATABASE WritingExample;
```

4. Once you press the **Execute Query** button, the window will split and you will see the results of your query on the right:

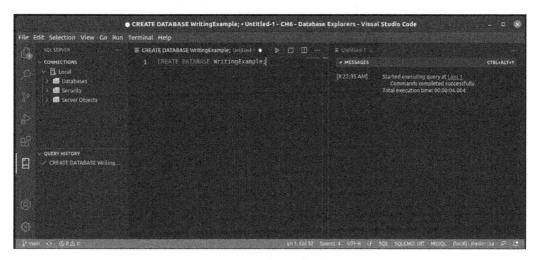

Figure 6.17 – Create database

That's it, we've successfully created a database! If you open the **Databases** folder in the **SQL SERVER** extension panel, you won't immediately see your new **WritingExample** database. Right-click on the **Databases** folder and click **Refresh** and you will see it:

Figure 6.18 – Databases folder contents

Now that we have created a database, if we expand it, we can see the tables, views, and other standard SQL Server database content.

Expanding the database

We should add some content to our new database to make it more useful. Let's start with a table to contain our writing instruments. We will create fields in the database to hold **Name** and **Description**, as well as a primary key named Id:

1. Right-click on the **WritingExample** database and click **New Query**:

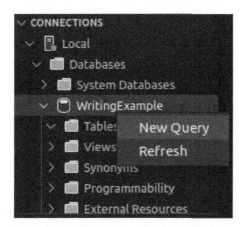

Figure 6.19 – New database query

Once again, we will get a new empty query window with **Execute Query** and **Cancel Query** buttons in the top-right corner.

2. Now we can create our table, with all the fields and primary key information. In the query window, add the following SQL (it's also in the dbo. WritingInstrument.sql file in the repository) and press the **Execute Query** button:

```
CREATE TABLE [dbo].[WritingInstrument] (
    [Id]          INT            NOT NULL IDENTITY,
    [Name]        VARCHAR (250)  NOT NULL,
    [Description] VARCHAR (MAX)  NULL,
    PRIMARY KEY CLUSTERED ([Id] ASC)
);
```

3. In the **SQL SERVER** extension panel, right-click on the **WritingExample** database, and click **Refresh** and you will see your new table. Expand it and you can see **Columns**, **Keys**, and so forth:

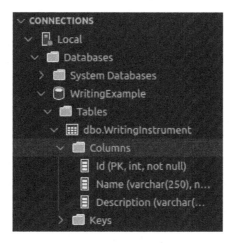

Figure 6.20 – WritingInstrument table

4. Now let's add some data to the table. We'll add a row for each of our
    `WritingInstrument` classes: `Crayon`, `Pencil`, `Marker`, and `Pen`. Right-click
    on the `WritingExample` database and click **New Query**. Enter the following SQL
    into the query window and press the **Execute Query** button:

```
USE WritingExample;
go
INSERT INTO WritingInstrument(Name)
VALUES ('Crayon'),
       ('Pencil'),
       ('Marker'),
       ('Pen');
```

5. Right-click on the **WritingInstrument** table and click **Select Top 1000**:

Figure 6.21 – Select Top 1000

You will see the rows you just added in a nice tabular display:

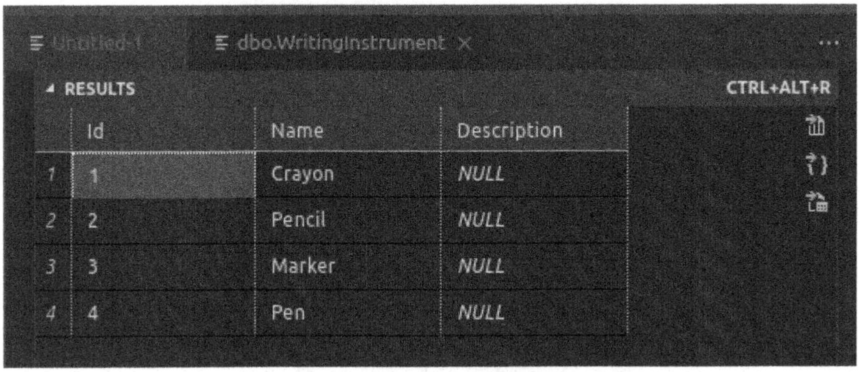

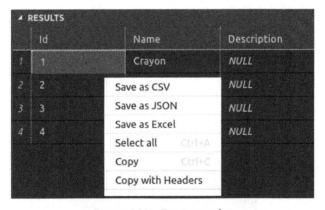

Figure 6.22 – Top 1000 rows

You can also edit the query and press the **Execute Query** button to filter or update your results.

6. Another great feature of this view is the ability to export results. Right-click on the **RESULTS** view and you will be presented with the ability to save the results in various formats, including CSV, JSON, and Excel:

Figure 6.23 – Export results

Now that you have the tools, you're ready to tackle any database project you come across!

Summary

In this chapter, we discussed the creation of a database, a database table, and data rows in **SQL Server Object Explorer**. Having this functionality inside Visual Studio 2019 for Windows allows us to make quick design and data changes without leaving our development tools, saving time and energy.

We also accomplished the same tasks of creating a database and a database table and adding data rows using the **SQL Server** extension for VS Code. One of the best things this extension brings to us is the ability to run quick queries and view data in the database without having to launch another tool.

In the next chapter, we will discuss compiling, debugging (including remote debugging), and versioning.

7
Compiling, Debugging, and Versioning

It has been said that up to 80% of coding is debugging, and the other 20% is writing bugs! So, no matter how you look at it, we spend a lot of time either debugging our own code or assisting someone else to debug a difficult issue. At other times, we need to test different configurations and items or use distinct options for compilation. For debugging purposes, it is also helpful to make sure we have numbered versions so that we can identify various builds and ensure the correct version is in a particular environment.

In this chapter, we will discuss the various ways to set options, how to debug both locally and remotely, and the versioning of applications and libraries.

In this chapter, we will cover the following topics:

- Exploring compilation flags and options
- Investigating advanced debugging techniques
- Discovering application versioning

Technical requirements

In order to run the remote debugging exercises in this chapter, you will need to install Docker on your machine. Docker can be downloaded for free from `https://www`. `docker.com`. If you do not want to install Docker, then you can simply read through the advanced content in the *Remote debugging Docker in Visual Studio 2019* section of this chapter. However, containerized development has become pretty mainstream. If you are not familiar with Docker, consider using this chapter as a way to help you get started. For readers that do not have Docker installed already, detailed instructions are provided later on.

Additionally, the sample project in this chapter is primarily designed to target the use of VS Code. However, you can still use VS for Windows if you prefer. If you have not done so already, it would be a good idea to clone the repository for this book. The code for this chapter is available on GitHub at `https://github.com/PacktPublishing/Visual-Studio-2019-Tricks-and-Techniques/tree/main/`.

Please visit the following link to check the CiA videos: `http://bit.ly/3oxE5QM`.

> **Warning**
>
> Please read the following if you receive an error while cloning the repository. Starting in Git 2.28, `git init` will look to the value of `init.defaultBranch` when creating the first branch in a new repository. If that value is unset, `init.defaultBranch` defaults to `master`. Because this repository uses `main` as its default branch, you may have to run the following code from Command Prompt or Git Bash to avoid the error:
>
> **$ git config --global init.defaultBranch main**

Installing Docker

There can be a few gotchas related to installing Docker, and getting started can be intimidating for some developers. In this section, we will try to walk through some common errors and help you to work through them. If you do not plan on doing the advanced remote debugging exercise in this chapter, then you can skip this content. Otherwise, please follow these steps, and we will try to navigate through it together:

1. Navigate to `https://www.docker.com`.

2. Click on the **Get Started** button on the home page, and then click on the **Download for Windows** button near the **Docker Desktop** option. Downloads are available for both Windows and Mac.

3. For Windows, open the `Docker Desktop Installer.exe` file once the download completes. Now you must decide whether to use **Windows Subsystem for Linux 2 (WSL 2)** or not:

Figure 7.1 – Installing Docker Desktop

> **WSL 2**
>
> WSL 2 is architecturally different from the legacy version in that it is a full Linux kernel built by Microsoft. This has the benefit of allowing Linux containers to run natively without emulation, which enables users to leverage Linux workspaces and avoid having to maintain both Linux and Windows build scripts. For more information, please refer to `https://docs.docker.com/docker-for-windows/wsl/`.

To update to WSL 2, you must be running Windows 10 with these requirements:

- For x64 systems: Version 1903 or higher and Build 18362 or higher
- For ARM64 systems: Version 2004 or higher and Build 19041 or higher
- It is recommended that you use the Windows Update Assistant to update your version of Windows if you are running a version lower than 18362, which does not support WSL 2.

Click on the **OK** button once you have decided whether or not to keep the checkbox for **Install required Windows components for WSL 2** checked.

4. A **reboot** of the computer will be required once the installation completes.

5. If you did enable the WSL 2 backend, upon rebooting Windows, you may be greeted by the following **Docker Desktop** dialog:

Figure 7.2 – The WSL 2 installation is incomplete warning

6. If so, follow the link at https://aka.ms/wsl2kernel, and then *download and install the kernel update*. For x64 machines, the download is named wsl_update_x64.msi. If you have an ARM64 machine, then a separate download package is available.

7. Once the WSL update setup program completes, click on the **Restart** button on the **Docker Desktop – Install WSL 2 kernel update** dialog (please refer to the preceding screenshot). You may receive a **Docker is starting** notification:

Figure 7.3 – The WSL 2 backend is starting notification

8. Once Docker starts, feel free to either start or skip the **Get started with Docker** tutorial that pops up in the Docker dialog when it appears. You're done!

Exploring compilation flags and options

Controlling the compiler allows us to decide how the build works, and to make decisions about the output and compilation flow. All of the Visual Studio flavors have options to do advanced compilations. This ranges from adding conditional compilation symbols and constants all the way to setting target platforms that overrides default compilation options.

Visual Studio 2019 for Windows

In Visual Studio 2019, we can set compilation properties in the **Build** tab of the **Project Designer** (navigate to **View | Property Pages**, or right-click on the project and select **Properties**). The following screenshot shows the part of the **Build** tab in **Property Pages** and some associated compile options:

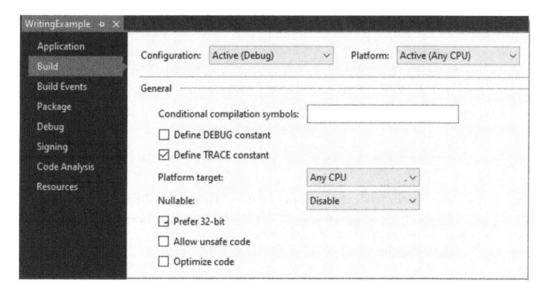

Figure 7.4 – The Visual Studio Build tab

Advanced compilation in Visual Basic.NET

In Visual Basic, the compilation settings are contained in the **Compile** page of the **Project Designer**. Pre- and post-build events can also be set on this page.

Visual Studio Code

In VS Code, compilation options are still available, but we must set them manually. These compilation options live in the **Build** task section of the `tasks.json` file. The sample code for this chapter contains a project named `remotedebug`. If you open that project, and then open the `tasks.json` file inside the `.VS Code` folder, this is what you will see:

```
"version": "2.0.0",
  "tasks": [
    {
      "label": "build",
      "command": "dotnet",
      "type": "process",
      "args": [
        "build",
        "${workspaceFolder}/remotedebug.csproj",
        "/property:GenerateFullPaths=true",
        "/consoleloggerparameters:NoSummary"
      ],
      "problemMatcher": "$msCompile"
    },
```

Note that in the preceding code the compiler property, **GenerateFullPaths**, has its value set to true, and the console logger parameter is set to `NoSummary`. Any compile options we need to add can be set in this file and will run on each compilation. This is where compilation options live for VS Code, but what about VS for Mac?

Visual Studio 2019 for Mac

On the Mac, compilation options are contained in the **Build** section of the **Project Options** window. You can view this window by right-clicking on the project and selecting **Options** or using **Project | <projectname> Options**:

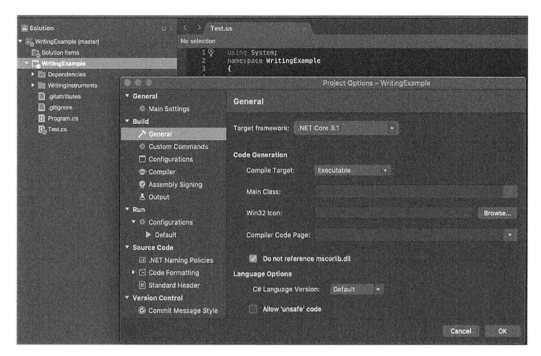

Figure 7.5 – Visual Studio Mac Project Options

The preceding screenshot shows the options available for compilation in Visual Studio 2019 for Mac using the `WritingExample` project from *Chapter 3, IDE Tips and Tricks*.

Conditional compilation

Preprocessor directives in C# can be used in various scenarios to turn on or off sections of code. You might use this technique, for example, to include or exclude features from different versions of an application (for instance, a trial version versus a full-featured version). Or, in a Xamarin mobile application, you might have a shared code file that uses `IPHONE` or `ANDROID` symbols to determine which block of code to run. However, one of the most common compilation options you will use is the `DEBUG` constant.

You may not realize it, but when you compile using the **Debug** profile, the IDE automatically sets this constant for us, and we can use it in our code to make compilation decisions. Note that a symbol can be defined either with the `#define` directive at the top of a source file or with the `-define` compiler option. Let's look at how we can use this to control our build.

In the next code example, you will see that we have wrapped a simple `Console.Writeline()` statement in an `#if DEBUG` preprocessor directive. This instructs the compiler to include the `Console.Writeline()` call in the compilation only if the `DEBUG` constant is set. If we are compiling using the **Release** profile, the compiler will skip the call. That is unless we enable the checkbox next to **Define DEBUG constant** in the **Build** tab of the project properties (which would not make sense):

```
#if DEBUG
                Console.WriteLine("I'm Debugging!!!");
#endif
```

In addition to the `DEBUG` and `RELEASE` constants, the IDE adds additional constants for us to use, such as the IDE version, the OS version, the OS platform, and more. We can use these constants to do some pretty intricate stuff, as you can see here:

```
#if DEBUG
...
#elif RELEASE
..
#elif (!DEBUG && VC_V10)
...
#else
...
#endif
```

To learn how to use these directives, along with a list of predefined preprocessor symbols that represent different target frameworks, please refer to https://docs.microsoft.com/en-us/dotnet/csharp/language-reference/preprocessor-directives/preprocessor-if.

Sometimes, we want to use our own custom constants, in addition to the ones that the IDE defines. In this case, we can define them at the top of the code file (before any using namespace or other statements) using a `#define` call. Here, we define a constant called `MYCONSTANT` and use it in the code as follows:

```
#define MYCONSTANT
#if MYCONSTANT
...
#endif
```

Using conditional compilation, we can choose what code is included in each build, make decisions about how the code is built based on the OS it is being built on, and even make completely different compilations based on any combination of this target.

To make things a little more flexible, there is also an #undef directive. This should also appear at the top of a source file and, just like the #define directive, adjust any compilation options for the entire file. The #undef directive is the opposite of the #define directive and allows you to undefine a symbol. If you later use the undefined symbol as the expression in an #if directive, then that expression will always evaluate to false. Consider the example code shown in the following screenshot, which undefines the myCustom1 symbol:

```
#define myCustom1
#define myCustom2
#undef myCustom1

using System;
namespace versioning.core
{
        0 references | Aaron Cure, 82 days ago | 1 author, 1 change
        internal class Program
        {
                0 references | Aaron Cure, 82 days ago | 1 author, 1 change
                private static void Main(string[] args)
                {
#if myCustom1
                        Console.WriteLine("myCustom1 enabled");
#elif myCustom2
                        Console.WriteLine("myCustom2 enabled");
#elif myCustom3
                        Console.WriteLine("myCustom3 enabled");
#endif

#if myCustom1
                        Console.WriteLine("myCustom1 again!");
#else
                        Console.WriteLine("myCustom1 is not enabled");
#endif
                }
        }
}
```

Figure 7.6 – Using the #undef directive

The preceding code example demonstrates the use of the #elif (else if) and #else directives. As you may be able to tell from the editor's highlighting of enabled and disabled code, the preceding program will have the following output:

Figure 7.7 – Example of an undefined directive output

As you can imagine, this code can get out of hand pretty quickly as the compile options increase. Let's examine a way to organize your code to make it a little more readable, as well as add the ability to collapse it in the editor.

Regions

The #region block can be used to define blocks of code that can be expanded or collapsed using the outlining feature of the IDE. Regions are defined using the #region tag and are finalized with the #endregion tag.

In the following example, you will see that we are defining a region, called Conditional Output, that we can hide and show at will:

```
#region Conditional Output
#if DEBUG
Console.WriteLine("I'm Debugging!!!");
#endif
#endregion
```

To make it even clearer where things start and end, we can optionally add the name of our region to the #endregion tag, as follows:

```
#region Conditional Output
...
#endregion Conditional Output
```

Using regions, we can really make things easier to read, especially when we expand or collapse regions. Take a look at the expanded regions in the following screenshot, and just imagine if there were 200 lines, or so, of code in the region:

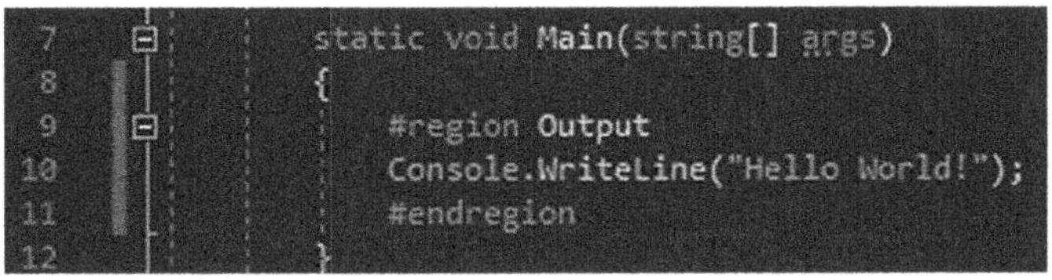

Figure 7.8 – The Visual Studio region – expanded

Now take a look at the same code after we have collapsed the region:

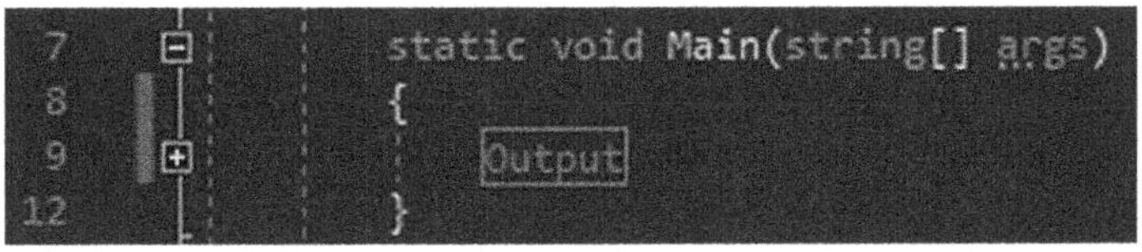

Figure 7.9 – The Visual Studio region – collapsed

The beautiful thing is that regions work identically in Visual Studio 2019 for Windows, Visual Studio 2019 for Mac, and even VS Code.

Are regions evil?

Beware that some developers really hate C# regions. When they were first introduced back in 2003, they really served a purpose. However, advancements in the Visual Studio IDE and developer standard of living since then have made them less relevant.

You see, there was no such thing as multiple 32" curved gaming monitors as standard issue for developers back in the day. Heck, I even recall a green and amber monochrome monitor! Anyway, the point is that you had one screen and it was much smaller. Also, at the time, Visual Studio did not have a way to collapse code blocks such as if structures, for loops, methods, classes, namespaces, and more. It did, however, have collapsible regions, and that was a welcome feature.

In short, try to use regions sparingly, and do not use them to hide large sections of code that should really be refactored into smaller pieces. A software metric known as **cyclomatic complexity** exists to provide a metric that indicates the complexity of a program. This concept is touched on in *Chapter 13, CodeMaid Is Your Friend*. For now, just know that if you find the need to incorporate regions inside of methods, then that is a code smell indicating your cyclomatic complexity for that method is high. In that case, you should probably refactor it into smaller, more manageable methods.

That was more than you needed to know about regions. Next, let's consider actions that you can trigger to happen before and after your code compiles.

Pre-build and post-build events

One of the compilation options we use frequently is the **pre-build** and **post-build** events, which can be accessed in the **Project Properties | Build Events** tab. These events execute immediately before, or after, the build. They give us the opportunity to run scripts before the build, such as generating transforms (please refer to the *Discovering Versioning* section), copying files, and other configuration tasks. The following screenshot depicts a **post-build** event, which is designed to execute only if the current configuration (for example, Debug or Release) is set to Publish. Although we could directly include many lines of code here, this event will, instead, launch a PowerShell script containing those lines of code. As you can imagine, this opens up a lot of possibilities:

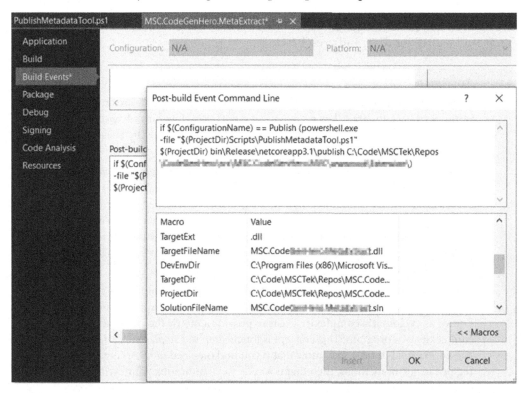

Figure 7.10 – Example post-build event

If you examine the preceding screenshot, you may notice that a few parameters get passed to the PowerShell script. Some of these, such as `ProjectDir`, come from the **macros** that are available for use by default. The bottom part of the screenshot shows a number of these available macros, such as `$(DevEnvDir)` and `$(ProjectDir)`. We can use these macros instead of hardcoding pathnames and other items to make the project more portable and the build more resilient. Additionally, as previously mentioned, the PowerShell script only runs if the build configuration is set to `Publish`. This is achieved by using the `$(ConfigurationName)` macro.

We will come back to using these tasks in the *Discovering versioning* section of this chapter.

Investigating advanced debugging

Becoming a skilled debugger can be the difference between fixing a bug in 5 minutes or 5 hours. Knowing how to step through code, inspect it at various points, and find that little copy and paste error you (or someone else!) injected is critical to being successful. Let's discuss a few strategies that you can use to be more successful.

Breakpoints

One of the most useful things you can use while debugging is a **breakpoint**.

To set a breakpoint, click on a line of code and hit *F9* (or click in the margin to the left of the line number), and a red dot will appear. When the debugger reaches this line, it will stop and wait for your next command. Notice the **breakpoint** on *line 14* in the following screenshot:

```
 9      static void Main(string[] args)
10      {
11          var assyVersion = Assembly.GetEntryAssembly().GetName()
12          var fvi = FileVersionInfo.GetVersionInfo(Assembly.GetEx
13          string fileVersion = fvi.FileVersion;
14          Console.WriteLine($"Assembly Version: {assyVersion}");
15          Console.WriteLine($"File Version: {fileVersion}");
```

Figure 7.11 – The VS Code breakpoint

An advanced version of this technique is the **conditional breakpoint**. Set a breakpoint, right-click on it, and then click on **Conditions** (in Visual Studio Code and Visual Studio 2019 for Mac, it's called **Edit Breakpoint**). This will present you with an editor to define the condition, or what must be satisfied for the breakpoint to be activated and the debugger to stop, as you can see in the following screenshot:

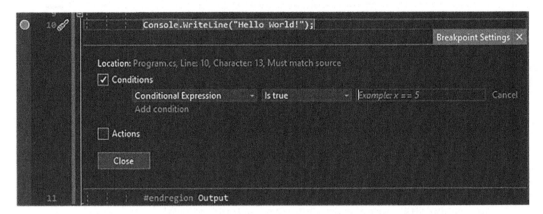

Figure 7.12 – The Visual Studio 2019 for Windows conditional breakpoint

If you enter `fileVersion.StartsWith("1.0")` as a value for the **Conditional Expression**, then that instructs the debugger to only stop when the `fileVersion` variable, set on line 13, contains a string starting with `1.0`, as shown in the following screenshot:

```
 9              static void Main(string[] args)
10              {
11                  var assyVersion = Assembly.GetEntryAssembly().GetName(
12                  var fvi = FileVersionInfo.GetVersionInfo(Assembly.GetE
13                  string fileVersion = fvi.FileVersion;
14                  Console.WriteLine($"Assembly Version: {assyVersion}");
    Expression  v   fileVersion.StartsWith("1.0")|
15                  Console.WriteLine($"File Version: {fileVersion}");
```

Figure 7.13 – The VS Code conditional breakpoint

This can be a very powerful way to stop the debugger in loops or in instances where a particular value or condition is making it difficult to troubleshoot.

> **Debugging extensions**
>
> If you really want to take debugging to the next level, then the Ozcode Visual Studio extension might be worth investigating. It has specific search and predictive capabilities for looping structures. An overview of this paid extension is given in ~~Chapter 16,~~ *Other Popular Productivity Extensions.*
> *the Appendix, p.329*

More powerful features that are worth examining include how Visual Studio helps us to quickly determine the value of variables, and even change them, while code is executing. How to do this is discussed next.

The Immediate window

Once the debugger has stopped on one of the breakpoints we have set, it is possible to inspect the value of variables in the **Immediate window**. For example, in the **Debug Console**, as shown in the following screenshot, while stopped at a debug point, we can type in `fileVersion` and hit **Enter**, and the current value of the `fileVersion` variable will be returned. We can also type in `fileVersion = "1.1.1.1"` and it will change the value of that variable. Similarly, entering a Boolean condition such as `fileVersion == "1.0.0.0"` will return `true` or `false`:

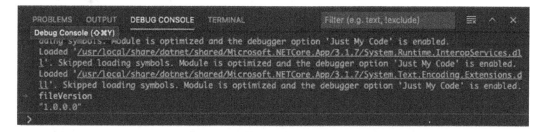

Figure 7.14 – The Immediate window

In addition to the **Immediate window**, we can use **watches** to inspect and interact with variables and objects.

Who's watching?

When the debugger is stopped at a breakpoint, we can hover over a variable and view its contents. This might be a simple string or a full object. Either way, we can inspect the value, its properties, child objects, and more. The following screenshot shows code stopped at a breakpoint. By using the mouse to hover over the `fileVersion` variable, its current value of **1.0.0.0** gets displayed as a tooltip:

```
static void Main(string[] args)
{
    var assyVersion = Assembly.GetEntryAssembly().GetName()
    var fvi = Fil "1.0.0.0"  o.GetVersionInfo(Assembly.GetEx
    string fileVersion = fvi.FileVersion;
    Console.WriteLine($"Assembly Version: {assyVersion}");
    Console.WriteLine($"File Version: {fileVersion}");

}
```

Figure 7.15 – Quick Watch for a simple variable

Sometimes, hovering over an item and viewing its value is not enough. Perhaps it's a complex object, with multiple child objects and children of those children. In this case, hovering over a variable will cause a chevron to appear along with the tooltip. You can click on the chevron to expand the properties of that variable. Alternatively, to open a **Quick Watch** dialog, use the *Shift + F9* keyboard shortcut, as shown here:

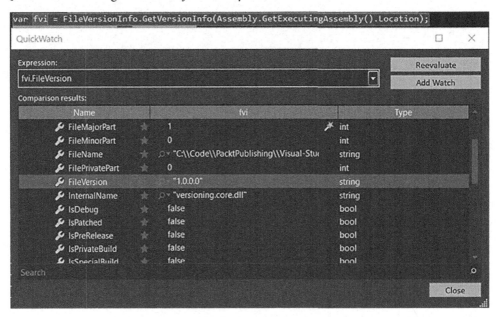

Figure 7.16 – Quick Watch for a complex object

Navigating to an item of interest in a popup over the course of multiple debugging attempts gets cumbersome. If only we could pin this object to a window somewhere, and see the updated value every time the debugger hits a breakpoint. This can be done by using the **Watch Window**.

There are two ways that we can add items to this window: by right-clicking on an item and hitting **Add Watch**, or in the **Watch Window**, we can type in a variable or object name in an empty row (in Visual Studio) or hit the + button and type in the variable or object name (in VS Code):

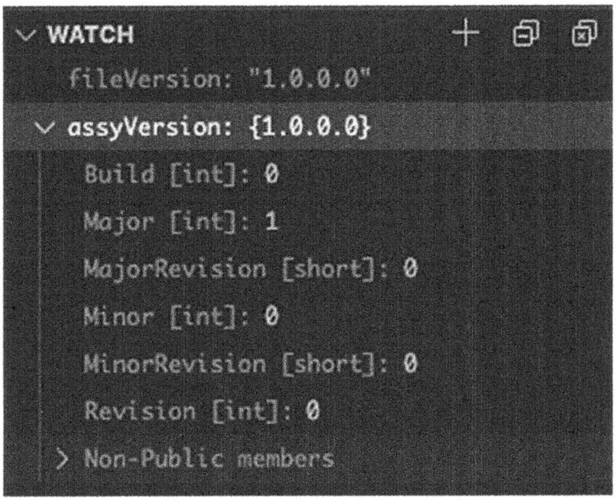

Figure 7.17 – Watching variables in VS Code

In the preceding screenshot, we added the `assyVersion` variable to the **Watch Window** and have expanded it to show all its properties. Next, we are going to go beyond our local machine and examine debugging code that is running elsewhere.

Remote debugging

Remote troubleshooting has always been a chore. You create a project locally, build it, deploy it, and it doesn't work. Add in the difficulty of developing on one OS and deploying to another, and suddenly, things get more challenging. Luckily, there is a solution!

The idea of remote debugging allows us to connect to a running application on another system and step through the code just as if it was running locally.

One very common task today is the use of containerized development using Docker, which deploys our application to isolated environments. Let's create a new project, add it to a Docker container, and remotely debug the project. We'll discuss this for each of the Visual Studio flavors.

> **Advanced topic alert**
>
> Getting Docker up and running does involve a bit of time and effort. As important as knowing how to use containers is, if this is not something you want to tackle right now, then feel free to just read along.

Remote debugging Docker in Visual Studio 2019 for Windows

Visual Studio 2019 for Windows has the ability to attach to a remote debugger (on another process or another machine). To do this, we will need to ensure that at least one of two workloads is enabled.

> **Enabling Docker in Visual Studio 2019 for Windows**
>
> You will need either the Web Development Azure Tools workload or the .NET Core cross-platform development workload. These can be installed using the Visual Studio Installer. One easy way to start the installer from within Visual Studio is via the **Tools | Get Tools and Features...** menu item.

In the following screenshot, you can see the selection of .NET Core cross-platform development workloads that we will use:

Figure 7.18 – The Visual Studio Installer workload

Let's create an application and a Docker container to house it, and then deploy it to our Docker server and remotely debug it:

1. Open Visual Studio and create a new `Console App (.NET Core)` project. Name the project whatever you like, perhaps `remotedebug`, set any desired project location, and then click on the **Create** button.

2. Right-click on the project file and select **Add**, as shown in the following screenshot. Then, select **Docker Support...**:

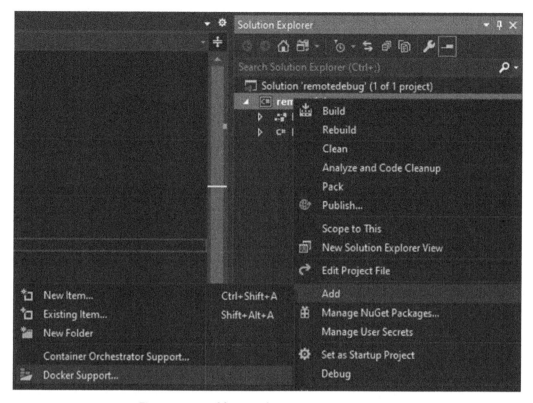

Figure 7.19 – Adding Docker Support… – Windows

3. When the **Docker File Options** prompt appears, select the target OS that you want to use. By default, Docker Desktop installs to use Linux containers. If, however, you would prefer to use Windows containers instead, please follow the instructions listed after *Step 15*:

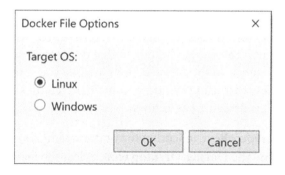

Figure 7.20 – Choosing Target OS

4. Visual Studio will create a `Dockerfile` file for your project.

5. Set a breakpoint on `Console.Writeline("Hello World!");` (line 9) of the `Program.cs` file.

6. Hit *F5* to start the debugger, which will download the .NET Core Docker image (if you don't already have it locally), build the application on the image, and then start the application with remote debugging enabled. Your breakpoint should be hit, stopping the debugger. Press *F10* or click on the **Step Over** debug icon *once* (don't close the program).

7. Open the Docker Desktop application and you should see your application running. In the following screenshot, a project, named `ConsoleApp1`, is being run in the container, and you can see the **Hello World!** output in the bottom-right corner:

Figure 7.21 – The Hello World console output

Congratulations! You have just remotely debugged an application running in a Docker container!

Using Windows containers

If you would like to switch between Windows and Linux containers, instructions on how to do so are provided for convenience. From the Docker Desktop menu, choose either Linux or Windows to have the Docker CLI talk to that daemon. Docker Desktop, by default, uses Linux containers, so these instructions assume you want to switch to using Windows containers. Note that using Windows containers requires enabling the Hyper-V Windows feature, which is described as follows:

1. Click on the **up-arrow chevron icon** in the bottom-right corner of your screen. Then, right-click on the **Docker Desktop icon**. Select the **Switch to Windows containers…** menu item:

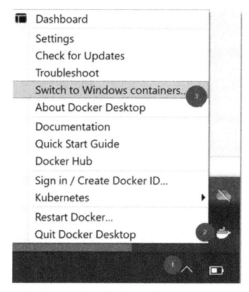

Figure 7.22 – Switch to Windows containers…

2. At this point, you may be prompted to confirm a warning dialog that says existing containers (if any) will continue to run, but you will not be able to manage them until switching back. Confirm the change by clicking on the **Switch** button:

Figure 7.23 – Existing containers warning

If you do not already have Hyper-V running on your machine, then you may see a second warning that an error has occurred. This means the next hurdle you have to jump over is to enable that Windows feature:

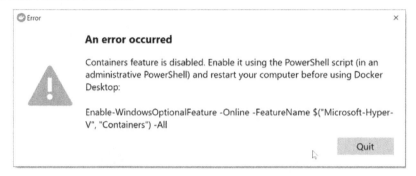

Figure 7.24 – Hyper-V not enabled warning

Here are the steps:

1. To enable Hyper-V, open a Windows PowerShell console in Administrator mode. Next, paste in and execute the following command:

    ```
    Enable-WindowsOptionalFeature -Online -FeatureName
    $("Microsoft-Hyper-V", "Containers") -All
    ```

    Note that this action requires a reboot of the computer:

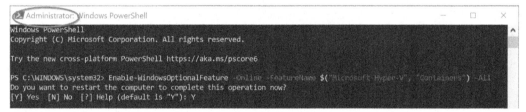

Figure 7.25 – Existing containers warning

Once Hyper-V is installed and you have rebooted, you will again have to repeat the same actions as *step 1*.

2. Click on the up-arrow chevron icon in the bottom-right corner of your screen, then right-click on the **Docker Desktop icon**. Select the **Switch to Windows containers…** menu item. This time, you should get a notification that reads: **Docker Desktop is switching…This may take some time**.

3. Return to the project created earlier, run it using the Windows container, and you should get the same result.

Let's examine how remote debugging works in VS Code.

What about remote debugging in VS Code?

VS Code has the ability to remotely debug projects, too. The steps are very similar to its Windows cousin.

In VS Code, you need to have the Docker extension installed. This extension is developed by Microsoft, and the current version (as of this writing) is shown in the following screenshot:

Figure 7.26 – Docker VS Code extension

Debugging Docker in Visual Studio Code on the Mac

If you are running this code on a Mac, you need to tell Docker where to find the .NET Core libraries. Open Docker and navigate to **Preferences | Resources | FILE SHARING**, and then add an exported directory link to `/usr/local/share/dotnet/sdk/NuGetFallbackFolder`.

The following screenshot shows the **Resources** tab of the **Preferences** window in Docker:

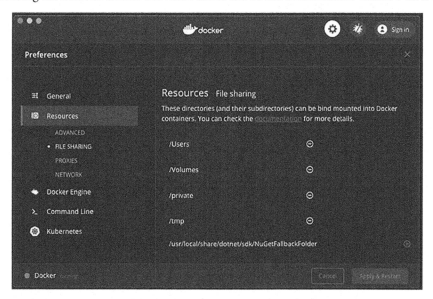

Figure 7.27 – The Docker add .NET Core path

Let's create our remote debugging project in Visual Studio Code and debug it remotely:

1. First, create a folder called `remotedebug`. Then, create a new .NET console project (`dotnet new console`) inside it.

2. Open the project in VS Code, wait for the **Required assets to build and debug are missing from…** notification, and then select **Yes**.

    If you do not get this popup (because you do not have the C# tools installed), you can run it via pressing *F1*, and then typing in `.NET Generate Assets for Build and Debug` after installing the C# tools.

3. Open the **Command Palette** (*Shift + Ctrl + P/Shift + Command + P*) and select **Docker: Add Docker Files to Workspace** to dockerize our app, as shown in the following screenshot:

Figure 7.28 – VS Code Add Docker Files

4. Select **.NET Core Console**.

5. Select **Linux** on Mac or Linux or **Windows** on a Windows box. Though, on Windows, you can run either Linux or Windows containers out of the box (please refer to the previous section).

6. When you are prompted with **Include optional Docker Compose files?**, select **No**.

7. Set a breakpoint on `Console.Writeline("Hello World!");` (line 9) of the `Program.cs` file.

8. *Ensure your debugger is set to use the Docker container.* Next, hit *F5* to start the debugger, which will download the .NET Core Docker image (if you don't already have it locally), build the application on the image, and then start the application with remote debugging enabled.

Visual Studio 2019 for Mac, too!

You can also remotely debug applications on a Mac using the full Visual Studio 2019 for Mac IDE. Once again, you will notice that the steps are very similar.

> **Enabling Docker in Visual Studio 2019 for Mac**
>
> You will also need either the Web Development Azure Tools workload or the .NET Core cross-platform development workload. These can be installed using the Visual Studio installer.

As you might have guessed, we're going to create our remote debugging project in Visual Studio 2019 for Mac, too:

1. When Visual Studio starts, create a new project, and then select **Console Application – Web and Console |App | General application**.

2. Select **.NET Core 3.1** as the **Target Framework**.

3. Name the project remotedebug, set any desired project properties, and then select **Create**.

4. Right-click on the project file, select **Add**, and then select **Docker Support**, as shown in the following screenshot:

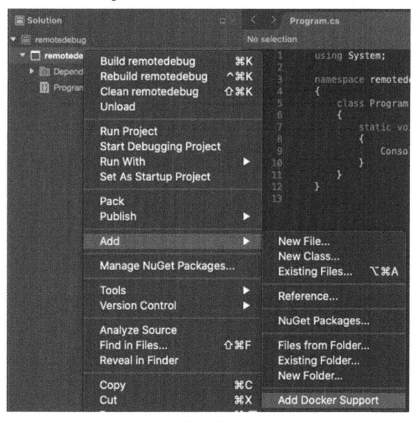

Figure 7.29 – Add Docker Support – Mac

5. Visual Studio will create a `Dockerfile` and a **docker-compose** project.

6. Set a breakpoint on `Console.Writeline("Hello World!");` (line 9) of the `Program.cs` file.

7. Hit *F5* to start the debugger, which will download the .NET Core Docker image (if you don't already have it locally), build the application on the image, and then start the application with remote debugging enabled.

Discovering versioning

One of the best ways in which to tell our various binary builds apart is to ensure that it has a unique version number. We can control this versioning in a number of ways, depending on the platform.

The version number has four parts, separated by dots. These parts are the **major version**, the **minor version**, the **build number**, and the **revision** parts, and they look like this:

```
<major version>.<minor version>.<build number>.<revision>
```

Let's look at how to control these in both the full framework and .NET Core projects.

Versioning in traditional full framework .NET projects

Let's start by creating a new full framework project in Visual Studio:

> **Time saver tip**
>
> If the following code is too much to type, there is a completed `Versioning.FullFramework.sln` solution available in the sample code for this chapter that contains the final solution. You can copy and paste code from there.

1. Create a **Console App (.NET Framework)** project and name it `versioning`. Remember, it is important that you *select the .NET Framework project template, as opposed to .NET Core*; otherwise, the later steps in this exercise will not work.

2. Open the `Program.cs` file, and add the following code in the `Main` method:

```
var assyVersion = Assembly.GetEntryAssembly()
    .GetName().Version;
var fvi = FileVersionInfo.GetVersionInfo(Assembly
    .GetExecutingAssembly().Location);
```

```
string fileVersion = fvi.FileVersion;
Console.WriteLine($"Assembly Version: {assyVersion}");
Console.WriteLine($"File Version: {fileVersion}");
Console.WriteLine("\nPress any key to exit.");
Console.ReadKey();
```

References required

You will need to add using statements for System.Diagnostics and System.Reflection.

---

3. Open the Properties\AssemblyInfo.cs file and find the [assembly:
    AssemblyVersion("1.0.0.0")] line. This line controls the version number
    and is what we will modify in order to change the version of our assembly.

AssemblyFileVersion

You may notice another property in the AssemblyInfo.cs file,
AssemblyFileVersion. This is used for deployment by setup programs
to mark assemblies that have the same AssemblyVersion property but are
generated from different builds.

---

4. Hit *F5* to start the debugger, and you will see the following output:

```
Assembly Version: 1.0.0.0
File Version: 1.0.0.0
```

We can control the build number by providing an (*) in place of an absolute
number, which makes the compiler change the build and revision numbers every
time you build. The actual method for generating these numbers varies based on the
version of Visual Studio and MSBuild that is used.

5. Update the Properties\AssemblyInfo.cs file, and change the line to read:
    [assembly: AssemblyVersion("1.0.*")].

6. Hit *F5* to start the debugger, and you will see a build error:

```
error CS8357: The specified version string contains
wildcards, which are not compatible with determinism.
Either remove wildcards from the version string, or
disable determinism for this compilation
```

While this error is cryptic and a little strange, the fix is really simple. Microsoft added a **Deterministic** compilation to ensure that builds are byte-to-byte identical if the inputs haven't changed.

7. To use our versioning strategy, all we have to do is open the `versioning.csproj` file and set the `Deterministic` compilation flag to `false`:

```
<Deterministic>false</Deterministic>
```

8. Hit *F5* to start the debugger, and you will see the following output:

```
Assembly Version: 1.0.XXX.XXX
File Version: 1.0.0.0
```

If you're like me, then you won't be too thrilled about disabling the **Deterministic** compilation just for versioning. Fear not; there is another way!

9. Update the `Properties\AssemblyInfo.cs` file and comment out the `AssemblyVersion` and `AssemblyFileVersion` lines:

```
//[assembly: AssemblyVersion("1.0.*")]
//[assembly: AssemblyFileVersion("1.0.0.0")]
```

10. Next, let's create a T4 template file to automatically increment our build numbers. Create a new file in the `Properties` folder, called `Assy.tt`. Alternatively, use the **Project | Add New** menu item and find and select the **Text Template** item. Note that you may get a security warning about running text template files. If so, you can click on the **Cancel** button for now.

11. Be sure to delete any code/text that Visual Studio adds by default to new T4 files so that we can start with an empty file before adding the following code.

12. Add the following code to the top of the new `Assy.tt` file, telling the compiler we will output a `.cs` file and that we will need to use `System.IO` and `System.Text.RegularExpressions`:

```
<#@ template debug="true" hostspecific="true"
    language="C#" #>
<#@ output extension=".cs" #>
<#@ import namespace="System.IO" #>
<#@ import namespace="System.Text.RegularExpressions" #>
```

13. Next, we will create the code that finds the `Assy.cs` file, then finds current `AssemblyVersion`, and splits it into groups to use as the parts of our version:

```
<#
   var incBuild = 0;
   var incRevision = 1;

try {
    var currentDirectory = Path.GetDirectoryName(
        Host.TemplateFile);
    var assemblyInfo = File.ReadAllText(
        Path.Combine(currentDirectory,"Assy.cs"));
    var pattern = new Regex("AssemblyVersion\\(\"\\
        d+\\.\\d+\\.(?<build>\\d+)\\.(?<revision>\\
        d+)\"\\)");
    var matches = pattern.Matches(assemblyInfo);
    build = Convert.ToInt32(matches[0].Groups["build"].
        Value) + incBuild;
    revision = Convert.ToInt32(matches[0].
        Groups["revision"].Value) + incRevision;
    }
    catch( Exception ) { }
#>
```

14. Next, we create the output text for our replacement `Assy.cs` file using the groups that we assigned to `build` and `revision` in the previous code sample:

```
using System.Reflection;

// Version information for an assembly consists of the
// following four values:
//    Major Version
//    Minor Version
//    Build Number
//    Revision
[assembly: AssemblyVersion("1.0.<#= this.build #>.<#=
    this.revision #>")]
[assembly: AssemblyFileVersion("1.0.<#= this.build #>.<#=
    this.revision #>")]
```

15. Finally, we initialize the variables that will hold the values of our build and revision numbers:

```
<#+
    int build = 0;
    int revision = 0;
#>
```

> **Note for the GitHub repository**
>
> If you are using the source code from the GitHub repository, you will need to uncomment the lines that contain `AssemblyVersion` and `AssemblyFileVersion` in the `Assy.tt` template.

16. In the project, add a **Pre-build** event to run the **TextTransform** tool on every build:

```
"$(DevEnvDir)\TextTransform.exe" -a
!!$(ConfigurationName)!1 "$(ProjectDir)Properties\Assy.
tt"
```

Note that the *preceding code must be contained on a single line* or you will get an error.

17. Hit *F5* to start the debugger, click on the **OK** button if you get a warning about running the template, and you should see the following output:

```
Assembly Version: 1.0.0.1
File Version: 1.0.0.1
```

> **Unable to locate Assy.tt**
>
> If you get an error message stating, **Unable to locate specified template file....\ Properties\Assy.tt**, please make sure you have placed the `Assy.tt` file inside the `Properties` folder. Otherwise, you will need to adjust the script for the location where you placed the `Assy.tt` file (for instance, the project root).

Now, every time you run a build, you will see the build number increment automatically. You have full control of the template code that generates the build numbers and can customize it any way you prefer! For example, if you wanted to change the major build number, you could alter lines 28 and 29 in the `Assy.tt` file:

```
[assembly: AssemblyVersion("1.0.<#= this.build #>.<#= this.
revision #>")]
[assembly: AssemblyFileVersion("1.0.<#= this.build #>.<#= this.
revision #>")]
```

Note that the script is currently written to keep the revision numbers of both the `AssemblyVersion` and `AssemblyFileVersion` values in sync. You could change this behavior, too, if desired. Next, let's explore how we can do something similar with .NET Core.

Versioning in .NET Core

Similar to the full framework version, we can add versioning information to a project and have it automatically generate our versions. Let's walk through how to create a new console project and set up versioning:

1. Open a **Command Window** and then create a new directory, named `versioning.core`. Change your current directory to this new directory.

2. Create a new .NET Core console project by running `dotnet new console`.

3. Open the project in VS Code, and in the `Program.cs` file, add the following code inside the `Main` method:

```
var assyVersion = Assembly.GetEntryAssembly()
    .GetName().Version;
var fvi = FileVersionInfo.GetVersionInfo(Assembly
    .GetExecutingAssembly().Location);
string fileVersion = fvi.FileVersion;
Console.WriteLine($"Assembly Version: {assyVersion}");
Console.WriteLine($"File Version: {fileVersion}");
```

> **References required**
>
> You will need to add using statements for `System.Diagnostics` and `System.Reflection`.

4. Hit *F5* to start the debugger, and you will see the following output:

```
Assembly Version: 1.0.0.0
File Version: 1.0.0.0
```

5. Open the `versioning.csproj` file, and in `<PropertyGroup>`, right after the `<TargetFramework>`...`</TargetFramework>` tags, add the following:

```
<VersionSuffix>1.0.0.$([System.DateTime]::UtcNow.
ToString(mmff))</VersionSuffix>
```

```
    <AssemblyVersion Condition=" '$(VersionSuffix)' == ''
">0.0.0.1</AssemblyVersion>
    <AssemblyVersion Condition=" '$(VersionSuffix)' != ''
">$(VersionSuffix)</AssemblyVersion>
    <Version Condition=" '$(VersionSuffix)' == ''
">0.0.1.0</Version>
    <Version Condition=" '$(VersionSuffix)' != ''
">$(VersionSuffix)</Version>
```

6. Hit *F5* to start the debugger, and you will see the following output:

```
Assembly Version: 1.0.0.XXX
File Version: 1.0.0.XXX
```

We now have full control of the versioning and can change it any way we want. However, what if we want to do it the full framework way – with wildcards? No problem.

7. Remove the code we added previously, and add the following:

```
<AssemblyVersion>1.0.*</AssemblyVersion>
<FileVersion>1.0.0.0</FileVersion>
```

8. Hit *F5* to start the debugger, and you will see a build error:

```
error CS8357: The specified version string contains
wildcards, which are not compatible with determinism.
Either remove wildcards from the version string, or
disable determinism for this compilation
```

Fear not. Just like with the full framework, Microsoft added a **Deterministic** compilation to ensure that builds are byte-to-byte identical if the inputs haven't changed.

To use our versioning strategy, all we have to do is add the `Deterministic` compilation flag and set it to `false`.

9. Open the `versioning.csproj` file, and in `<PropertyGroup>`, right after the `<TargetFramework>`...`</TargetFramework>` tags, add the following:

```
<Deterministic>false</Deterministic>
```

10. Hit *F5* to start the debugger, and you will see the following output:

```
Assembly Version: 1.0.XXX.XXX
File Version: 1.0.0.0
```

It's as easy as that!

Summary

In this chapter, you picked up some experience of installing Docker. We then discussed several ways in which compilation flags and options can be used to control how a compiler builds an assembly. We discussed using regions in code, and you also learned a little about **pre-** and **post-build** events. You learned how to use breakpoints, the **Immediate window**, and the **Watch Window** to make debugging easier. Even better, you learned how to perform remote debugging using both the full .NET Framework and the .NET Core framework.

We finished up the chapter by discussing versioning assemblies, and we demonstrated techniques to control the build number. That way, it is easy to identify various builds so that you know which assemblies are actually deployed in each environment.

In the next chapter, we will embark on a journey to learn how project and item templates can save time and effort.

Section 2: Customizing Project Templates and Beyond

In this section, we cover everything you ever wanted to know about project and item templates, starting with their core function. After a quick primer on what exactly they are, we leap into creating our own complex, custom, multi-project templates. Finally, we see what it takes to package and deploy our custom templates to a broader audience.

This section has the following chapters:

- *Chapter 8, Introduction to Project and Item Templates*
- *Chapter 9, Creating Your Own Templates*
- *Chapter 10, Deploying Custom Templates*

8
Introduction to Project and Item Templates

Section 1, Visual Studio IDE Productivity Essentials of this book covered necessary basics such as shortcuts and snippets that speed up your everyday coding at a micro level. By now, we hope you have already picked up a few helpful tips and tricks. This chapter kicks off *Section 2, Customizing Project Templates and Beyond* of the book, where we take things up a notch. Project and item templates accelerate the creation of classes, and even entire projects. The techniques examined are quite valuable, yet underutilized among developers.

In this chapter, we will cover material aimed at the following topics:

- Understanding item templates
- Knowing when to use project templates
- Looking at a sample scenario
- Valuing templates

The majority of .NET developers use templates all day, but did you know that you can also create your own? After introducing the concept of templates, you will work with a couple of pre-built templates to expand upon a sample project. Then, in the next chapter, you will learn how to create your own project templates.

> **Note**
>
> As a hint of what is to come in *Section 3, Leveraging Extensions For the Win* of this book, we will demonstrate how to combine what you learn in this section with code generation, to have entire multi-tiered solutions up and running in a flash. Perhaps you can think of this progression as walk, run, and fly.

Technical requirements

To run the sample application in this chapter, you will need to have the **.NET desktop development** workload installed. This can be installed using the Visual Studio Installer. One easy way to start the installer from within Visual Studio is via the **Tools | Get Tools and Features…** menu item. The **.NET desktop development** workload is shown in the following screenshot:

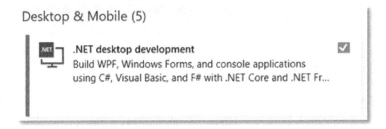

Figure 8.1 – .NET desktop development workload

If you have not done so already, it would be a good idea to clone the repository for this book. The code for this chapter is available on GitHub at `https://github.com/PacktPublishing/Visual-Studio-2019-Tricks-and-Techniques/tree/main/`.

Please visit the following link to check the CiA videos: `http://bit.ly/3oxE5QM`.

> **Warning**
>
> Please read the following if you receive an error while cloning the repository. Starting in Git 2.28, `git init` will look to the value of `init.defaultBranch` when creating the first branch in a new repository. If that value is unset, `init.defaultBranch` defaults to `master`. Because this repository uses `main` as its default branch, you may have to run the following code from a Command Prompt or Git Bash to avoid the error:
>
> **$ git config --global init.defaultBranch main**

> **Visual Studio 2019 for Windows focus**
>
> This chapter focuses on understanding and using templates in the Visual Studio 2019 for Windows flavor. Know that similar things are possible in other **integrated development environment** (IDE) flavors, but they work differently. For example, Visual Studio Code does not include the **File | New Project** dialog or prepackaged project templates. Instead, you install additional components and scaffolders that are like the workloads concept of the Visual Studio Installer but are more targeted. Tools such as Yeoman and the npm package manager are used to install modules and scaffold projects.

Understanding item templates

The easiest way to understand project items is to simply open any solution in Visual Studio and either use the *Ctrl + Shift + A* keyboard shortcut or right-click in **Solution Explorer** and choose **Add | New Item…** from the context menu. When you do this, a dialog containing a variety of project item templates ready to add to your project will appear. The following screenshot shows some item templates that come installed by default with the **.NET desktop development** workload such as **Class**, **Interface**, **User Control (WPF)**, **Resource Dictionary (WPF)**, and **Application Configuration File**:

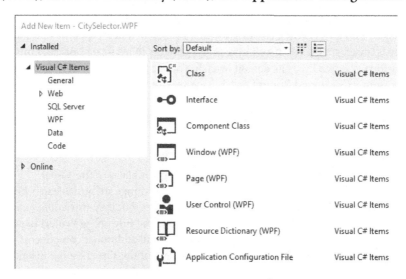

Figure 8.2 – Project item templates

Other project types, such as a web project, will have different item types including **Razor Component**, **API Controller**, and **Content Page**. As you will soon see, we are not limited to just what comes out of the box. Visual Studio provides excellent support for creating your own templates. This can be a great way to accumulate blueprints that can be reused from one project to the next with great speed and consistency.

Whereas item templates can be as simple as crafting a single class file with dependency injection, project templates can be more complex to scaffold out many code and configuration files all at once. We will look at project templates next.

Knowing when to use project templates

Full-time employees often work on multiple applications that use the same technology stacks. In these cases, having some consistency between them can be beneficial. Project templates provide a way to save time up front, provide guidance to junior developers, and make maintenance easier down the road. For example, microservices has become a trend and, by definition, this may require setting up the same structure repeatedly. That kind of work not only wastes time but is not much fun either. Instead, you could make a Visual Studio template that sets everything up—such as logging, Entity Framework, Swagger, and so on—and is ready to go in a flash.

Personally, as a consultant/contractor, I code on several projects every year. I find myself doing similar things between different applications and clients. My next project often uses a similar "stack" or group of technologies used on a prior project. Typically, a few months have passed since I last had to do all the setup work for a target architecture. That means I cannot easily remember how a solution should be structured or how logging and security were configured, or even particular patterns I prefer to follow when coding a certain type of class file.

If I still have access to that prior code base it is possible to use it as a reference, but that approach can get messy. A lot of time is wasted analyzing all the items that need to be removed, changing namespaces, and so on. Alternatively, if I start from scratch then I must think through things; mistakes get made and time is lost having to search the web to find forgotten material.

A much better approach is to use my own custom project templates to get up and running in an instant. For understanding, chances are good that *you already use project templates*. When you add a new project or add a new file to an existing project, Visual Studio displays a dialog that allows you to search for and select one of the installed templates, as shown here:

Figure 8.3 – Project templates

Azure Resource Manager (ARM) templates and Azure Blueprints

The kinds of templates we are going to cover in the coming chapters are neither related to ARM templates nor Azure Blueprints. However, if you are working with cloud deployments, I recommend you check out those topics as well. They are a little more Azure-focused and beyond the scope of this book about Visual Studio. The following are a couple of links to get you started:

ARM template documentation: https://docs.microsoft.com/ en-us/azure/azure-resource-manager/templates/

What is Azure Blueprints?: https://aka.ms/whatareblueprints

Visual Studio for Windows does an excellent job of providing developers with numerous templates from the get-go. When creating your own templates, you will often start with one of the out-of-the-box items, layer in your own customizations, and ultimately export to create your own templates. Then, the next time you want to make a similar project or class, simply select the template you created from the same dialog and you are off to the races.

Template tags

With so many project templates to choose from, how do you find the right one? The answer is that the template author can include template tags in the metadata. Tags appear under the template description in the **New Project** dialog box and allow search and filter functions. Exactly how this works will become clearer in the next chapter when we create our own template and examine its `.vstemplate` **Extensible Markup Language (XML)** file content.

Visual Studio 2019 leverages the following three different types of tags to facilitate searching:

- **Language**: C#, F#, C++, JavaScript, and so on

- **Platform**: Windows, Android, iOS, Linux, and so on

- **Project type**: Cloud, console, games, mobile, web, and so on

In the following screenshot, the user is searching for templates whose metadata contains a keyword of web. The arrows point to areas that show how a project-type tag can be used to filter template selections via one of the dropdowns that are located above the list of templates:

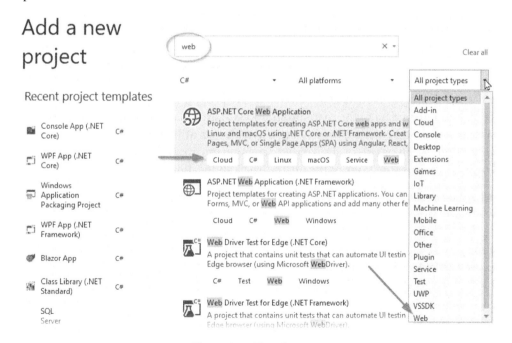

Figure 8.4 – Template tags

Note that you are not limited to the template tags built in to Visual Studio. It is possible to create your own custom template tags and Visual Studio will pick up on them.

When to use templates

Consider making your own *item template* whenever you find yourself copying and pasting the same class files either within the same project or across different projects. Likewise, consider making a *project template* whenever you find that you need to create a new project that uses similar technologies and structures to a past project.

Now that we understand the template concept, let's move on to an imaginable case that illustrates how custom templates can be used effectively.

Looking at a sample scenario

In this part, we provide a hypothetical situation that allows us to introduce a sample **City Selector Windows Presentation Foundation (WPF)** utility program, provided in the code that accompanies this book. We will use this sample program in multiple chapters, so it is good to become familiar with it here.

In a hypothetical work scenario, you have developed a tiny desktop application that integrates with a separate off-the-shelf product. Analogous to a microservice, the custom WPF app provides a very simple function that can be invoked by this other third-party application. Although we do not have its source code, the third-party application is designed with extension points on several screens. These extension points will call out to external utility programs such as ours. Each utility program should perform a discrete function and return data to the main program via standard output and the clipboard. Because business stakeholders loved your **City Selector** utility so much, they want you to make another dozen or two of similar, but separate, mini applications just like it. Each one will tie in to various functions of the off-the-shelf application.

So, what does your first custom utility do? The **City Selector** utility program constrains user input by using dependent drop-down lists in a hierarchy of **Country | State | City**. Once the user selects a country in the first dropdown, the second one populates with only the states that are valid for that country. Likewise, once a state is selected, only valid cities are available for selection. It simply prevents invalid and misspelled user input. The following screenshot shows an extract of the utility program:

Figure 8.5 – City Selector sample utility

Although the other tools you must develop will have different user inputs, processing, and outputs, there are several aspects of this original tool that need to be repeated in the other applications as well, including the following:

- WPF technology

- Flexibility to use either remote or local data sources

- Ability to record how long remote **application programming interface** (**API**) calls take and log any errors

- The output of user-selected data to the Windows clipboard or console (standard output—so that a calling application can then read it)

To satisfy the second bullet point, you will use *dependency injection* and interfaces to make swapping out the data source a breeze. Then, to meet the third bullet point, you want *logging* set up and configured. The fourth bullet-point requirement, returning data via the console, requires some trickery that is *simply not part of Visual Studio's out-of-the-box WPF project template* when we create new projects. Have a look at the following screenshot:

```
CitySelector.WPF.csproj
    1  <Project Sdk="Microsoft.NET.Sdk.WindowsDesktop">
    2
    3    <PropertyGroup>
    4      <OutputType>Exe</OutputType>
    5      <TargetFramework>netcoreapp3.1</TargetFramework>
    6      <UseWPF>true</UseWPF>
    7      <StartupObject>CitySelector.WPF.Program</StartupObject>
    8    </PropertyGroup>
```

Figure 8.6 – Project file output is Exe (console) versus WinExe (WPF)

Do you remember how it was done? You may vaguely recall that, when originally coded, the custom **City Selector** application project output type that had to be changed and the startup object was set to our custom `Program` class instead of using a `StartUri` value in **Extensible Application Markup Language** (**XAML**). There were a few other things such as special code to hide the console window at startup, but what are you forgetting?

No worries—instead of taking the time to remember each and every customization step, in the next chapter we are going to make a project template out of this example. That way, we do not have to manually repeat all the steps where time was originally invested to get it all just how we need it!

Running the project

In this exercise, we are going to walk through the details of the sample application that we will template in the next chapter. We will start by running the sample project and pointing out some of the aspects that make it unique, as follows:

1. Using Visual Studio, open the `CitySelector.WPF.sln` solution file from the sample code that accompanies this chapter.

2. Press *F5* to run the solution in **Debug** mode.

3. Make some random choices in the drop-down controls for country, state, and city. Notice that a unique identifier corresponding to each dropdown displays the underlying value corresponding to each of your choices, as illustrated in the following screenshot:

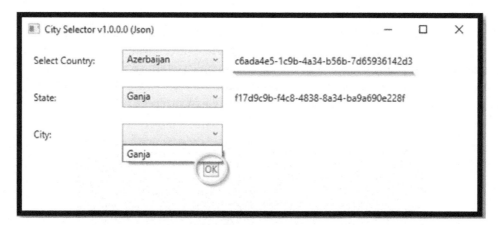

Figure 8.7 – Making country, state, and city selections

4. The **OK** button is disabled until you have selected a city. Once you have selected a city, click the **OK** button.

5. Open a text editor such as Notepad and press *Ctrl + V* to paste the value contained in the Windows Clipboard. The **globally unique identifiers** (**GUIDs**) that you see, separated by colons, correspond to the key values of the selections made in the tool, as illustrated in the following screenshot:

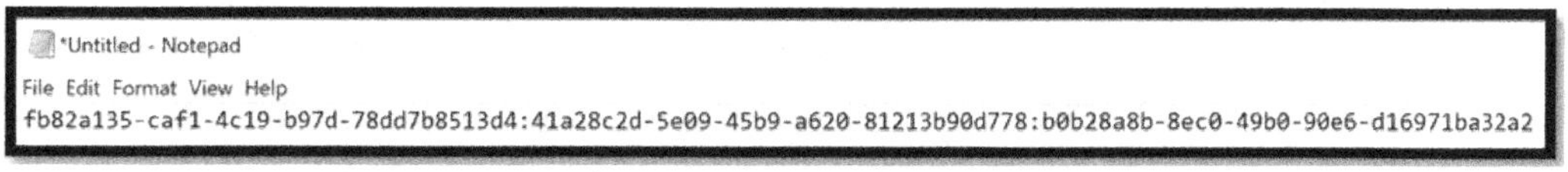

```
*Untitled - Notepad
File  Edit  Format  View  Help
fb82a135-caf1-4c19-b97d-78dd7b8513d4:41a28c2d-5e09-45b9-a620-81213b90d778:b0b28a8b-8ec0-49b0-90e6-d16971ba32a2
```

Figure 8.8 – Sample City Selector output

Now, let's move on to the next section.

Examining the project

Now that you can see what the project does, we will examine a few of the bits that we want to clone into all those future projects we have to create, as follows:

> **Not a WPF programmer?**
>
> It's OK if you are not a WPF programmer. We are about to cover a couple of very specific facets of WPF programming that are important only in as much as they emphasize that our project is special. In other words, this is not the typical code you would get by using existing templates that come pre-installed with the Visual Studio desktop development workload. The key takeaway is that we have a reason why we want to be able to repeat this project architecture. What we do to template this desktop application can just as easily be done with web and mobile projects as well.

1. Open `Program.cs` and notice the use of `STAThread`, which replaces the use of a `StartupUri` value. This is part of what allows us to run as a console application and communicate data to the calling application via `StdOut`. In fact, the out-of-the-box WPF template does not even have a `Program.cs` class file. The `Program.cs` class file is shown in the following screenshot:

```
public class Program
{
    public static IServiceProvider ServiceProvider { get; internal set; }
    public static IServiceCollection ServiceCollection { get; private set; }

    [STAThread]
gma warning disable IDE0060 // Remove unused parameter
    public static void Main(string[] args)
gma warning restore IDE0060 // Remove unused parameter
    {
        var app = new App();
        app.InitializeComponent();

        var builder = new HostBuilder()
            .ConfigureServices((hostContext, services) =>
            {
                ServiceCollection = services;
                services.AddSingleton<ICitySelectorService,
                    CitySelectorMockService>();
                services.AddSingleton<MainWindow>();

                //Add Serilog
                var serilogLogger = new LoggerConfiguration()
                        .WriteTo.RollingFile("CitySelector.WPF.log")
                        .CreateLogger();

                services.AddLogging(x =>
                {
                    x.SetMinimumLevel(LogLevel.Information);
                    x.AddSerilog(logger: serilogLogger, dispose: true);
                });
            });
```

Figure 8.9 – Program.cs class file

2. Further down, see how dependency injection is configured.

3. A final point of interest is that logging to a file is also being configured.

4. View the NuGet packages that are being used by expanding **Dependencies |
    Packages**, as illustrated in the following screenshot:

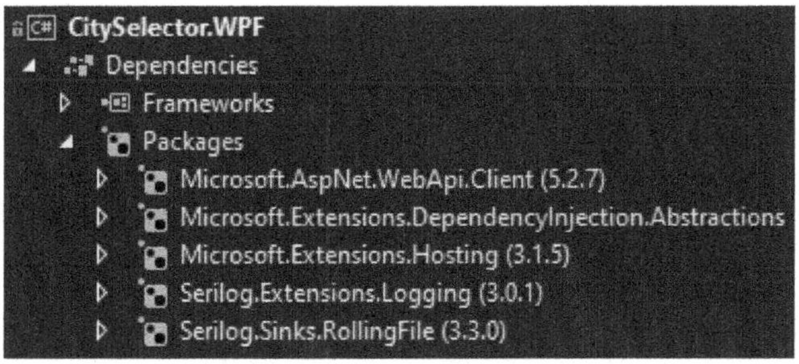

Figure 8.10 – Sample City Selector output

Including NuGet packages in project templates

When templating a project, you have the option to include NuGet packages.
If you choose to omit them from your template package, the developer using
your template must manually import them into the project. On the other hand,
if you include them, some are sure to be out of date by the time the template is
being used and will probably require updates. Details on how to include NuGet
packages are covered in *Chapter 10, Deploying Custom Templates*.

---

5. Let's continue with examining key aspects of our sample project. Open the `App.
    xaml.cs` code-behind file located underneath the `App.xaml` file and examine the
    `Application_Startup` method.

    Notice the little trick to hide the console window that would normally appear in
    a console application (remember the project output type has been changed).

More importantly, we are using a configuration setting, `DataProvider`, to determine which of multiple service classes we want to use with dependency injection, as illustrated in the following screenshot:

```csharp
private void Application_Startup(object sender, StartupEventArgs e)
{
    string msgBadDataProviderConfig = $"Please specify a DATAPROVIDER configuration value of 'API', 'JSON', or 'MOCK'";
    var dataProvider = ConfigurationManager.AppSettings[CONFIG_DATAPROVIDER];
    if (string.IsNullOrWhiteSpace(dataProvider))
    {
        throw new ApplicationException(msgBadDataProviderConfig);
    }

    HideConsoleWindow();
    IServiceCollection services = Program.ServiceCollection;
    Log.Logger.Information($"Using {dataProvider} as a data provider.");
    switch (dataProvider?.ToUpperInvariant())
    {
        case "API":
            services.Replace(ServiceDescriptor.Singleton<ICitySelectorService, CitySelectorApiService>());
            break;

        case "JSON":
            services.Replace(ServiceDescriptor.Singleton<ICitySelectorService, CitySelectorJsonService>());
            break;

        case "MOCK":
            services.Replace(ServiceDescriptor.Singleton<ICitySelectorService, CitySelectorMockService>());
            break;

        default:
            throw new ApplicationException(msgBadDataProviderConfig);
            // break;
    }

    Program.ServiceProvider = services.BuildServiceProvider();
    var myWindow = Program.ServiceProvider.GetRequiredService<MainWindow>();
    myWindow.Show();
}
```

Figure 8.11 – Application_Startup method

6. In this step, we experiment with switching between different service implementations. This ability to easily change the implementation in one area of an application while leaving the rest of the application untouched is a key benefit of using dependency injection.

    Change the `DataProvider` configuration value in the `App.config` file between `API`, `JSON`, and `MOCK`.

    Set a breakpoint on the `switch` statement in `Application_Startup`.

    Set a breakpoint on the `CitySelectorService` setter in the constructor of the `MainWindowViewModel` class located in the `ViewModel` folder.

Debug the application and verify that different service implementations are, indeed, used, as illustrated in the following screenshot:

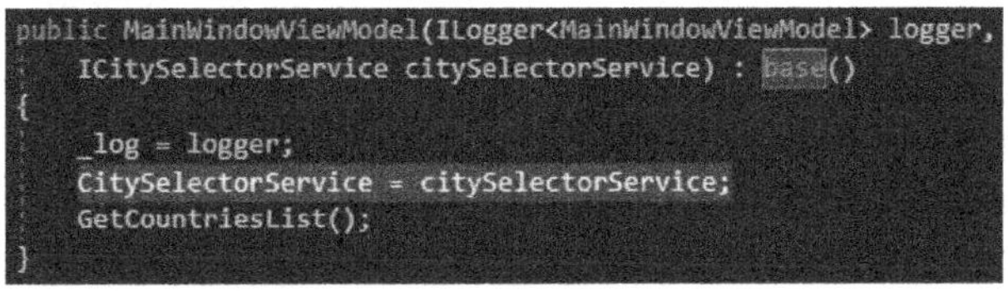

```
public MainWindowViewModel(ILogger<MainWindowViewModel> logger,
    ICitySelectorService citySelectorService) : base()
{
    _log = logger;
    CitySelectorService = citySelectorService;
    GetCountriesList();
}
```

Figure 8.12 – MainWindowViewModel constructor

In this sample project, we can easily switch between using the following:

- **Mock** data that is hardcoded into the application via the `SampleData.cs` file
- **JSON** data that is read from the `SampleData.json` file
- **API** data that is retrieved from a web API whose implementation is assumed to exist outside of this project

Other items to explore, if you are interested, include the custom `IEqualityComparer` implementations in the `Comparers` folder, as well as a couple of utility classes located in the `Infrastructure` folder.

Now that you understand the sample project that we will be working with in the next couple of chapters, let's take a moment to put what we are about to do into perspective.

Valuing templates

Have you ever started a new project and thought this? *OK—this is just like when we did X. Do I still have that source code? I should probably review it to see how it was set up and reuse some of that infrastructure.* Developers who typically work on multiple projects per year certainly encounter these situations. Likewise, if you are inclined to switch jobs, your resume tends to be attractive to prospective employers with needs that are similar to the technology stack(s) you have experience with already. Imagine two candidates are interviewing for the same position:

- The first candidate says, *Oh yes, I've done <fill in the blank> [Blazor, Model-View-Controller (MVC), WPF, Xamarin, APIs, and so on] before.*
- The second candidate says, *Not only have I done that, but I have a library of my own reusable templates that have proven to work on past projects. If you would like to see a demonstration, I could show you how they can really save time.*

Which job candidate do you think differentiated themselves and is more likely to make a great impression? Of course, that impression might be different if the intellectual property associated with those templates belongs to the developer's former employer!

Similarly, if you want to be paid more as a developer then you need to be able to justify why companies should view you as worth it. One way to do that is by getting things done faster, and both item and project templates can help. You should not have to reinvent the wheel on each new project. Furthermore, organizations tend to want multiple applications to have comparable structures and follow similar patterns to standardize things and reduce maintenance burdens. This can be one of the biggest value propositions for using templates.

Summary

This chapter laid the conceptual foundation for project item templates and project templates. The use of template tags for searching and filtering was covered, along with an explanation of when to use templates. It is important to recognize when this technique makes sense. To this end, we ran and examined a sample application that will be used in the next chapter to create our own custom template.

This sample application made use of dependency injection, a significant programming principle. After an exercise to demonstrate swapping out the data provider, the value of templates was also emphasized. We stated that it does not matter if the example project used for demonstration does not exactly match your own needs. Once you see how simple it is to create templates, you can easily apply these techniques to your own classes and projects.

Personally, I have been on project teams where we had to create the numerous API controllers, mappers, repository classes, interfaces, and so on, for literally hundreds of tables. This work, even with copy-paste, is very tedious and error-prone. Likewise, as your career progresses, the chances of needing to craft a project that is quite similar to the one you did last month/quarter/year increase greatly. If you are not using a code generator for this kind of work, then item templates and project templates are the next best thing.

In the next chapter, we will expand on what was learned here and create our own templates.

Further reading

If you want to explore project templates offered by third parties, here are a couple of links to get started: `https://marketplace.visualstudio.com/search?term=project%20template&target=VS` (for Visual Studio) and `https://marketplace.visualstudio.com/search?term=project%20template&target=VSCode` (for VS Code).

9
Creating Your Own Templates

Having completed *Chapter 8, Introduction to Project and Item Templates*, you can appreciate the power and speed project templates bring to the creation of a new project. Instead of starting with a blank slate, within seconds developers can have an entire working project that is nicely organized and preconfigured with best-practice code, and often has many sample screens. While there are a number of great templates available online, sometimes we just want to do it "our way," and a custom template makes perfect sense.

In this chapter, we will shift our attention to turning our **City Selector** sample **Windows Presentation Foundation** (**WPF**) application into our own custom project template. By the end of the chapter, you will have gained the basic skills it takes to make repeatable application architectures that work the same way as the built-in Visual Studio templates.

Here, we will put the concepts learned into practice, as we will be doing the following:

- Exporting and importing custom project templates to/from Visual Studio
- Identifying and fixing issues with our custom template
- Reimporting the fixed template
- Exporting project items

> **Repeating architectures**
>
> The key point of learning how to create your own templates is to encourage
> you to leverage the hard work that goes into crafting a robust, tested solution.
> Making a solution architecture that works and is extensible can take a lot of
> time and energy. Then again, when you do it right, it tends to be possible to
> reuse those same technologies and patterns to solve the next business problem,
> even if the problem domain is different. The exercises in this chapter give you
> the knowledge and skills required to reclaim some of that investment made in
> the original solution. You will see just how easy it is to carry the core structure
> from one project to the next, saving both time and money.

Technical requirements

The code examples in this chapter have been tested with Visual Studio 2019 and the full
.NET Framework v4.7.2. Also, to follow along, make sure to clone the repository for this
book. The code for this chapter is available on GitHub at `https://github.com/`
`PacktPublishing/Visual-Studio-2019-Tricks-and-Techniques`.

So, for this, let's begin by exporting a custom template of the project.

Please visit the following link to check the CiA videos: `http://bit.ly/3oxE5QM`.

Exporting a custom project template

In this exercise, we are going to make a project template using the sample application that
we introduced in the last chapter. Proceed as follows:

1. Use Visual Studio to open the `CitySelector.WPF.sln` solution file that is
    included in this chapter's folder within the source repository for this book.

2. Build and run/debug the application just to make sure it works.

3. Launch **Export Template Wizard** from the top menu bar in Visual Studio by
    selecting the **Project | Export Template...** menu item, as illustrated in the following
    screenshot:

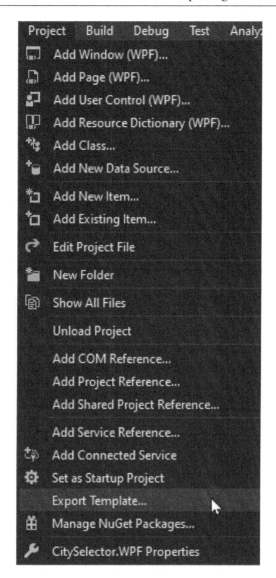

Figure 9.1 – Export Template menu

4. Ensure that the **Project template** radio button option is selected in the **Export Template Wizard**. The `CitySelector.WPF` project should be the only option for creating a template. Click the **Next** button.

5. On the second page of the dialog, **Select Template Options**, enter a template name of `WPF Console Starter` and a description of `A project for creating a console-initialized WPF application with dependency injection, logging, and basic MVVM patterns.`, as shown here:

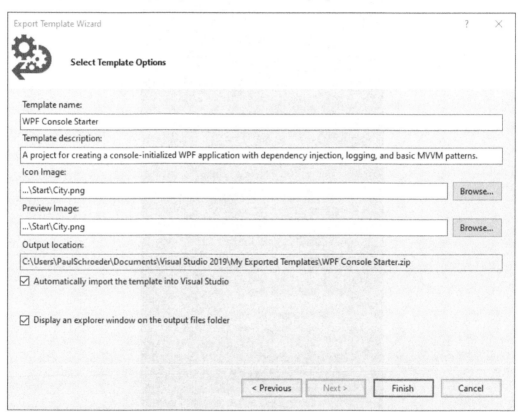

Figure 9.2 – Completed Select Template Options screen

After completing the template name and description fields, you may optionally choose icon or preview images. For your convenience, a `City.png` icon file has been included at the root of the start directory in the provided code files. You can select this file as either the icon image or preview image, or both if you like.

Note that preview images appear next to the template description when someone is searching in the **Add New Project** dialog. Similarly, the icon image is what appears in **Solution Explorer** next to that project type.

6. To wrap up this exercise, either make a mental note of the **Output location** specified or copy and paste the value into a text editor. We will edit the output file generated by the **Export Template Wizard** in a later exercise. Leave the **Automatically import the template into Visual Studio** checkbox checked, as well as the **Display an explorer window on the output files folder** checkbox. Click the **Finish** button.

That is all it takes to create a new project template to use when adding projects to a solution. In the next exercise, we will see how we can put this template to use.

Manual project template creation

Using the **Export Template Wizard** is by far the easiest way to create project templates. However, it is worth mentioning that it is also possible to manually create project templates. This can be done by adding all the required project files into a folder and then creating a `.vstemplate` **Extensible Markup Language** (**XML**) file that lists the files to include with the template, as well as the standard descriptive metadata elements. Much of this more advanced approach is covered in the next chapter.

Now that we have used the wizard, in the next section we will learn how to create a new project using this freshly exported custom project template.

Using the exported project template

In this exercise, we are going to create a new project using the template that we exported in the last exercise. You will see just how quickly we can replicate our original project using the template file Visual Studio created in our last exercise.

Restarting Visual Studio

Even though we told the **Export Template Wizard** to automatically import our template into Visual Studio, that change is not immediate. If you try to add a new project to the solution right after exporting a template, it may not be available. Either close and restart Visual Studio or open a second instance to remedy this issue.

Follow these steps to create a new project

1. Open a second instance of Visual Studio.

2. Click on the **Create a new project** button from the **Start** screen or use the **File |
New | Project** menu, or use the *Ctrl + Shift + N* keyboard shortcut to launch the
new project dialog. The former option is shown in the following screenshot:

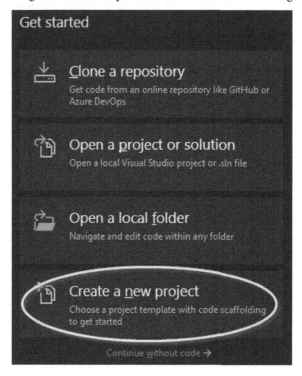

Figure 9.3 – Create a new project

3. Press *Alt + S* or click inside the template search textbox and type starter. Our
custom template should appear as an option. Select the **WPF Console Starter**
project and click the **Next** button, as illustrated in the following screenshot:

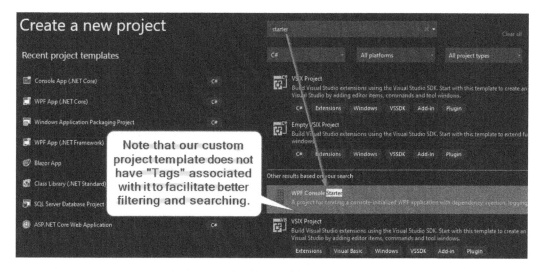

Figure 9.4 – Search for imported project template

Project template search notes

We could also search for our project template by typing in other keywords such as WPF, Console, logging, or MVVM. In addition to searching the template tags we learned about in *Chapter 8, Introduction to Project and Item Templates*, Visual Studio also searches template title and description metadata for matches. Unfortunately, by default, our exported project template does not include tag metadata for the language, platform, and project type to enable filtering.

4. *It is important that we change the default project name* from WPF Console Starter1 to SampleApp.MyCompany.WPF (no spaces). Your entry here will set both the default namespace and the assembly name for the project.

5. Choose a directory location to place the code and provide a solution name. Click the **Create** button to generate the solution and project files.

6. Open a few random class files and notice that all the namespace entries have been adapted to match the user-provided project name.

7. Build and debug or run the project to ensure it works just like the original sample application.

So, now that we have seen our imported template work successfully, let's see next how problems might arise.

Identifying issues with the project template

For this topic, we want to repeat the same exercise we just completed, with one exception—retain the default project name as WPF Console Starter1. You may continue using the solution from the previous exercise, if desired, by adding another project to the existing solution, as follows:

1. Click the **Add a New Project** button from the **Start** screen or use the **File | New | Project** menu. Alternatively, use the *Ctrl + Shift + N* keyboard shortcut or right-click on the solution and choose **Add | New Project** to launch the new project dialog.

2. Press *Alt + S* or click inside the template search textbox and type starter. Our custom template should appear as an option. Select the **WPF Console Starter** project and click the **Next** button, which will take you to the following screen:

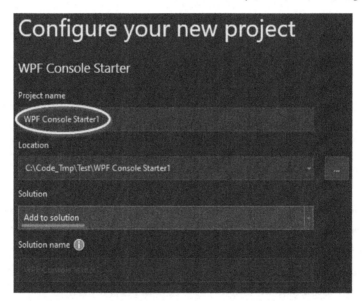

Figure 9.5 – Add new project using the default project name

3. It is important that if we are using the same solution from the prior exercise, change the **Solution** option to **Add to solution**. Be sure to leave the default project name as WPF Console Starter1. Your entry here will set both the default namespace and the assembly name for the project.

4. Choose a directory location to place the code and provide a solution name. Click the **Create** button to generate the solution and project files.

5. Try to build and run the new project. You should see the following error message in the **Build Output** window:

```
error MC6029: 'WPF Console Starter1' name is not valid in
the default namespace 'WPF Console Starter1'. Correct the
RootNamespace tag value in the project file.
```

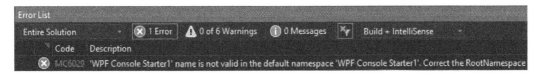

Figure 9.6 – Error using default project name

Well done—you have successfully failed! Next, let's understand why this happened and then see how we can fix this problem.

Fixing problems in the template definition

The reason we received a build error in the prior exercise is because, by default, the wizard we used previously to export project templates does not include a `<RootNamespace>` element in the bundled project file. One terrible option would be to tell users of our template to manually edit the generated `.csproj` project file to insert a line, such as the following, for the missing element:

```
<RootNamespace>WPF_Console_Starter1</RootNamespace>
```

A better option is to tweak our template bundle a bit to avoid the issue altogether, and that is what we will cover in the next exercise.

> **Time saver**
>
> If you prefer to skim the following detailed steps for fixing the template issues, you may simply skip to the next exercise and use the `WPF Console Starter Fixed.zip` file that is provided in the `Completed` folder alongside the code for this chapter. It contains the fixes that we walk through in this exercise.

Of course, as long as we are going to adjust our template bundle, we might as well add those missing tags that help with searching and filtering as well. Let's get started, as follows:

1. Close all instances of Visual Studio.

2. Use **Windows Explorer** to locate the Project Templates directory and therein the project template that we auto-imported as part of the first exercise from the *Exporting a custom project template* section of this chapter. The imported file can typically be found in this folder location:

```
C:\Users\<your username>\Documents\Visual Studio 2019\
Templates\ProjectTemplates
```

3. Once found, simply *delete* the WPF Console Starter.zip file as we do not need it.

   Warning: We are going to use the file located in the My Exported Templates directory. Do not delete that copy of the file.

   The file to be deleted is shown in the following screenshot:

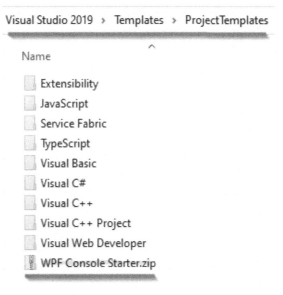

Figure 9.7 – Delete original imported project template

4. Navigate to the **My Exported Templates** directory. Here, you should find a copy of the `WPF Console Starter.zip` file at the following location:

```
C:\Users\<your username>\Documents\Visual Studio 2019\My
Exported Templates
```

5. Right-click on the `WPF Console Starter.zip` file and choose **Extract All...**. Then, extract the compressed file's content into a working directory and then open that directory. The process is illustrated in the following screenshot:

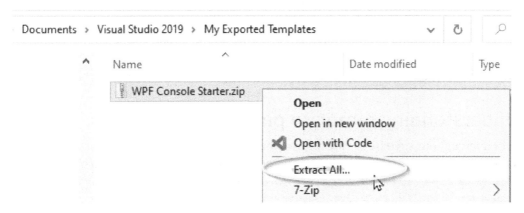

Figure 9.8 – Extract project template file

6. Open the `CitySelector.WPF.csproj` file in your favorite text editor such as **Visual Studio Code (VS Code)** and insert the following lines of text inside the first `<PropertyGroup>` element:

```
<RootNamespace>$safeprojectname$</RootNamespace>
<AssemblyName>$safeprojectname$</AssemblyName>
```

Withstanding the note that follows, Visual Studio has traditionally defaulted the default namespace and assembly names for new projects to the value of the `$projectname$` token. By explicitly specifying the use of the `$safeprojectname$` token instead, characters such as spaces will be replaced with underscore characters. This can prevent compiler issues with newly scaffolded projects, such as the one seen in the prior exercise.

Differences between .NET Core and full .NET Framework v4.7.2

Note that this step may no longer be necessary, depending on your version of Visual Studio and/or target framework. The previous step was necessary in versions of Visual Studio 2019 prior to v16.6.3 when using exported project templates that target .NET Core. However, the same project template targeting the full .NET Framework already had these elements set.

---

7. Save the changes and compare your project XML to that of the following screenshot:

```
CitySelector.WPF.csproj ⊠
```

```xml
<Project Sdk="Microsoft.NET.Sdk.WindowsDesktop">

  <PropertyGroup>
    <OutputType>Exe</OutputType>
    <TargetFramework>netcoreapp3.1</TargetFramework>
    <UseWPF>true</UseWPF>
    <StartupObject>$safeprojectname$.Program</StartupObject>
    <RootNamespace>$safeprojectname$</RootNamespace>
    <AssemblyName>$safeprojectname$</AssemblyName>
  </PropertyGroup>
```

Figure 9.9 – Insert RootNamespace and AssemblyName elements

You can see that the variables have thus been added.

Understanding template parameters

Let's interrupt our exercise to explain what we see in *Figure 9.9*. As we discussed earlier, `$safeprojectname$` is a special keyword. It instructs Visual Studio to remove unsupported characters such as spaces from the namespace or assembly name during new project scaffolding. This is an example of a template parameter.

Template parameters such as this provide substitution tokens for identifiers such as class names and namespaces at the point in time when Visual Studio generates code using the files in our template bundle.

For a list of reserved template parameters, visit https://docs.microsoft.com/en-us/visualstudio/ide/template-parameters?view=vs-2019.

> **Custom template parameters**
> Know that it is possible to specify your own template parameters and values. For more information, see the `CustomParameters` element documentation found here: https://docs.microsoft.com/en-us/visualstudio/extensibility/customparameters-element-visual-studio-templates?view=vs-2019.

With that brief aside out of the way, we will now return to fixing the issues found with our template definition. Next, we will add tags to the definition that enable Visual Studio to search and filter our custom template in the **New Project** dialog shown in the first exercise of this chapter. To do so, proceed as follows:

1. Open the `MyTemplate.vstemplate` file in your favorite text editor such as Notepad++ and insert the following lines of text inside the `<TemplateData>` element:

    ```
    <LanguageTag>C#</LanguageTag>
    <PlatformTag>windows</PlatformTag>
    <ProjectTypeTag>console</ProjectTypeTag>
    <ProjectTypeTag>desktop</ProjectTypeTag>
    <ProjectTypeTag>TipTrick</ProjectTypeTag>
    ```

2. Save the changes. Your file should match what is shown in the following screenshot:

```
MyTemplate.vstemplate

<VSTemplate Version="3.0.0" xmlns="http://schemas.microsoft.com/
  <TemplateData>
    <Name>WPF Console Starter</Name>
    <Description>A project for creating a console-initialized WPF
    <ProjectType>csharp</ProjectType>
    <LanguageTag>C#</LanguageTag>
    <PlatformTag>windows</PlatformTag>
    <ProjectTypeTag>console</ProjectTypeTag>
    <ProjectTypeTag>desktop</ProjectTypeTag>
    <ProjectTypeTag>TipTrick</ProjectTypeTag>
    <ProjectSubType>
    </ProjectSubType>
    <SortOrder>1000</SortOrder>
    <CreateNewFolder>true</CreateNewFolder>
    <DefaultName>WPF Console Starter</DefaultName>
    <ProvideDefaultName>true</ProvideDefaultName>
    <LocationField>Enabled</LocationField>
    <EnableLocationBrowseButton>true</EnableLocationBrowseButton>
    <CreateInPlace>true</CreateInPlace>
    <Icon>__TemplateIcon.png</Icon>
    <PreviewImage>__PreviewImage.png</PreviewImage>
  </TemplateData>
  <TemplateContent>
```

Figure 9.10 – Insert tags for language, platform, and project type

Take a moment to realize that the tag elements we just inserted are what Visual Studio will later be used to enable filtering and sorting. Examine the `<TemplateContent>` element and appreciate that these `<Folder>` and `<ProjectItem>` elements are what Visual Studio uses to scaffold the new project.

Now that we have addressed both our default namespace naming issue and our lack of search/filter tag elements in the definition, we want to prepare to reimport our work. Visual Studio understands and can import project templates whose file contents and metadata definitions are bundled into a single compressed ZIP file. The next and final step in this exercise does just that.

3. Back in **Windows Explorer**, select all the files from within the directory containing the template files. Right-click and choose **Send to | Compressed (zipped) folder**. Name the created ZIP file WPF Console Starter Fixed.zip. The process is illustrated in the following screenshot:

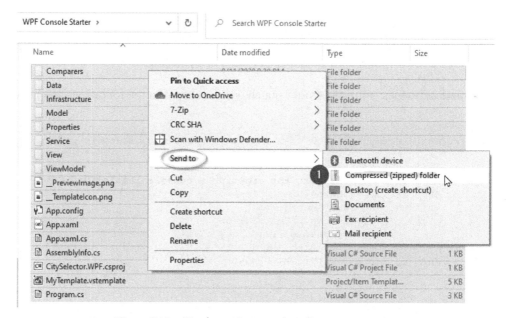

Figure 9.11 – Zip the project template directory contents

Zip the files, not the folder

Do not zip the folder itself and create a .zip file whose first level of content is a single top-level folder. Be sure that the .zip file contains all the files at the root level, as shown in the preceding screenshot. Otherwise, when we perform the next step to import the template into Visual Studio and then try to use the project template when creating a new project, it will not be found.

You have now performed the modifications necessary to fix the lack of filter and search tags as well as the potential compilation issue for new project creation using our custom template.

Reimporting the fixed template

In the previous exercise, we addressed a couple of custom template issues. However, we did not test the result to see whether our updates to the custom project template work. At the start of the last exercise, we deleted the template that was originally imported. All we must do now is provide Visual Studio our updated version. So, let's see how this is done, as follows:

1. Back in **Windows Explorer**, copy the WPF Console Starter Fixed.zip file created in the previous exercise. Paste that copied file into the Visual C# folder located within the ProjectTemplates folder at this path:

   ```
   C:\Users\<your username>\Documents\Visual Studio 2019\
   Templates\ProjectTemplates\Visual C#
   ```

   > **Keeping templates organized**
   >
   > Note that previously, Visual Studio auto-imported our project template file to the ProjectTemplates directory. We could have placed our updated file in that directory and it would have worked just fine. However, you can also take advantage of the subfolders such as Visual C# to organize and separate your custom template files. This becomes more useful as the number of custom template files you create and import grows.

   Believe it or not, simply copying that ZIP file into the correct folder is all that Visual Studio requires to *import* or pick up on the new project template the next time it restarts.

2. Reopen Visual Studio and then open the solution file we were using in this chapter's previous exercises. If the build errors are still present and they bother you then either unload the faulty project or remove it from the solution altogether.

3. Add a new project to the solution. This time, search for tip or open the **All project types** dropdown and filter by **TipTrick**, as shown in the following screenshot:

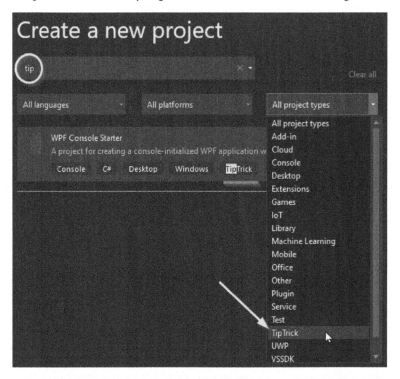

Figure 9.12 – Custom project type and filter tags

Notice how the tags such as **Console**, **C#**, **Desktop**, **Windows**, and even **TipTrick** now appear beneath our custom project template item. In previous exercises, nothing appeared in this space. Seeing these tags indicates that our new project template has been successfully imported for use by Visual Studio.

4. Go ahead and keep the default project name, such as WPF Console Starter2, and then create the new project. Previously, those spaces caused us a compilation error. However, this time you should not see a compilation error, as a result of our updated project template.

If you examine the project properties for our new project, you will see that our addition of the $safeprojectname$ namespace value in the <RootNamespace> element had the effect of adding underscores to our default namespace for the project.

The following screenshot depicts the resulting assembly name and default namespace, which contain underscores instead of spaces, because we used the $safeprojectname$ template parameter:

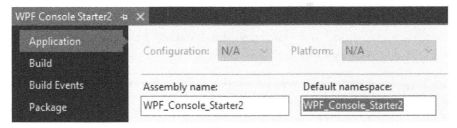

Figure 9.13 – Result of using $safeprojectname$

You now know how to export entire projects, but what if you only want a few files from a given project and not the whole thing? That is where project item templates are useful.

Exporting project items

Visual Studio is not limited to only working with entire projects when it comes to template support. If you only want a couple of files then simply choose the **Item template** option from the same **Export Template Wizard** dialog instead of **Project template**, as shown here:

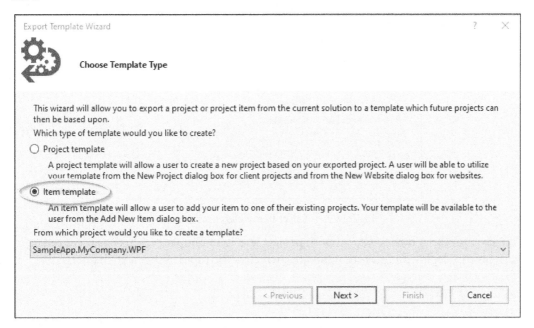

Figure 9.14 – Exporting an item template

The remainder of the item template experience parallels the procedures we just followed for project templates. One key difference is that, to import your template's .zip file, place it in the ItemTemplates directory instead of the ProjectTemplates directory, as illustrated in the following code snippet:

```
C:\Users\<your username>\Documents\Visual Studio 2019\
Templates\ItemTemplates
```

The other key difference is that you will be prompted to choose references that must be included for your item template to work:

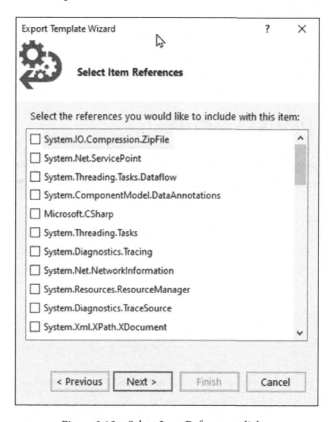

Figure 9.15 – Select Item References dialog

You have now seen how to export both project and item templates. This has prepared us to learn how to deploy our custom templates, which is the topic of the next chapter.

Summary

Visual Studio comes with many project template options out of the box. However, knowing when and how to use your own custom templates can be a very powerful and valuable weapon for developers to have in their arsenal.

In this chapter, we made a project template using our own custom WPF project that was already configured for things such as dependency injection, logging, multi-service implementation (mock, **JavaScript Object Notation (JSON)**, or **application programming interface (API)** data), and special output requirements. Keep in mind that things that can be done for project templates can also be done for individual files within a project.

By knowing how to export, import, use, and modify project template definitions, you have gained the skills needed to repeat successful architectures across multiple problem domains. This technique can result in achieving important benefits such as standardization across multiple projects, which eases learning curves, reduces maintenance costs, and makes enterprise architects happy. Additionally, using templates saves research and coding time, which can directly translate into cost savings on new projects.

In the next chapter, we are going to close out this theme with the distribution of our custom templates for broad use by other developers.

10
Deploying Custom Templates

Have you ever been tasked with creating a new application that is similar to one you previously created? What do you do in such situations? A common option is to locate that previous solution, copy/paste it, and then furiously search through it to change namespaces, remove obsolete code, and delete other project-specific configuration data.

This chapter is going to demonstrate an alternative approach, using an extremely powerful capability of Visual Studio—the deployment of custom templates. The prior two chapters on project and item templates have been building up to this point. Now that you understand project and item templates and have seen how to make your own, we are going to take things to a level beyond simple copying and refactoring an existing solution.

For context, in the last chapter, you learned how to use Visual Studio's built-in **Export Template Wizard**. This technique allowed us to easily create a `.zip` file containing everything Visual Studio needs to import and use templates that generate a single project. In many cases, such as templates designed solely for internal use, that may be all you will need. If so, sharing the `.zip` file for manual import may be sufficient. This chapter, however, is going to demonstrate the power of creating an extension (VSIX file, where **VSIX** stands for **Visual Studio Extension**) for Visual Studio. The extension that we create will be designed to provide a seamless installer for our custom template.

In this chapter, we will learn about the following topics:

- Introducing the client-server project

- Creating the VSIX deployment package

- Using the VSIX deployment package

- Publishing to the Visual Studio Marketplace

- Distribution instructions for the dotnet core **command-line interface (CLI)**

> **Advanced topic alert**
>
> The topic of creating and deploying multi-project templates, covered in this chapter, is a rather advanced one. Not every developer will have an immediate need to deploy custom templates to a broad audience. However, it is important that you understand this Visual Studio capability exists. If you are short on time, feel free to peruse the content and exercises in this chapter rather than focusing on mastering everything covered right now. When the right time comes, you will know what needs to be done and have this book as a reference.

Technical requirements

The code examples in this chapter have been tested with Visual Studio 2019 version 16.8.2 and the full .NET Framework version 4.7.2. Also, to follow along, make sure to clone the repository for this book. The code for this chapter is available on GitHub at https://github.com/PacktPublishing/Visual-Studio-2019-Tricks-and-Techniques/.

Please check the following link for CiA videos: http://bit.ly/3oxE5QM.

> **Warning**
>
> Please read the following if you receive an error while cloning the repository. Starting in Git 2.28, `git init` will look to the value of `init.defaultBranch` when creating the first branch in a new repository. If that value is unset, `init.defaultBranch` defaults to `master`. Because this repository uses `main` as its default branch, you may have to run the following code from Command Prompt or Git Bash to avoid an error:
>
> ~~$ git config --global init.defaultBranch main~~
>
> `Microsoft.VisualStudio.TemplateWizard` was updated in the version 16.8 release of Visual Studio. If you are using a version of Visual Studio prior to 16.8 then you may need to remove and re-reference the `Microsoft.VisualStudio.TemplateWizardInterface` assembly in the `CitySelector.Wizard` project to use version 8.0.0.0 instead of version 16.0.0.0. This can be done either through the **Solution Explorer** window or by changing this line in the `CitySelector.Wizard.csproj` file:
>
> ```
> <Reference Include="Microsoft.VisualStudio.
> TemplateWizardInterface, Version=8.0.0.0,
> Culture=neutral, PublicKeyToken=b03f5f7f11d50a3a,
> processorArchitecture=MSIL" />
> ```

The components required to create extensions for Visual Studio do not get installed by default out of the box. If you want to dig in and experiment with the exercises in this chapter then you need to install the **Visual Studio software development kit (SDK)** component.

Installing the Visual Studio SDK component

The easiest approach to ensure we can create a VSIX project is to run the Visual Studio Installer and install the Visual Studio SDK. To do this, navigate to the **Tools | Get Tools and Features...** menu item in Visual Studio. When you run the installer, ensure that the **Visual Studio extension development** workload is checked and installed, as shown in the following screenshot:

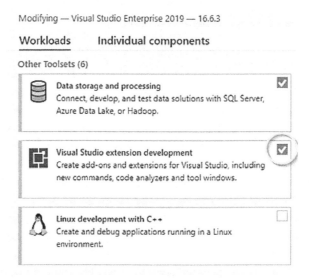

Figure 10.1 – Adding the Visual Studio extension development feature

> **What is a VSIX package?**
>
> A **VSIX package** is a file with a .vsix extension that contains one or more Visual Studio extensions. These packages also typically contain *assets* (discussed later) as well as metadata Visual Studio uses to search, filter, and install the extensions.

Introducing the client-server project

You are already familiar with the common single-project templates that Visual Studio ships with and makes available in the **Add New Project** dialog. But did you know that it is possible to have multiple coordinated projects in a single template? This multi-project template capability is what we work with in this chapter.

We are going to take a sample client-server application that consists of two related projects and use it as the basis for our multi-project template. So, the goal here is to develop a custom *client-server* project template that, when invoked from Visual Studio's **New Project** dialog, creates not one but *two* related projects, as follows:

- The first (*client-side*) project is basically the `CitySelector` **Windows Presentation Foundation** (**WPF**) application that we are already familiar with from prior chapters.

- The second (*server-side*) project is a Web API project designed to provide data to the WPF application.

Of course, your designs do not have to be limited to only two projects. Depending on your architecture, there could be a separate data access layer project, a business objects project, and so on.

Client-server sample code

The multiproject template examined in this chapter is based on our `CitySelector` sample application. In this section, we are going to take a brief look at that application to provide some context for the rest of this chapter's content.

Note that the clientside WPF project remains unchanged from prior chapters. As such, we will not go into detail on this one here. We do, however, want to open the solution and take a look at just a few noteworthy items in the new Web API project that has been added. Proceed as follows:

1. Open the `CitySelector.ClientServer.sln` solution that is located in the `Start` folder for this chapter. Compile the solution by navigating to the **Build | Build Solution** menu or by pressing the *F6* shortcut key. This will download and install referenced NuGet packages that satisfy the design-time editor.

2. Open the `CountryStateCityController.cs` class file found in the `Controllers` folder of the `CitySelector.API` project.

3. Find and navigate to the `LoadSampleData()` method. This method generates mock data that, in turn, is used by the action methods in this controller to return data from the Web API project to the WPF application.

The following screenshot shows an extract of the code:

```
private static List<CitySelectorDataItem> LoadSampleData()
{
    var retVal = new List<CitySelectorDataItem>();

    for (int i = 1; i < 10; i++)
    {
        Guid countryId = Guid.NewGuid();
        string countryName = $"Sample Country {i}";

        for (int j = 1; j < 10; j++) [...]
    }

    return retVal;
}
```

Figure 10.2 – LoadSampleData code extract

4. Open the Web.config file located at the root of the CitySelector.API project. For future reference, notice that there is a myDBConnectionString connection string setting in here, as shown in the following screenshot. As you will see in a later exercise, this value will be set dynamically when our template is invoked:

```
<connectionStrings>
  <add name="myDBConnectionString" connectionString="This is just a test connectionstring!" />
</connectionStrings>
```

Figure 10.3 – myDBConnectionString setting in web.config

5. Open the Index.cshtml page under the Views\Home folder. This page is written to display the following:

Name of the API project in an <h1> element, hardcoded in this version of the file

File version of the assembly

Value of the myDBConnectionString setting mentioned previously, using a ViewBag property

Note that the <h1> element will actually be switched to use a special parameter named $safeprojectname$ in the project template used in a later exercise, as illustrated in the following screenshot:

```
<div class="jumbotron">
    <h1>$safeprojectname$</h1>
    <h2>Version @ViewBag.Version</h2>
    <h3>DB Connection: "@ViewBag.DBConn"</h3>
</div>
```

Figure 10.4 – Index.cshtml templated to use $safeprojectname$

Because of this $safeprojectname$ parameter, the file that gets scaffolded using our template will instead contain whatever name is provided to the project by the user in the **Add Project** dialog.

6. Right-click on the CitySelector.ClientServer solution in **Solution Explorer | Set Startup Projects….** Choose the **Multiple startup projects option** and ensure that both the CitySelector.API and CitySelector.WPF projects both have their action set to **Start**, as illustrated in the following screenshot:

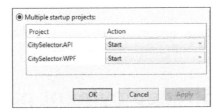

Figure 10.5 – Multiple startup projects

7. Try running or debugging the solution. If the solution is configured to start multiple projects, both the Web API and the WPF projects should launch and you should see something like the following:

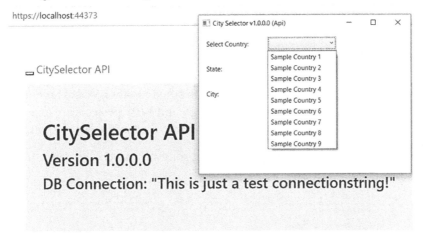

Figure 10.6 – Running the sample application

In the preceding screenshot, the server-side Web API page is shown launched in the background and the WPF client-side application is shown in the foreground, toward the upper right.

8. If you want to test it works as intended, select a country, then a state, then a city, and click the **OK** button. Open a text editor such as Notepad and press *Ctrl + V* to paste the contents to the clipboard. Depending on your selections, you should see something like this:

```
58128261-e9f8-455e-89f4-39f46f5620d3:c51b3181-1739-4b21-
883f-9c1712c121ea:c4af13a6-9948-40e3-a0f7-a11e824cbbac
```

All this output is meant to represent is three unique identifiers, separated by colons, each corresponding to one of your selections.

9. Stop the running application and close the `CitySelector.ClientServer. sln` solution.

Now that you are at least familiar with the original solution that our multi-project template is based upon, we can move into preparing our VSIX deployment package.

Creating the VSIX deployment package

Visual Studio extensions are installed using code packages that are commonly referred to as VSIX files, due to their file extension. Some extensions install **user interface** (**UI**) controls or add entirely new functionality to the **integrated development environment** (**IDE**), as we will see in later chapters. In this chapter, however, we will show the pieces required to make a deployment package that contains a project template capable of reproducing the custom solution from the prior section, using the **Add Project** dialog in Visual Studio.

Because creating a multi-project template could be a small book unto itself, a pre-built multi-project template is provided in the sample code. Our focus here will be what it takes to generate the VSIX file that can be broadly distributed to other Visual Studio users. As such, we start at a point after both the Web API and WPF projects are exported as templates. This project export technique was demonstrated in the last chapter.

To get started, let's walk through the deployment solution contents to gain a further understanding.

Open the `CitySelector.Deploy.sln` solution found in the `Template` folder of the sample code. Note that this solution consists of the following three projects:

1. `CitySelector.Deploy`: This creates the VSIX installation file.

2. `CitySelector.Template`: This contains the exported template projects for easy reference.

3. `CitySelector.Wizard`: This contains classes that implement `IWizard` and present a dialog during new project creation to collect the database connection string from the user.

> **Helpful sample code**
>
> Readers who want to apply this practice of creating multi-project solutions in their own endeavors can save many hours by leveraging and customizing this pre-built solution!

Reviewing the deployment project

In this section, we are going to review the key pieces that the deployment project needs in order to generate a working VSIX installation file. Proceed as follows:

1. With the `CitySelector.Deploy.sln` solution open, double-click on the `source.extension.vsixmanifest` file in the `CitySelector.Deploy` project and click on the **Assets** tab, as illustrated in the following screenshot:

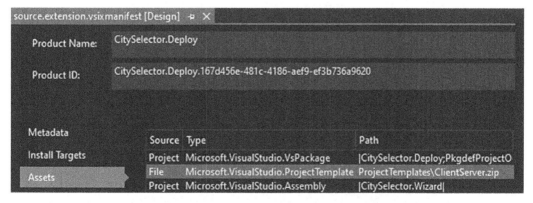

Figure 10.7 – Assets tab of the source.extension.vsixmanifest file

You should see three assets listed in the **Assets** tab, as follows:

When you create a new VSIX deployment project, the project itself is included by default as an asset. In the preceding screenshot, this is shown as the first asset.

The second asset shown in the preceding screenshot, `ClientServer.zip`, is a *file* type asset, as opposed to a *project* asset. This asset was added with a type of `ProjectTemplate` and was made by compressing the contents of the `CitySelector.Template` project.

The third and final asset, `CitySelector.Wizard`, is another *project* asset located in this solution and was added with a type of `Assembly`. Including this asset enables `.vsTemplate` files to reference code that can perform various actions during installation. As you will see, our installation will trigger code that copies a `ReadMe.md` file and also presents a dialog to the user requesting a database connection string for the Web API project to use.

2. Expand the `Pkgs` folder and look at the several NuGet packages whose actual `.nupkg` files are included in the `CitySelector.Deploy.vsix` output file that the `CitySelector.Deploy` project creates when it builds. The reason for this, as we will see later, is that all these NuGet packages are needed and referenced by our server-side Web API project. The packages can be seen in the following screenshot:

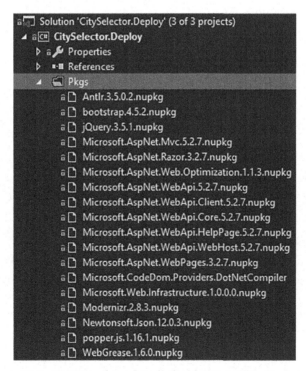

Figure 10.8 – NuGet packages bundled with CitySelector.Deploy.vsix

You might wonder why this approach is taken when many, if not all, of the referenced NuGet packages can be readily downloaded from nuget.org. There are a couple of basic explanations for this. The first reason is that we may want to bundle custom—possibly proprietary or non-public—NuGet packages that are not available for download from nuget.org. Another reason is that our solution has been tested with particular versions of each package. If a specific package version were no longer available or the user retrieved the latest release of a package that contained breaking changes, that would cause trouble. This approach allows us to bundle all the required dependencies for our solution in one package, akin to containerized development practices.

Including NuGet packages for classic packages.config

Be aware that projects using the classic packages.config approach to referencing NuGet packages should include those packages as part of the installation. As with all full framework ASP.NET projects, this *specifically applies to our Web API project*. Including these packages as a part of VSIX saves the user having to manually add these references to resolve compiler errors during that first build.

In contrast, this step is not strictly necessary for projects that use the newer PackageReference format, as *demonstrated by our WPF project* (which uses PackageReference).

In the next section, *Examining the template project*, we will see how another component, the NuGet.VisualStudio.TemplateWizard component, actually adds our referenced packages to the new project being generated.

3. Back in the CitySelector.Deploy project, expand the ProjectTemplates folder and locate the CitySelector.zip file that corresponds to the file asset described in the first step of this exercise. The important thing to understand here is that this file was manually created by compressing the contents of the CitySelector.Template project. If you are so inclined, go out to the filesystem, copy the file somewhere, extract the archive, and scan the output.

4. If you have not done so already, build the solution, then use Windows Explorer to navigate to the output directory of our deploy project's directory, Template\CitySelector.Deploy\bin\Debug. Sort by date modified, descending, and look for the CitySelector.Deploy.vsix file that gets generated. The whole point of this CitySelector.Deploy project is to generate this VSIX installation file.

> **Error – path too long**
>
> Because the name of the GitHub repository for this book is so long, you may receive the following error: `VSSDK1300: An error occurred while attempting to extract the vstemplate zip files. The specified path, file name, or both are too long. The fully qualified file name must be less than 260 characters....` If you do get this error, simply close the solution, navigate to the repository location on your local drive, and rename the folder from `Visual-Studio-2019-Tricks-and-Techniques` to VSTT. Then, you can reopen the `CitySelector.Deploy` project and try again.

5. The VSIX installation file generated by the `CitySelector.Deploy` project is really a compressed `.zip` file. Rename this file to have a `.zip` extension and extract its contents using Windows Explorer. Alternatively, you may use a utility such as 7-Zip to open the archive and inspect its contents, which are displayed in the following screenshot:

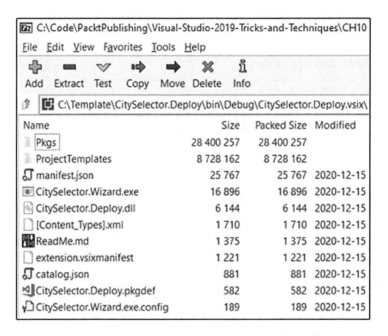

Figure 10.9 – Contents of the CitySelector.Deploy.vsix installation file

Notice that the bulk of the VSIX file size is due to the inclusion of the NuGet packages in the `Pkgs` folder, discussed previously. This is followed in size by our project templates directory, which contains the `ClientServer.zip` file. You may notice that all the files associated with Bootstrap, jQuery, and things such as Popper.js (a positioning engine for elements) take up a lot of space. None of these is strictly required for a pure Web API project and could be eliminated if size were a concern. Likewise, there are other ways to reference NuGet packages; for additional details, see `https://docs.microsoft.com/en-us/nuget/visual-studio-extensibility/visual-studio-templates`.

Also, see that a `CitySelector.Wizard.exe` file gets bundled in this VSIX package, which corresponds to the last asset mentioned in the first step of this exercise. We will explain what this executable does in the *Making template wizards* section coming up later in this chapter. Finally, note that there is a `ReadMe.md` file bundled into this VSIX package. There will be some code called out in our wizard implementation later that uses this file.

Now that we have a good idea about the deployment project, we will next review the template project that provides the actual content we intend to deploy.

Examining the template project

Let's return to Visual Studio and turn our attention to the `CitySelector.Template` project. This project contains all of our template files. I want to explicitly call out that this project is designed to contain *two* project templates, one in the `WebApi` folder and one in the `WPF` folder. These are glued together using the `Root.vsTemplate` file, which we will discuss momentarily.

If you have a simple template then it is not strictly necessary to create a separate project as we have done with the `CitySelector.Template` project. In simple scenarios, you have the option of using a single VSIX project and simply adding itself as a `ProjectTemplate` asset. For basic template scenarios, read the *Deployment* section of this documentation: `https://docs.microsoft.com/en-us/visualstudio/extensibility/creating-custom-project-and-item-templates?view=vs-2019`.

Refer to the following steps to examine the template project

1. Open the `Root.vsTemplate` file in the `CitySelector.Template` project that was mentioned earlier. The `<TemplateData>` element contents should look familiar by now, from prior chapters.

There is a <Name> element that, along with the <LanguageTag>, <PlatformTag>, and <ProjecTypeTag> elements, is used by Visual Studio for search and filtering user options in the **New Project** dialog.

We can use the value of the <Name> element, **Client Server WPF / Web API Application Template**, later to locate and select this project template for review and testing. Other elements, such as <Icon> and <PreviewImage>, are covered in a previous chapter.

2. In the screenshot that follows, look at the <ProjectCollection> element inside the <TemplateContent> element. By the way, the <SolutionFolder> elements are optional and are used here to illustrate how projects can be organized within solution folders—Server and Client, in this example:

```
</TemplateData>
<TemplateContent>
  <ProjectCollection>
    <SolutionFolder Name="Server">
      <ProjectTemplateLink ProjectName="$safeprojectname$.WebApi">
        WebApi\WebApi.vstemplate
      </ProjectTemplateLink>
    </SolutionFolder>
    <SolutionFolder Name="Client">
      <ProjectTemplateLink ProjectName="$safeprojectname$.WPF">
        WPF\WPF.vstemplate
      </ProjectTemplateLink>
    </SolutionFolder>
  </ProjectCollection>
</TemplateContent>
<WizardExtension>
  <Assembly>
    CitySelector.Wizard, Version=1.0.0.0, Culture=Neutral, PublicKey
  </Assembly>
  <FullClassName>CitySelector.Wizard.RootWizard</FullClassName>
</WizardExtension>
</VSTemplate>
```

Figure 10.10 – VSTemplate TemplateContent and WizardExtension XML file

The <ProjectCollection> element is the key to making a multi-project template. As shown previously, we are using multiple <ProjectTemplateLink> elements to instruct the project creation process to look for corresponding child .vstemplate files, specifically WebApi\WebApi.vstemplate and WPF\WPF.vstemplate.

3. Locate and open the child `WebApi\WebApi.vstemplate` and `WPF\WPF.vstemplate` files inside of their respective folders within the same project. Notice how their content is almost the same as that created in the prior chapter.

Near the bottom of the `WebApi.vstemplate` file, we have a few distinctions to consider, as follows:

- The first element to examine is the `<WizardExtension>` element. With a full class name of `NuGet.VisualStudio.TemplateWizard`, this gets added by default new project scaffolding. Recall from the *Reviewing the deployment project* section that this is the process responsible for locating and installing NuGet packages contained in the `<packages>` element. Have a look at the following screenshot:

```
</TemplateContent>
<WizardExtension>
    <Assembly>NuGet.VisualStudio.Interop, Version=1.0.0.0, Culture=neutra
    <FullClassName>NuGet.VisualStudio.TemplateWizard</FullClassName>
</WizardExtension>
<WizardExtension>
    <Assembly>CitySelector.Wizard, Version=1.0.0.0, Culture=Neutral, Publ
    <FullClassName>CitySelector.Wizard.WebApiWizard</FullClassName>
</WizardExtension>
<WizardData>
    <packages repository="extension"
              repositoryId="CitySelector.Deploy.167d456e-481c-4186-aef9-e
        <package id="Antlr" version="3.5.0.2" targetFramework="net472" />
        <package id="bootstrap" version="4.5.2" targetFramework="net472" />
        <package id="jQuery" version="3.5.1" targetFramework="net472" />
        <package id="Microsoft.AspNet.Mvc" version="5.2.7" targetFramework=
```

Figure 10.11 – WebApi.vstemplate XML elements

There is a second wizard shown in the preceding screenshot to consider. This one, created specifically for this project template, contains code that will be invoked during Visual Studio's add new project scaffolding process.

- The second `<WizardExtension>` element, with a full class name of `CitySelector.Wizard.WebApiWizard`, is representative of how to instruct the new project scaffolding process to invoke our custom code (described in the next section).

Technically, it is the `CitySelector.Wizard.RootWizard` element, referenced in the `Root.vstemplate` file, that will be invoked for our multi-project template that, in turn, invokes the `WebApiWizard` code, but you get the idea.

- Finally, the `<packages>` element is used by that NuGet wizard extension described previously. It contains metadata to instruct the process in which NuGet packages should be installed. The `repository` and `repositoryId` attributes indicate that we have bundled those packages into our VSIX deployment project.

- In case you are wondering, the value of the `repositoryId` attribute comes from the `Product ID` value of the `source.extension.vsixmanifest` file in our `CitySelector.Deploy` deployment project, as illustrated in the following screenshot:

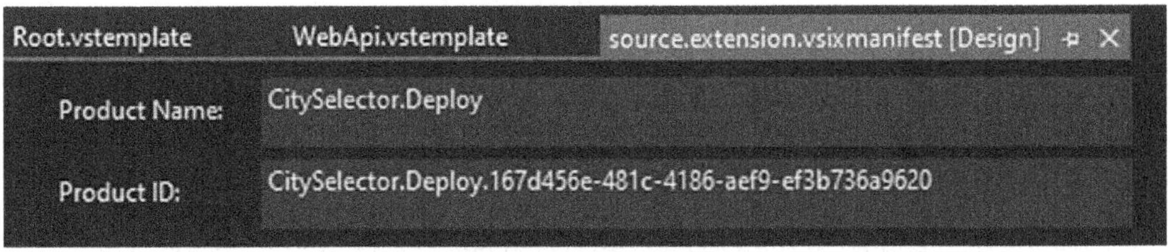

Root.vstemplate	WebApi.vstemplate	source.extension.vsixmanifest [Design] ₽ ✕
Product Name:	CitySelector.Deploy	
Product ID:	CitySelector.Deploy.167d456e-481c-4186-aef9-ef3b736a9620	

Figure 10.12 – Source.extension.vsixmanifest product ID

> **Caveat for referencing NuGet packages inside template files**
>
> If you were to inspect the `CitySelector.Template.csproj` project file inside the compressed `ClientServer.zip` template file of the `CitySelector.Deploy` project, you would notice that an additional directory level (`..\`) has been added to the `<HintPath>` elements: `<HintPath>..\..\packages\`. This is just something to keep in mind if you find yourself battling compiler issues, indicating that the NuGet references in your custom template cannot be resolved.

That wraps up what you need to know with respect to the template project. The final project in this sample solution, `CitySelector.Wizard`, contains code that will display a custom UI during project scaffolding. The page presented is designed to collect user input that can be used by the scaffolding process. In this case, we will prompt the user for a database connection string that will find its way into a `web.config` configuration file.

Making template wizards

When a user selects a new project to create, the Visual Studio process looks for assemblies referenced by the `<WizardExtension>` element contents (covered in the previous section). In our sample project, the `CitySelector.Wizard.RootWizard` wizard extension element is located at the bottom of the `Root.vstemplate` file in the `CitySelector.Template` project.

Open the RootWizard.cs class file found in the CitySelector.Wizard project. This is the class being referred to by that <WizardExtension> element in the previous *Examining the template project* section. Notice that the RootWizard class implements the **IWizard** interface, described next.

IWizard interface

The IWizard interface contains method signatures designed to be invoked at specific points in the project creation/scaffolding lifecycle. Two of these methods are leveraged by our custom multi-project template, as follows:

- RunStarted is the first IWizard interface method we will consider. It is invoked at the beginning of a template wizard run, as illustrated in the following screenshot:

```
public void RunStarted(object automationObject,
    Dictionary<string, string> replacementsDictionary,
    WizardRunKind runKind,
    object[] customParams)
{
    _dte2 = (DTE2)automationObject;
    _templateName = Path.GetFileNameWithoutExtension((string)customParams[0]);
```

Figure 10.13 – IWizard interface implementation of the RunStarted method

- RunFinished is the other method we will implement in this project. This method gets invoked once the wizard has completed all tasks and is illustrated in the following screenshot:

```
public void RunFinished()
{
    // Add ReadMe file to solution folder.
    var solution = (Solution2)_dte2.Solution;
    solution.AddSolutionFolder("Solution Items");

    // Copy the readme file to the solution directory.
    var sourceReadMePath = GetTemplateReadMeFilePath(_templateName);
    var destReadMePath = GetDestReadMeFilePath(solution, _templateName);
    if (!string.IsNullOrWhiteSpace(destReadMePath))[...]

    // Set startup project(s).
    if (_templateName == Consts.ProjectTemplates.Root)[...]
}
```

Figure 10.14 – IWizard interface implementation of the RunFinished method

With the `RootWizard.cs` class file open, notice how we cast the `automationObject` parameter to an instance of the `EnvDTE80.DTE2` class. By capturing this object in the `_dte2` module-level variable, we can use it later in the `RunFinished()` method.

Also noteworthy is that the first item in the `customParams` array is the name of the template that is executing—`Root.vstemplate` in this case.

This is the code responsible for invoking the `GetConnectionStringUserInput()` static method in the `WebApiWizard` class. That is the code designed to open a form to prompt our user for a database connection string, as illustrated in the following screenshot:

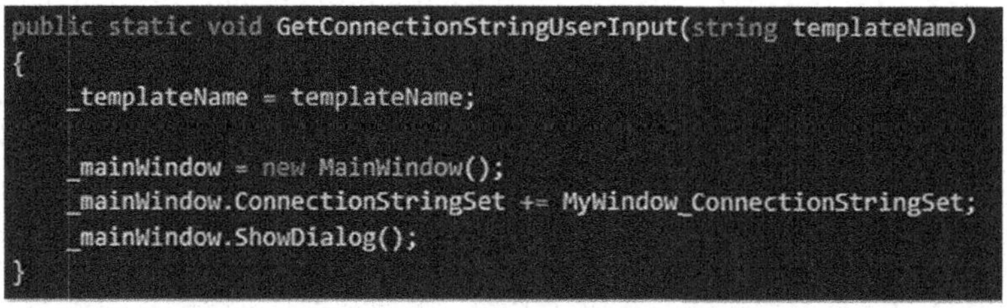

```
public static void GetConnectionStringUserInput(string templateName)
{
    _templateName = templateName;

    _mainWindow = new MainWindow();
    _mainWindow.ConnectionStringSet += MyWindow_ConnectionStringSet;
    _mainWindow.ShowDialog();
}
```

Figure 10.15 – Static GetConnectionStringUserInput method in WebApiWizard.cs

There is just a little bit of trickery going on to make this work, with a flow that includes the following:

- Subscribe to a custom `ConnectionStringSet` event.
- When the event gets triggered, the `MyWindow_ConnectionStringSet()` method contains code to take the user-input value on the displayed form and place it into a `RootDictionary` object.
- The stored value can later be pulled out of the `RootDictionary` object and placed in a local `replacementsDictionary` object. This occurs in the `RunStarted()` method of the `WebApiWizard` class.

As a minor note, we use the `ShowDialog()` call instead of `Show()`. This ensures that our project creation code will wait here until the user finishes their input and closes the modal form.

> **Sharing custom data between wizards**
>
> This is demonstrating an advanced technique that enables sharing of data/ user input between multiple child template wizards. If your needs are not that complex then it is possible to do away with the `RootDictionary` object and simplify the `WebApiWizard` code. In case it is not obvious, the `WebApiWizard` class also implements the IWizard interface.

At this point, we have dissected the template project, seen how custom code can be launched during add new project scaffolding, and reviewed the deployment project. Now, let's see all of this work in action.

Using the VSIX deployment package

In prior chapters, we had to take steps to manually install our custom project and item templates. Because we are using a VSIX extension installation project, we no longer need to manually import our template. Instead, simply running the `CitySelector.Deploy` project will make our template available for testing in Visual Studio's *experimental instance*.

If you are unfamiliar with using the experimental instance, it is basically a shadow copy of Visual Studio made automatically for you during installation. This copy is then used by developers to experiment with code in a way that does not affect your main instance. If anything gets corrupted, simply run the **Reset the Visual Studio 2019 Experimental Instance** app and a new, fresh, shadow copy is made.

As you will see in a moment, debugging launches a second—separate—instance of Visual Studio. This action is controlled by specifying a command-line argument of `/rootsuffix Exp` in the **Debug** menu of the `CitySelector.Deploy` project properties, as illustrated in the following screenshot:

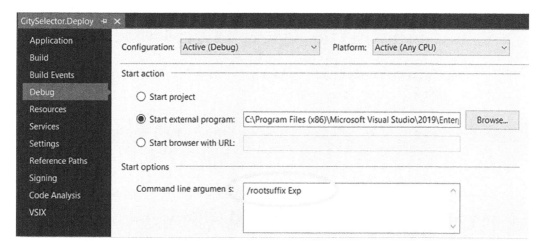

Figure 10.16 – Command-line argument to launch the Visual Studio experimental instance

For more information on the experimental instance, see `https://docs.microsoft.com/en-us/visualstudio/extensibility/the-experimental-instance?view=vs-2019`.

Testing the project template

Let's run our deployment project and see if we can create a new project! Proceed as follows:

1. If the `CitySelector.Deploy` project is not already set as the default project to run, set it as the startup project. Make sure the solution builds and then choose **Start Without Debugging** (*Ctrl + F5*). If all goes well, the experimental instance of Visual Studio should open.

2. Click the **Create New Project** button from the start page or choose **File | Add | New Project** from the menu. It may take a minute for Visual Studio to load project templates.

3. Once the templates are available, locate and select the **Client Server WPF / Web API Application Template** project. After selecting the template, click the **Next** button to continue, as illustrated in the following screenshot:

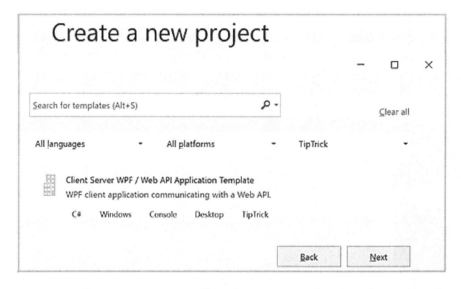

Figure 10.17 – Creating a new project: Client Server WPF / Web API Application Template

4. Give the project a name/location and then click the **Create** button, as illustrated in the following screenshot:

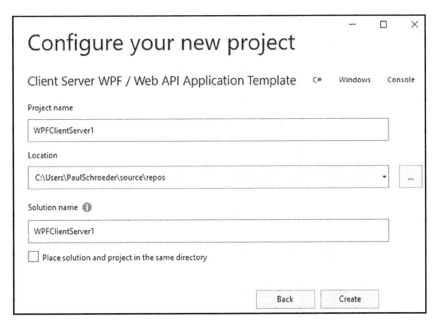

Figure 10.18 – Configuring a new project

5. A window titled **VS Tips and Techniques - Project Template Wizard** should display, prompting you to enter a database connection string. Enter some text into the input field.

It really does not matter what you enter here as we are using mock data in the Web API project and will not be connecting to a live database. However, be sure to remember what you enter because we will want to verify it gets used momentarily. For example, the `Server=myServerAddress;Database=myDataBase;User Id=myUsername;Password=myPassword;` value was used in the following screenshot. Click the **OK** button:

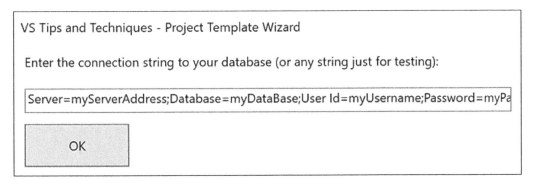

Figure 10.19 – Entering text to simulate gathering user input

6. If everything worked as designed after the project creation dialog closes, you should find yourself looking at a ReadMe.md file, as illustrated in the following screenshot:

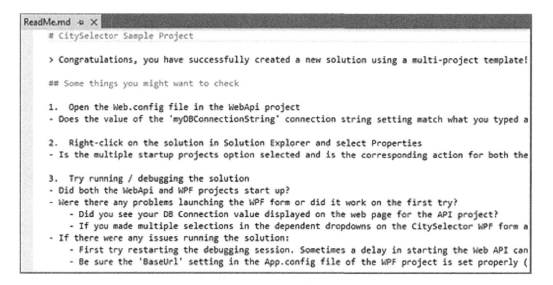

```
ReadMe.md  ₽ X
   # CitySelector Sample Project

   > Congratulations, you have successfully created a new solution using a multi-project template!

   ## Some things you might want to check

   1.  Open the Web.config file in the WebApi project
   - Does the value of the 'myDBConnectionString' connection string setting match what you typed a

   2.  Right-click on the solution in Solution Explorer and select Properties
   - Is the multiple startup projects option selected and is the corresponding action for both the

   3.  Try running / debugging the solution
   - Did both the WebApi and WPF projects start up?
   - Were there any problems launching the WPF form or did it work on the first try?
       - Did you see your DB Connection value displayed on the web page for the API project?
       - If you made multiple selections in the dependent dropdowns on the CitySelector WPF form a
   - If there were any issues running the solution:
       - First try restarting the debugging session. Sometimes a delay in starting the Web API can
       - Be sure the 'BaseUrl' setting in the App.config file of the WPF project is set properly (
```

Figure 10.20 – ReadMe.md file following new project scaffolding

Follow the instructions in the ReadMe.md file to inspect and run the application without debugging (*Ctrl + F5*). Depending on how your instance of **Internet Information Services Express** (**IIS Express**) was set up, you may receive a warning message, as follows:

> This project is configured to use SSL. To avoid SSL warnings in the browser you can choose to trust the self-signed certificate that IIS Express has generated. Would you like to trust the IIS Express SSL certificate?

If you get the preceding warning, you may want to check the **Don't ask me again** checkbox and click the **Yes** button. Then, confirm that you want to install the certificate on the next dialog that pops up. Alternatively, you should be able to run the following command from a developer Command Prompt (two dashes before trust):

```
Dotnet dev-certs https --trust
```

> **What is going on? You're blowing my mind!**
>
> Developers not accustomed to developing extensions and/or project templates may not be very familiar with the experimental instance of Visual Studio. At this point, with the application running, we have our original instance of Visual Studio that is running the `CitySelector.Deploy` project in the experimental instance of Visual Studio. Then, in the experimental instance, we are running code for a newly created project. Well, technically, our template created two projects, a Web API and a WPF project; we are running both. So, two instances of Visual Studio are running and two of our executables are running. Clear?

7. When you run the application, two windows should open, as shown in the following screenshot. One window shows the hosted Web API running, and the second window is the WPF application. The rest of the application behaves as demonstrated in previous chapters:

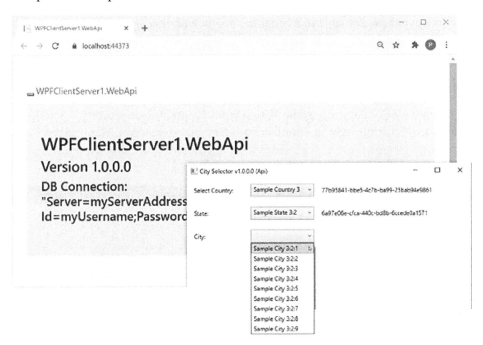

Figure 10.21 – Running the scaffolded CitySelector application using a Web API

> **Tip of the iceberg**
>
> Pause for just a moment to appreciate the power and potential of what just happened. With our custom template, we were able to scaffold out multiple coordinated projects that work together right out of the box. We demonstrated collecting user input, a connection string, during new project creation, and had that value automatically inserted into the `Web.config` file of the `WebApi` project.
>
> This is just the proverbial tip of the iceberg when it comes to what is possible. We could easily create advanced forms to gather additional user input and then use that information to dynamically change the code that gets scaffolded. For instance, the ASP.NET Core web application project template has all kinds of options to scaffold out an API, web application, Angular, or React project, with additional options for different authentication schemes and even Docker support.

So, now that we have a working multi-project template that can be deployed using a VSIX file, how do we make it available to a broader audience of developers? That is the topic of discussion in the final sections of this chapter.

Publishing to the Visual Studio Marketplace

Publishing your VSIX extension to the Visual Studio Marketplace is pretty straightforward. Basically, you can publish and manage extensions using `https://marketplace.visualstudio.com/vs`, as illustrated in the following screenshot:

Figure 10.22 – Publishing extensions to the Visual Studio Marketplace

Click the **Publish extension** link, fill in the basic information—information about you (the publisher)—and upload your VSIX file. Be aware that by publishing to the Visual Studio Marketplace, you are agreeing to Microsoft's 12-page legal agreement as well.

Distributing instructions for the Dotnet Core CLI

Just like we have done with our full framework projects, using .NET Core you can create and deploy templates that generate projects. Installing the .NET Core SDK will give you access to numerous built-in templates for creating projects and files. To see a list of the templates you have installed, open **Visual Studio Developer Command Prompt** and type the following:

```
dotnet new -l
```

You should see a list of project templates similar to the following:

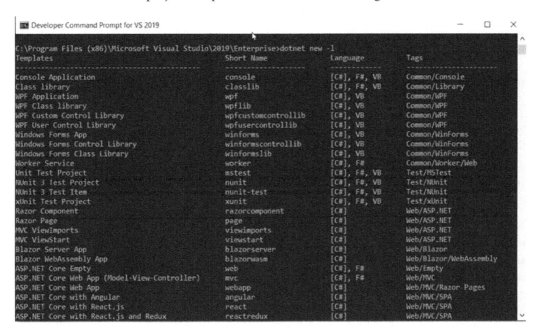

Figure 10.23 – List of .NET Core project templates

If you would like to see how you can make your own templates for the dotnet CLI, see https://docs.microsoft.com/en-us/dotnet/core/tools/custom-templates.

Even more interesting is that you can install custom templates from either a hosted NuGet package (that is, `nuget.org`) or by referencing a local filesystem folder/file that contains `.nupkg` files (which contain your template). For more information on how to do this, see the *Packing a template into a NuGet package (nupkg file)* section here: `https://docs.microsoft.com/en-us/dotnet/core/tutorials/cli-templates-create-project-template`.

That was quite an introduction to deploying your custom templates—let's wrap up.

Summary

This was the final chapter on an advanced productivity feature of Visual Studio, deploying multiproject templates. In this chapter, we gave an overview of a sample client-server application, `CitySelector`, which consists of a WPF application retrieving data from a Web API serving sample data. We walked through a recipe for creating VSIX deployment packages. The ingredients we covered included a deployment project, a template project, and a custom code project.

By implementing the `IWizard` interface, we were able to launch a form during new project creation to gather user input for use by our Web API project template. Finally, we rounded off the chapter with information on how to publish and distribute project templates in the Visual Studio Marketplace. As highlighted in the last section, you can also create project templates for use with the `dotnet new` command. These can even be packaged as NuGet files for easy installation.

Not every developer will find an immediate use for crafting their own project templates, yet knowing this capability exists is great information to have for when the right situation arises. Specifically, these skills apply in situations where you want to make new solutions similar to a proven one. Likewise, if you design an amazing architecture and want to share it, VSIX files are a very easy way for developers to install your templates.

Hopefully, you now have both the knowledge and the confidence to create your own project items and templates, as the need arises. Even if you do not see yourself creating your own custom templates anytime soon, you may now better appreciate knowing the inner workings of how Visual Studio itself accomplishes this feat for its own built-in templates.

In the next couple of chapters, we are going to take things down a notch and provide an overview of both Visual Studio 2019 and Visual Studio Code extensions. Once that foundation is set, we will again raise the bar and dive into some more advanced content with the CodeGenHero™ and PumaScan extensions.

Section 3: Leveraging Extensions for the Win

Extensions play a vital role in improving the developer experience and providing niche capabilities that are simply not available in the standard product. This section ensures that you do not miss out on the power that Visual Studio extensions have to offer. After preparing you with concise overviews, we dive into the details of three diverse extensions that really exemplify what is possible. You will learn how to clean, generate, and secure code. We close out the book with an overview of 15 favorite extensions for you to try.

This section has the following chapters:

- *Chapter 11, Overviewing Visual Studio 2019 Extensions*
- *Chapter 12, Overviewing VS Code Extensions*
- *Chapter 13, CodeMaid Is Your Friend*
- *Chapter 14, Be Your Team's Hero with CodeGenHero™*
- *Chapter 15, Secure Code with Puma Scan*
- *Chapter 16, Other Popular Productivity Extensions*

11
Overviewing Visual Studio 2019 Extensions

While Visual Studio 2019 is an amazing **integrated development environment (IDE)**, sometimes we find ourselves wanting to do things with it that it just doesn't support. Maybe we want to edit Markdown files, connect to other database backends, or perform myriad other tasks. Whatever the task is, if it's not a built-in Visual Studio function, extensions are probably the answer.

In this chapter, we will discuss the following topics:

- What are extensions?
- Visual Studio Marketplace
- Creating extensions
- Roslyn analyzers

By the end of this chapter, you will be able to find and create your own extensions for Visual Studio.

Technical requirements

The code for this book is available on GitHub at: `https://github.com/PacktPublishing/Visual-Studio-2019-Tricks-and-Techniques/tree/main/`.

Please check the following link for CiA videos: `http://bit.ly/3oxE5QM`.

What are extensions?

Visual Studio extensions allow you to add new functionality to the already amazing Visual Studio 2019 IDE. Adding new features or augmenting existing ones makes your overall experience more enjoyable, and often makes the development process smoother, quicker, and easier.

Extensions in Visual Studio 2019 are managed using the **Manage Extensions** functionality. On Windows, you can show the window using the **Extensions | Manage Extensions** menu, as illustrated in the following screenshot:

Figure 11.1 – Extensions menu (Windows)

On the Mac, you use **Visual Studio | Extensions…**, as illustrated in the following screenshot:

Figure 11.2 – Extensions menu (Mac)

Selecting these menu options will show the **Manage Extensions** window, as depicted in the following screenshot:

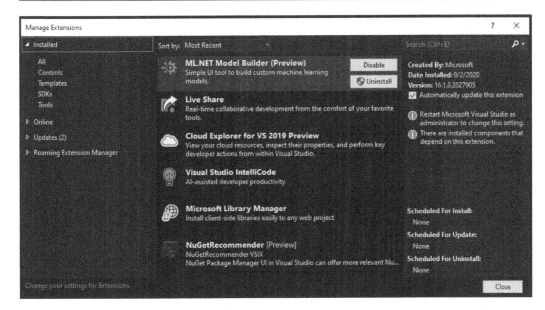

Figure 11.3 – Manage Extensions (Windows)

The **Extension Manager** functionality on the Mac has very similar options, as you will see in the following screenshot:

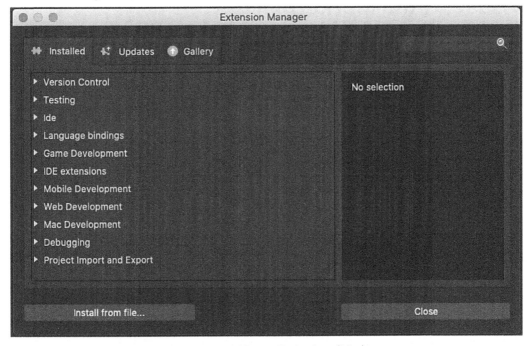

Figure 11.4 – Manage Extensions (Mac)

You will notice three primary categories of extensions, as follows:

- **Installed**: The **Installed** window shows all of the currently installed extensions. There are a number of categories for extensions, including **Controls**, **Templates**, **SDKs**, and **Tools**.

- **Updates**: If any of the installed extensions have been updated, they will show in the **Updates** window. Clicking an extension and selecting the **Update** button will update the selected extension, or use the **Update All** button to update all of the extensions with the updates available.

- **Online** or **Gallery**: The **Online** window (**Gallery** tab on macOS) takes you to **Visual Studio Marketplace**, which we'll discuss next.

> **Roaming Extension Manager**
>
> Visual Studio 2019 for Windows has an additional category named **Roaming Extension Manager** that allows you to install extensions across multiple development environments, such as your desktop and laptop, and keep them in sync.

Visual Studio Marketplace

This marketplace is the first place to look for an extension. Select this window and use the search box in the upper-right corner to find extensions, or browse through the hundreds of extensions that are already on the marketplace. Select one and hit **Download** (**Install** on macOS) and Visual Studio 2019 will download and install it, ready for you to use!

Creating extensions

So, what do you do when you want an extension but you can't find one in the marketplace that does what you want? Or, what if you find one but it doesn't do exactly what you want? It's simple—we're DEVELOPERS! We can just write our own.

Creating extensions in Visual Studio 2019 for Windows

To develop extensions in Windows, we need the **Visual Studio SDK (VSSDK)**. This can be installed using the **Visual Studio extension development** workload in the **Visual Studio Installer**, as shown in the following screenshot:

Figure 11.5 – VSSDK installation

There are a number of things we can extend in Visual Studio, including menus and commands, tool windows, languages and editors, projects, Visual Studio itself, and many other things. The **VSSDK** provides templates for menu commands, tool windows, editor extensions, basic VSPackages, and **Visual Studio Extension (VSIX)** projects.

Let's create a simple menu command that inserts a licensing header at the top of an open document, as follows:

1. Create a new **VSIX project**, and name it `HeaderInserter`. This will create our basic structure for the extension, including a base `HeaderInserterPackage.cs` C# code file and a `source.extension.vsixmanifest` file.

2. Right-click the project (not the solution). On the context menu, select **Add | New Item**.

3. Select the **Extensibility** section, and then choose **Command**.

4. In the **Name** field at the bottom, enter a filename such as `HeaderCommand.cs` and click **Add**.

5. Open the `HeaderInserterPackage.vsct` control file, and change the name of the button. Find the line that reads
    `<ButtonText>Invoke HeaderCommand</ButtonText>`
    and change it to
    `<ButtonText>Insert Code Header</ButtonText>`.

6. Execute the project using *F5*. This will start a new *experimental instance* of Visual Studio 2019 with the debugger attached. Choose **Continue without code** at the **Welcome** screen. Select **Tools | Insert Code Header** and you will see a message box, as illustrated in the following screenshot:

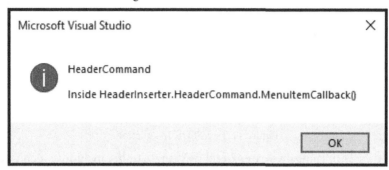

Figure 11.6 – Default HeaderCommand.cs

This is the default functionality of our command. Let's change that.

7. Stop your experimental instance of Visual Studio and edit the `HeaderCommand.cs` file. Replace the `Execute` method with the following code:

```
private async void Execute(object sender, EventArgs e)
{
    await ThreadHelper.JoinableTaskFactory.
        SwitchToMainThreadAsync();
    var dte = await this.ServiceProvider.
        GetServiceAsync(typeof(DTE)) as DTE;
    if (dte != null)
    {
        var activeDocument = dte.ActiveDocument;
        var doc = activeDocument.Object() as
            TextDocument;
        var header = "//\r\n// Copyright (c)
            Visual Studio 2019 Tips and Tricks. All
            rights reserved.\r\n// Licensed under the
            Creative Commons license. See LICENSE file in
            the project root for full license
            information.\r\n//\r\n\r\n";
        if (doc != null) doc.CreateEditPoint(doc.
            StartPoint).Insert(header);
    }
}
```

> **ActivePoint**
>
> This example inserts text at the top of the document (`doc.StartPoint`). If you want to insert text where the cursor is currently placed, you can use `doc.Selection.ActivePoint`.

8. You will also need to add a `using` statement at the top of the file, like this:

```
using EnvDTE;
```

9. Execute the project again. Choose **Continue without code** at the **Welcome** screen, then select **File | New File** and choose **Visual C# Class**.

10. Select **Tools | Insert Code Header** and you will see that this now inserts our licensing header at the top of the class, as illustrated in the following screenshot:

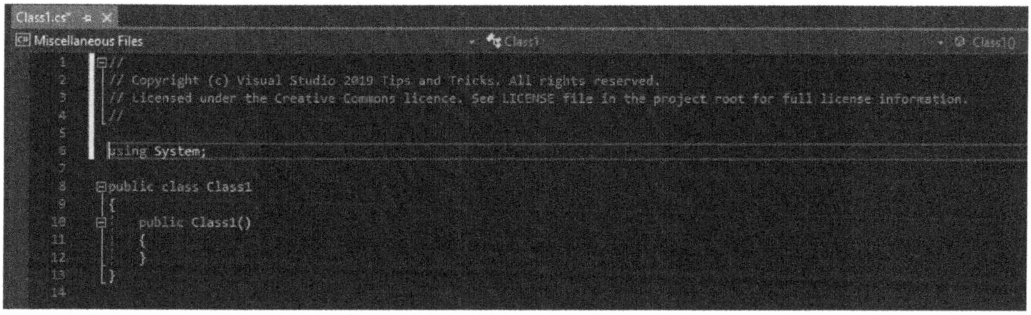

Figure 11.7 – Inserted header

> **Resetting the environment**
>
> If you run into issues with debugging or troubleshooting your VSIX extension, you can reset the experimental instance (the version of Visual Studio 2019 that is used to debug extensions) by using the **Reset the Visual Studio 2019 Experimental Instance** Windows Start menu item.

Now, let's look at how to create extensions for Mac.

Creating extensions in Visual Studio 2019 for Mac

macOS extension development requires the **AddinMaker** functionality. As with the **VSSDK**, **AddinMaker** will generate a basic extension for us to customize however we would like. **AddinMaker** is a Visual Studio 2019 extension itself and can be installed from the **Extension Manager**. It is located in the **Extension Development** section, as can be seen in the following screenshot:

Figure 11.8 – AddinMaker installation

Just as with Visual Studio 2019 for Windows, let's create a simple menu command that inserts a licensing header at the top of an open document, as follows:

1. Create a new **IDE Extension** project from the **Other | IDE Extensions** category in the **New Project** dialog.

2. Name the project `HeaderInserterMac` and click **Create**.

3. Edit the `Manifest.addin.xml` file in the `Properties` folder, and add `Command` and `CommandItem` to `ExtensionModel`. When you're done, it should look like this:

```xml
<?xml version="1.0" encoding="UTF-8"?>
<ExtensionModel>
    <Extension path="/MonoDevelop/Ide/Commands/Tools">
        <Command id="HeaderInserterMac.
            HeaderInserterCommands.InsertHeader"
            _label="Insert Code Header"
            defaultHandler="HeaderInserterMac.
            HeaderInsertHandler" />
    </Extension>
    <Extension path="/MonoDevelop/Ide/MainMenu/Tools">
        <CommandItem id="HeaderInserterMac.
            HeaderInserterCommands.InsertHeader" />
    </Extension>
</ExtensionModel>
```

This registers our `MacInserterMac.MacInserterHandler` method as the command that gets executed when the user clicks on the **Tools | Insert Code Header** menu item.

4. Right-click on the **HeaderInserterMac** project and click **Add | New File**. Add a new *empty enumeration* named Enums.cs. Replace the default enumeration with the following code:

```
public enum HeaderInserterCommands
{
    InsertHeader,
}
```

5. Right-click on the **HeaderInserterMac** project and click **Add | New Class**. Name the class HeaderInsertHandler.cs.

6. Replace the contents of the generated file with the following code:

```
using MonoDevelop.Components.Commands;
using MonoDevelop.Ide;

namespace HeaderInserterMac
{
    class HeaderInsertHandler : CommandHandler
    {
        protected override void Run()
        {
        }
        protected override void Update(CommandInfo info)
        {
        }
    }
}
```

7. Start the debugger by pressing *F5* and look at the **Tools** menu of the new experimental instance of Visual Studio 2019 for Mac that starts. To help you distinguish the running instances, the new instance that starts will be named **mono-sgen64** as compared to the original **Visual Studio** instance. You should see our **Insert Code Header** menu item. If you click on the menu item, you will see that it doesn't do anything. Let's add some code to make our extension more useful.

8. First, let's change the `Update` method to enable the add-in. In the
    `HeaderInserterHandler.cs` file, replace the `Update()` method with the
    following code:

```
protected override void Update(CommandInfo info)
{
    var textBuffer = IdeApp.Workbench.ActiveDocument.
        GetContent<ITextBuffer>();
    if (textBuffer?.AsTextContainer() is
        SourceTextContainer container)
        info.Enabled = container.GetTextBuffer() != null;
}
```

This code checks whether the current document is a text container (editor) and,
if so, enables the menu item.

9. You will also need to add two `using` statements at the top of the file, as follows:

```
using Microsoft.CodeAnalysis.Text;
using Microsoft.VisualStudio.Text;
```

10. Now, when you start the debugger (by pressing *F5*), create a new test *console
    application* (name this project whatever you like—it's just a test). Take a look at the
    Tools menu of the new experimental instance of Visual Studio 2019 for Mac that
    starts—you will see that our **Insert Code Header** menu item is enabled. Now,
    we can add some functionality to our add-in.

11. In the `HeaderInserterHandler.cs` file, replace the `Run()` method with the
    following code:

```
protected override void Run()
{
    var textBuffer = IdeApp.Workbench.ActiveDocument.
        GetContent<ITextBuffer>();
    var header = "//\r\n// Copyright (c) Visual Studio
        2019 Tips and Tricks. All rights reserved.\r\n//
        Licensed under the Creative Commons license.
        See LICENSE file in the project root for full
        license information.\r\n//\r\n\r\n";
    var insertPosition = 0;
    textBuffer.Insert(insertPosition, header);
}
```

> **Current position**
>
> This example inserts text at the top of the document (`insertPosition = 0`). If you want to insert text where the cursor is currently placed, you can set `insertPosition` to `textView.Caret.Position.BufferPosition.Position`.

12. Execute the project. Visual Studio 2019 will open a new experimental instance of Visual Studio with our add-in loaded.

13. Open the test console application you created earlier, and open the `Program.cs` file in the editor.

14. Click **Tools | Insert Code Header** and see our code execute and insert the code header at the top of the file!

Now, let's move on to our next topic, which is Roslyn analyzers—we're going to create a custom Roslyn analyzer.

Roslyn analyzers

With the advent of the **Roslyn** compiler, Microsoft has exposed a way for us to write our own custom rules (called **analyzers**) and have them executed by the compiler. We can now write rules that run as we type and show up in the IDE, just as with the built-in functionality such as undeclared variables, and we can even add code fixes for them!

To develop Roslyn rules in Visual Studio 2019 for Windows, we need the **.NET Compiler Platform SDK** functionality. This can be installed using the **Visual Studio Installer** by selecting it from the **Individual components** tab, under the **Compilers, build tools, and runtimes** category. You can easily get to the installer by selecting **Tools | Get Tools and Features** in Visual Studio. The following screenshot shows the **.NET Compiler Platform SDK** functionality:

Figure 11.9 – .NET Compiler Platform SDK

> **Roslyn in Visual Studio 2019 for Windows**
>
> This functionality was broken in Visual Studio 2019 for Windows prior to version 16.8.3. There are multiple open requests to fix the templates, and while there seems to be progress on the development side, it is not possible to create an analyzer using the **New Project** functionality. It is possible to work around this issue by creating an empty project, then adding a project to the solution via the solution manager.

Let's create a custom Roslyn analyzer to search for files that don't have our licensing header at the top, as follows:

1. Open Visual Studio 2019 for Windows and create a new **Analyzer with Code Fix (.NET Standard)** project.

2. Name the project `EnsureCodeHeaderExists` and click **Create**.

3. First, we need to create a method that searches each of the open files and checks for the header. Open the `EnsureCodeHeaderExistsAnalyzer.cs` file and search for the following lines:

```
// TODO: Consider registering other actions that act on
// syntax instead of or in addition to symbols
```

```
// See https://github.com/dotnet/roslyn/blob/master/
docs/analyzers/Analyzer%20Actions%20Semantics.md for more
information
```

```
context.RegisterSymbolAction(AnalyzeSymbol,
    SymbolKind.NamedType);
```

Instead of `SymbolAction`, we will use `SyntaxTreeAction` because we want to be able to examine the syntax tree (which will let us look at the code) instead. Replace the previous lines with the following code:

```
context.RegisterSyntaxTreeAction(AnalyzeComment);
```

4. Remove the `AnalyzeSymbol` method, as we will not use it.

5. Next, we need to add the `AnalyzeComment` method we registered previously. Create the method, and pass in `SyntaxTreeAnalysisContext`. This will give us access to the syntax tree we need to examine the code. The code for this is shown here:

```
private void AnalyzeComment(SyntaxTreeAnalysisContext
    context)
```

6. Now, we can get the text of the file, and check whether it starts with our licensing header. We can get the text of the file by calling `context.Tree.ToString()`, as follows:

```
var text = context.Tree.ToString();
if (!text.StartsWith("//\r\n// Copyright (c) Visual
    Studio 2019 Tips and Tricks. All rights reserved.\
    r\n// Licensed under the Creative Commons license.
    See LICENSE file in the project root for full license
    information.\r\n//\r\n\r\n"))
```

7. The last thing we need to do is create a **diagnostic**, which is what actually creates the notification in the IDE. We should also grab the filename to give the user a little more information about how to find the error, as follows:

```
var fileName = Path.GetFileName(context.Tree.FilePath);
...
var diagnostic = Diagnostic.Create(Rule, Location.
    Create(context.Tree, new TextSpan(0, 0)), fileName);
context.ReportDiagnostic(diagnostic);
```

Here, we are creating a new diagnostic using `Rule` (declared in the preceding code snippet) and a new `TextSpan` because we want our header to show up at the beginning of the file, and we pass in `fileName` so that we can use it in our description in the IDE.

8. That's it. Your finalized method should look like this:

```
private void AnalyzeComment(SyntaxTreeAnalysisContext
    context)
{
    var fileName = Path.GetFileName(context.Tree.
        FilePath);
    var text = context.Tree.ToString();

    if (!text.StartsWith("//\r\n// Copyright (c) Visual
        Studio 2019 Tips and Tricks. All rights
        reserved.\r\n// Licensed under the Creative
        Commons license. See LICENSE file in the project
        root for full license information.\r\n//\r\n\
        r\n"))
```

```
        {
            var diagnostic = Diagnostic.Create(Rule,
                Location.Create(context.Tree, new TextSpan(0,
                0)), fileName);

            context.ReportDiagnostic(diagnostic);
        }
    }
```

9. The last thing we need to edit is the `Resource.resx` file, because it contains all of our messages. Change `AnalyzerDescription` to `All files should contain licensing headers.`, `AnalyzerMessageFormat` to `The file '{0}' does not contain a licensing header.`, and `AnalyzerTitle` to `File Licensing Header`. This will give us reasonable messages as they appear in the IDE.

10. Let's see how we did! Set the `EnsureCodeHeaderExists.Vsix` project as the **Startup** project and press *F5* to start debugging.

11. When the new experimental instance of Visual Studio 2019 for Windows opens, load the `RoslynTestApp.sln` file from the Git repository. Open the `Program.cs` file and wait a few seconds (make sure you have **Warnings** enabled in **Error List**) and you should see a new warning that says **The file 'Program.cs' does not contain a licensing header**, as illustrated in the following screenshot:

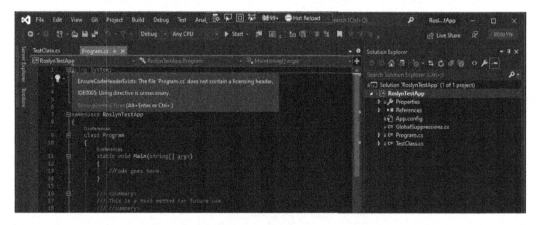

Figure 11.10 – Missing licensing header warning

> **Roslyn in Visual Studio 2019 for Mac**
>
> There is currently an open feature request to add custom Roslyn rule support in Visual Studio 2019 for Mac, but at this time it isn't possible to write custom rules for the Mac.

Now that we have the ability to write custom analyzers, there are all sorts of things we can automate and have run every time the compiler runs. We can even create custom fixes that will correct the code once we identify it!

Summary

In this chapter, we discussed Visual Studio extensions, how to manage them, and even how to write our own extensions in Windows and Mac. We also discussed Roslyn analyzers, and how we can use them to perform analysis of our code at runtime and even suggest fixes for the issues they find.

In the next chapter, we will discuss extensions in **Visual Studio Code** including how to add existing extensions from the marketplace, and even how to create your own.

12
Overviewing VS Code Extensions

While **Visual Studio Code (VS Code)** is a fantastic multi-language editing platform, we often find ourselves wishing that it could do additional tasks. Wouldn't it be great if we could view and edit GitHub tickets directly in VS Code? I would love to be able to edit MarkDown and create blog articles. If only I could connect to GitLab and see the latest status of my **Continuous Integration/Continuous Delivery (CI/CD)** pipeline. Wish no more! All these things and more are available as extensions to VS Code, and if there isn't an extension already, you can write your own to fill that void.

In this chapter, we will discuss the following topics:

- What are VS Code extensions?
- VS Code in Visual Studio Marketplace
- Creating an extension
- Publishing your extension

By the end of this chapter, you will be able to find and add extensions to VS Code, and even create your own and deploy them to the marketplace.

Technical requirements

Creating your own VS Code extensions requires the installation of Node.js (`https://nodejs.org`) and Git (`https://git-scm.com/`). You will also need the **Node Package Manager** (**npm**), which is installed with Node.js.

The code for this book is available on GitHub at: `https://github.com/PacktPublishing/Visual-Studio-2019-Tricks-and-Techniques/tree/main/`.

Please check the following link for CiA videos: `http://bit.ly/3oxE5QM`.

What are VS Code extensions?

Extensions in VS Code add functionality to the **integrated development environment** (**IDE**) that isn't built in. It can be something as small as a utility to insert a line of code, to a full-blown debugger/code formatter/syntax highlighter (that is, the C# for Visual Studio Code (powered by OmniSharp) extension that provides a full C# compiler and debugging environment). The functionality you can provide with an extension is virtually limitless.

In VS Code, we manage extensions using the **Extensions** view. We can access it using either the **View | Extensions** menu item or the **Extensions** icon on the sidebar, or through the *Ctrl + Shift + X* keyboard command (*Shift + Command + X* on a Mac). The **Extensions** view is shown in the following screenshot:

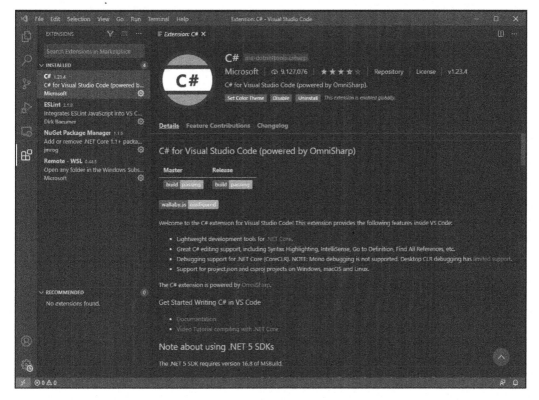

Figure 12.1 – Extensions view

This view lists all of the extensions currently in scope, as well as details about the extension in the right pane, and the installation status of the extension. There is a search box that allows you to find extensions as well.

> **To reload or not to reload**
>
> Some extensions can be applied in place, and some require the VS Code application to be reloaded. If a reload is required, a notification will be displayed in the **Details** pane. Simply click the **Reload** button, and VS Code will take care of the rest.

There are four additional views available in the **Extensions** view, as follows:

- The **Installed** view lists all of the currently installed extensions. If there is an update for an installed extension, it will be annotated as such in the list.

- The **Recommended** view shows all extensions that apply to tasks you have performed in the application. Say, for example, that you opened a Markdown document in VS Code—VS Code might then suggest the **Markdown** or **Markdown All in One** extension to make the development of Markdown documents easier.

- **Enabled** and **Disabled** views are just that: they show which extensions you have installed and which are currently enabled or disabled, depending on the view you have selected.

Now that we know how to view extensions in VS Code, let's talk about the Visual Studio Marketplace.

VS Code in the Visual Studio Marketplace

Unlike Visual Studio 2019, VS Code always shows extensions from the Visual Studio Marketplace. Searching for extensions is much like using the **Online** window or **Gallery** tab in Visual Studio 2019. Type your search criteria in the search box, select an extension to view the details, and if you like it click **Install**.

Creating an extension

What happens when you search and search but you still can't find the extension you want? Well, we are developers, after all, so let's just write our own! Everything we need to create an extension is available in a couple of **npm packages** all ready for us.

Generating a basic extension

Let's create an extension that inserts a licensing header at the top of an open document, as follows:

1. To get started, we will need to install the yo and generator_code npm packages. The yo package is a code scaffolder, which creates a basic project for us. The generator_code package contains the templates for the VS Code extensions. You can install them using the following command (on Windows, you will need to run this in an Administrator Command Prompt):

```
npm install -g yo generator-code
```

2. Once you have the required packages installed, we are ready to create our extension.

3. Start the creation of our extension by running yo code. This will ask **What type of extension do you want to create?**, as illustrated in the following screenshot:

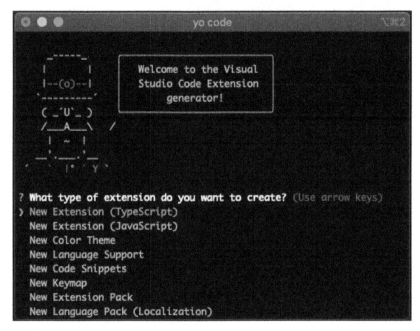

Figure 12.2 – Yo generator

4. Select **New Extension (TypeScript)**.

5. Name your extension HeaderInserterVSCode.

6. Leave the identifier blank, to use the default value headerinsertervscode.

7. Add a description, such as `Insert a Code Header into the current document`.

8. Don't initialize a Git repository (or do—your call). Neither choice will affect the creation or operation of our extension.

9. Don't bundle the source code with `webpack`.

10. Use the npm package manager.

11. When you finish making your selections, the extension generator should look like this:

```
aaron.cure@Aarons-MacBook-Pro-3: ~/Projects/Visual-Studio-2019-Tricks-and-Techniq...           ⌥⌘2


       |           |        ┌──────────────────────────┐
     |--(o)--|      │   Welcome to the Visual  │
     `---------'    │   Studio Code Extension  │
    ( _'U`_ )       │        generator!        │
    /___A___\   /   └──────────────────────────┘
     |  ~  |
   __'.___.'__
 ´   `  |° ´ Y `


? What type of extension do you want to create? New Extension (TypeScript)
? What's the name of your extension? HeaderInserterVSCode
? What's the identifier of your extension? headerinsertervscode
? What's the description of your extension? Insert a Code Header into the current document
? Initialize a git repository? No
? Which package manager to use? npm
```

Figure 12.3 – Yo generator (finished)

12. Navigate to the `headerinsertervscode` directory.

13. Open this folder in VS Code (from Command Prompt, use `code .`)

14. The generator created a large number of files for us, but the two we really need to be concerned with are `package.json` and `src/extension.ts`.

   The `package.json` file defines our function name and contains the structure to tell VS Code what to do with our extension. On *lines 2-4*, you will see the information we put into the `yo generator`:

```
"name": "headerinsertervscode",
"displayName": "HeaderInserterVSCode",
"description": "Insert a Code Header into the current
    document",
"version": "0.0.1",
```

15. The other item of interest to us right now in this file is the commands section. This is where the command name and title are defined. If you search for the headerinsertervscode.helloWorld command, you will see it is defined in the package.json file, as illustrated in the following code snippet:

```
"contributes": {
    "commands": [
        {
            "command": "headerinsertervscode.helloWorld",
            "title": "Hello World"
        }
    ]
},
```

16. The extension.ts file contains the actual implementation code for our extension. The two things we need here are the activate function and the registerCommand call, as illustrated in the following code snippet:

```
export function activate(context: vscode.
ExtensionContext) {
    ...
    let disposable = vscode.commands.registerCommand(
        'headerinsertervscode.helloWorld', () => {
    ...
        vscode.window.showInformationMessage('Hello World
            from HeaderInserterVSCode!');
    });
    context.subscriptions.push(disposable);
}
```

17. activate is called when the extension is instantiated in VS Code. This is where we register commands and perform initialization actions.

18. The registerCommand call defines the method/actions that will be performed when the extension is called. In this case, we register the headerinsertervscode.helloWorld command handler (remember this from the package.json file?) so that the function is called.

19. Let's see our extension in action! Press *F5*, which starts a new instance of VS Code with our extension running.

20. Open the **Command Palette** using *Ctrl + Shift + P* (*Shift + Command + P*) and enter the Hello World command, then press *Enter*. You should then see the following message:

Figure 12.4 – Hello World VS Code

Making our extension work for us!

Now that we know the extension works, let's make it do what we want, as follows:

1. First, let's update src/extension.ts. We need to get a TextEditor object so that we can make changes to the text. Then, we will use the editor, create a new insert position (line 0, character 0), and insert our text at that position. We will also change the name of the registered command from helloWorld to addCodeHeader. Replace your existing activate function with this function:

```
export function activate(context: vscode.
ExtensionContext) {
    const disposable = vscode.commands.registerCommand(
        'headerinsertervscode.addCodeHeader', () => {
        // Get the active text editor
        const editor = vscode.window.activeTextEditor;
        if (editor) {
            var header = "//\r\n// Copyright (c) Visual
                Studio 2019 Tips and Tricks. All rights
                reserved.\r\n// Licensed under the
                Creative Commons license. See LICENSE file
                in the project root for full license
                information.\r\n//\r\n\r\n";
            var insertPosition = new vscode.Position(
                0, 0);
            editor.edit(editBuilder => {
                editBuilder.insert(
                    insertPosition, header);
            });
        }
```

```
    });
        context.subscriptions.push(disposable);
    }
```

2. Now, we need to edit the `package.json` file. We need to make three changes here: in the `activationEvents`, we need to change the `onCommand` action to point to our `addCodeHeader` registered action. We also need to change the `command` and `title` properties to be more in line with our function, as follows:

```
"activationEvents": [
    "onCommand:headerinsertervscode.addCodeHeader"
],
"main": "./out/extension.js",
"contributes": {
    "commands": [
        {
            "command": "headerinsertervscode.addCodeHeader",
            "title": "Add Code Header"
        }
    ]
},
```

3. Now, if we run the code (*F5*), our new instance of VS Code will open again. Add a new file and open the **Command Palette** using *Ctrl + Shift + P* (*Shift + Command + P*). Enter the `Add Code Header` command and press *Enter*, and our extension will add a header at the top of the currently open document.

Editing selections

If we want to interact with text that is already there or a selection, we can use the `TextEditor` object we created earlier, like this:

```
const document = editor.document;
const selection = editor.selection;
const word = document.getText(selection);
editor.edit(editBuilder => { editBuilder.
replace(selection, replacement);
```

Now that we have a fully functional useful extension, we should share it with the world! Let's talk about publishing it to the marketplace.

Publishing your extension

Once you have your extension polished and ready to share, you need to push it to the marketplace. We will use **vsce** for this. Short for **Visual Studio Code Extensions**, vsce is a command-line tool for packaging, publishing, and managing VS Code extensions.

> **Prerequisites to packaging and publishing**
>
> Before you can publish, you will need to create a **personal access token** (**PAT**) and a publisher. This process requires you to have an Azure DevOps organization, which is free to create and use.
>
> More information on this process is available from `https://code.visualstudio.com/api/working-with-extensions/publishing-extension#publishing-extensions`.

Just like before, we will use npm to install the `vsce` package, like this:

```
npm install -g vsce
```

Once it's installed, we can use it to package and publish our extensions directly to the marketplace. To create a **vsix** package, we just need to move into the directory, run `package`, and then `publish`, by doing the following:

1. Navigate to the `headerinsertervscode` directory.

2. Before you can create a package or publish your extension, you will need to edit the `package.json` file and add a publisher name. Add your publisher name to the file, as follows:

    ```
    "publisher": "<your publisher name>"
    ```

    A sample of this change is shown in the following screenshot:

    ```
    {
        "name": "headerinsertervscode",
        "displayName": "HeaderInserterVSCode",
        "description": "Insert a Code Header into the current document",
        "version": "0.0.1",
        "publisher": "VisualStudioTipsAndTricks",
        "engines": {
    ```

Figure 12.5 – Adding a publisher name

3. If you want to package the extension to test or share with your friends, you can run `vsce package`. This will generate a `headerinsertervscode.vsix` file that can be installed to other VS Code instances with the `code --install-extension <your extension name.vsix>` command.

> **Missing repository**
>
> During the package or publish process, `vsce` may prompt you with a warning that states **A 'repository' field is missing from the 'package.json' manifest file.**, asking if you would like to continue. It is safe to enter y here, or alternately you can add a repository field to your `package.json` file.

4. Next, we run `vsce publish` and our extension goes to market!

We can also use `vsce` to search, retrieve metadata, and unpublish extensions. The `vsce --help` command will list all of the options available from the tool.

Summary

In this chapter, we discussed extensions in Visual Studio Code and how to locate and install them from the Visual Studio Marketplace. We also talked about creating extensions and made our own extension to put a licensing header at the top of a code file. Lastly, we created a `vsix` file to share our extension and discussed deploying it to the marketplace.

In the next chapter, we will cover the `CodeMaid` extension for Visual Studio and see how we can use it to clean up our code.

13
CodeMaid is Your Friend

Visual Studio, as amazing and mature as it is as an **integrated development environment (IDE)**, will never be everything to everyone right out of the box. What contributes greatly to its function is its open extensibility. This means that non-Microsoft developers can write code to do things that those developing the core Visual Studio product have not thought of, do not have the bandwidth to tackle, or simply choose to let others handle. The handful of custom extensions visited in the last few chapters are great examples of developers going beyond what is offered in the initial installation.

In the next few chapters, we are going to take a deep dive into interesting extensions that serve as diverse examples of what is possible. In this chapter, we will start with the CodeMaid extension.

The primary features of CodeMaid involve cleaning and organizing your code. Random spacing is made consistent, using statements can be sorted (or removed if unused), and class members are reorganized in alphabetical order. I have known people who refuse to develop without CodeMaid and install this extension immediately after a fresh install of Visual Studio, before writing any code.

There are several reasons why developers should care about the functionality CodeMaid provides. First and foremost, clean code is much easier to read and, thus, change. Similarly, inconsistent coding practices are a nightmare to maintain. Imagine walking into a grocery store and having all the products randomly placed throughout the floor. CodeMaid will reorganize your random placement of methods and properties so that each is grouped with its own kind and placed in alphabetical order. Similarly, it promotes randomly placed module-level variables to the top of class files.

These behaviors are akin to a grocery store placing vegetables together, or meats in one area. Just as it helps the shopper, organized code helps the maintainer. For those of you who use a Git-based version control, CodeMaid makes code reviews smoother because changes are easier for the difference engine to visualize. Over the long term, these practices will save you time and, in turn, money.

In this chapter, we will look at the following topics:

- A brief history of CodeMaid
- Learning about cleanup actions
- Exploring CodeMaid Spade
- Build Progress

> **Using your own projects**
>
> Instead of providing dirty sample-code examples in this chapter, we want to encourage readers to use CodeMaid with their own personal .NET solutions. It is recommended that you use a project that is already in source control so that you can better detect the before-and-after differences.

By the end of this chapter, you should have a much better understanding of the functions and features of the CodeMaid extension. You will appreciate how it can help you write better code that is more readable, maintainable, and testable. Finally, for those of you interested in writing your own extensions, you will also have a great resource as a reference example.

> **Installing the CodeMaid extension**
>
> The current 11.x version of CodeMaid supports Visual Studio versions 2019 and 2017. However, CodeMaid's VSIX installer can be downloaded from Visual Studio Marketplace at the following web page: `https://marketplace.visualstudio.com/items?itemName=SteveCadwallader.CodeMaid`.

Technical requirements

The code for this book is available on GitHub at: https://github.com/PacktPublishing/Visual-Studio-2019-Tricks-and-Techniques/tree/main/.

Please check the following link for CiA videos: http://bit.ly/3oxE5QM.

A brief history of CodeMaid

Steve Cadwallader, a developer hailing from Indiana, has maintained the CodeMaid open source project since its inception. This extension has been available since 2007 and there are versions still available all the way back to Visual Studio 2005! Over the years, Visual Studio's out-of-the-box functionality has gradually incorporated many features that once were only available through CodeMaid. Even so, if you ever want to create your own Visual Studio extension, it is worthwhile examining CodeMaid's open source code at the following web page: https://github.com/codecadwallader/codemaid.

> **Coding your own extension**
>
> There is much to be learned from this veteran project. More details, along with instructions on how to contribute, can be found at https://www.codemaid.net/.

Configuring CodeMaid

The ability to organize code consistently and automatically is where CodeMaid really shines. This Visual Studio extension works to clean up and simplify coding in over a dozen programming languages, including C# and JavaScript. As with most features in CodeMaid, the user can change options to configure which file types it should or should not process. There is even the ability to configure regular expressions to exclude files based on pattern matching.

The following screenshot shows the different file types CodeMaid can help with:

Figure 13.1 – CodeMaid file type options

There is an extensive set of configuration options available with this extension. To see all the configuration settings, navigate to **Extensions | CodeMaid | Options**, which will take you to the following screen:

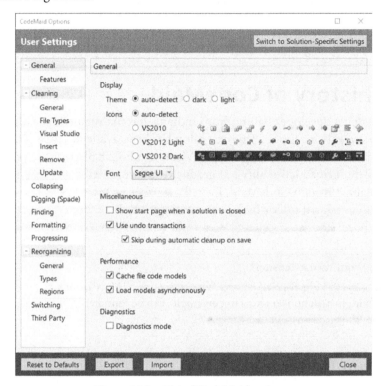

Figure 13.2 – List of CodeMaid options

With an understanding that CodeMaid is highly configurable, let's begin looking at some of the problems developers face that this extension can help with, starting with code reorganization.

Reorganizing to reduce merge conflicts

Any developer who has ever worked with a Git source control repository in a team environment can attest that resolving merge conflicts is not their favorite task. Often, the difficulty is that the difference comparison engine cannot correctly identify changes, additions, and deletions. This is particularly true when one developer moves methods or places properties in a different order from another developer who may have touched the same file. What CodeMaid does is *ensure each team member's code gets organized in a consistent fashion*. This has a direct and immediate impact on both reducing merge conflicts and making it much easier to isolate which code in a `pull` request actually changed.

The following screenshot of the configurable **Types** option in CodeMaid shows the default order followed to reorganize a document. Fields such as module-level variables come first, followed by constructors, then on through properties, methods, and – eventually – contained classes:

Figure 13.3 – CodeMaid Reorganizing | Types dialog

Beyond merge conflict reduction, CodeMaid virtually eliminates unconstructive team member behavior such as *churning code*. It's sad to say, but I have been on teams where a developer would simply move things around to make it look like a lot of work had been done when only a couple lines of code were truly different. And, no – I am not talking about refactoring. Requiring the team to use CodeMaid, which alphabetizes all the methods and properties, puts an end to this flavor of dysfunctional behavior.

Reducing noise in pull requests and code reviews

As depicted in *Figure 13.3*, item order can be customized in any way you like through simple drag-and-drop operations. Likewise, items can be combined, split, or even renamed. Changes to the ordering here control how the extension will reorganize code in project files. Of course, when changes are made you want those to persist somehow, and that is the job of user profile and solution settings, covered next.

User profile and solution settings

From the **Extensions | CodeMaid | Options** dialog, you can toggle between settings saved to your user profile and settings persisted to a solution-level file that can be added to your source control repository, as illustrated in the following screenshot:

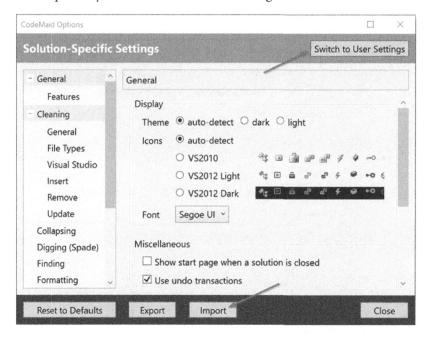

Figure 13.4 – Solution-specific or user-specific settings exported or imported

It is also possible to export and import the settings files that contain configuration differences from the default settings. In this manner, you can share your preferred settings with fellow developers.

Similarly, as depicted in the following screenshot, you can add the generated configuration files to source control. Having all team members share a single solution-level configuration file is how code remains organized in a consistent manner, regardless of who is doing the work:

Figure 13.5 – Adding a solution configuration file to source control

> **More reorganization features**
>
> There are a number of reorganization features we have not detailed, such as **Format comments**, **Join lines**, **Remove regions**, **Sort lines**, and **Switch file**. Although performing exercises on each feature would likely prove boring to our readers, we do encourage you to experiment with these on your own!

If reorganizing code were all CodeMaid did, it would still be useful. In the next section, we will see how this extension serves to also clean up our code files.

Learning about cleanup actions

Once the extension is installed, the **Extensions | CodeMaid** context menu does an excellent job of calling out the most used functions. Near the top of the following screenshot, we see several **CleanUp** menu items. These different options dictate whether the cleanup operation will occur on just the active document, all open documents, or the entire solution:

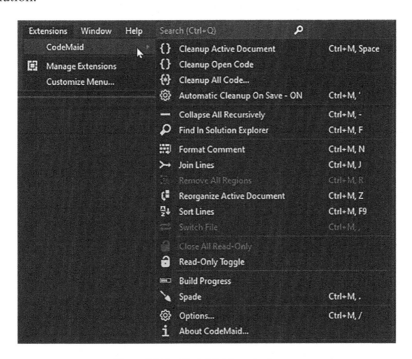

Figure 13.6 – CodeMaid context menu

When we talk about cleanup actions, we are primarily interested in things such as this:

- Removing unused `using` statements and sorting the rest alphabetically

- Removing extra whitespace or adding space in front of the method, between lines, or at the end of lines

- Formatting indentation and whitespace from one line to the next to match its level within the logic hierarchy or display tag structure

- Adding access modifiers to variables or methods where they are currently absent (are they private or internal by default?)

- Removing regions that have no content

Turning on automatic cleanup on save

Two highly recommended options, the first turned off by default, are given here:

- **Automatically run cleanup on file save**, found in the **Cleaning | General** options

- **Run reorganize at start of cleanup**, found in the **Reorganizing | General** options

---

The following screenshot shows a couple of checkboxes that you are recommended to enable:

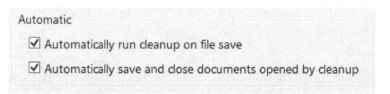

Figure 13.7 – Cleaning general options

Automatically running cleanup and reorganizing upon file save is a great way to ensure files are made or kept consistent. In fact, whenever I inherit someone else's code base where CodeMaid was not being used, *the very first commit/check-in I make is one where no new code is introduced. Instead, all I do is simply run the CodeMaid cleanup utility across the entire solution or project by project, depending on the solution size.*

Coffee-break warning

The previous recommendation has the effect of running the reorganize/cleanup process across all the code, for the enabled file types, in the solution. Although this action should not affect the logic or runtime results (of course be sure to test afterwards), it can take a very long time to run. Even individual files can take a long time to run if they have thousands of lines of code. For this reason, CodeMaid gives you the opportunity to change your mind before it embarks on cleaning the entire solution

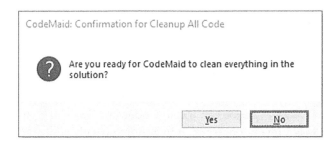

Figure 13.8 – Cleaning everything in the solution

Otherwise, if you do not reorganize the entire pre-existing solution, what happens is small changes can look like big changes. This is because the first time you go to edit/save a file CodeMaid will reorganize it. This reorganization and cleaning increase the number of differences detected compared to what is in source control beyond your actual edits. This can make it more difficult for a code reviewer to discern what really changed.

A truce for generated code

As the author of another Visual Studio extension, CodeGenHero, I appreciate that CodeMaid has support for a feature to exclude generated code files. Code that is generated should be idempotent regardless of how many times you regenerate that file (subsequent manual customizations aside).

Without support for bypassing files that are code-generated, what happens is generated files that do not exactly match the type order configured in CodeMaid end up getting reorganized upon a `save` operation. This causes source control to believe that files have changed when they have not. Rather, their code is just churning as an ongoing battle ensues between the code generator and the CodeMaid extension.

Including the phrase `<auto-generated>` in a document is all that is required for CodeGenHero to detect and skip that file. In fact, this technique will work even on files that are not the result of code generators, but I would not advocate that approach. It is probably best to go into the CodeMaid options and configure regular expressions with any files to skip, instead.

Now that we have an understanding of cleanup actions, let's talk about the functionality that Visual Studio 2019 for Windows already offers.

The narrowing gap

As mentioned previously, the gap between the functionality Visual Studio 2019 now offers and CodeMaid functionality has narrowed over time. Code cleanup is one of those areas where Visual Studio now has its own cleanup utility that CodeMaid ties into.

Besides reorganization and cleanup, there is one more piece to CodeMaid that we want to cover, and honestly, it could be an extension by itself – CodeMaid Spade.

Exploring CodeMaid Spade

CodeMaid Spade can be accessed either by using the **Extensions | CodeMaid | Spade** menu or via the *Ctrl + M + .* (period) shortcut. CodeMaid Spade has similar functionality to Visual Studio's **Class View** but presents it in a more visually appealing format. Spade also has a few extra bells and whistles included in its digging feature (Spade; digging – get it?), such as the following:

- Provide an overview of the code with easy mouse click navigation to each item
- Double-click on a method, property, or field to highlight that piece of code
- Right-click to delete entire methods, properties, or entire regions (everything within the region) or to find references for the given item
- Left-click on the plus/minus icon or middle-click on regions to open or collapse the region
- Sort either alphabetically or by file order
- Search functionality
- Simple drag and drop to reorder code items
- Perform multi-select using *Shift + click* or *Ctrl + click* to do multi-select

Using the Spade feature can make these common tasks a little easier and more pleasant. As we view these items, we can see just how complex our code is. In fact, CodeMaid has some functionality to help us gauge complexity.

McCabe Cyclomatic Complexity

Back in 1976, a person named Thomas McCabe aimed to capture the complexity of a module (that is, method) in a single number. For our purposes, this metric is roughly equivalent to one plus the number of conditional loops and if statements in each method or class. The basic premise is that high numbers are indicative of code that may be difficult to maintain or is a good candidate for refactoring along the lines of the **Single Responsibility Principle (SRP)**.

Something CodeMaid Spade does a nice job of is displaying the cyclomatic complexity of each item in an unobtrusive way, as shown in the following screenshot:

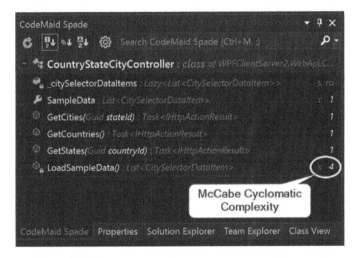

Figure 13.9 – CodeMaid Spade cyclomatic complexity

Also, in case you did not know, it is worth mentioning that Visual Studio has its own code analysis tools, which you can access and run from the **Analyze | Run Code Analysis** menu. You may want to give these a try on one of your own solutions to see if they can identify potential trouble areas. The following screenshot provides an example of these tools being run:

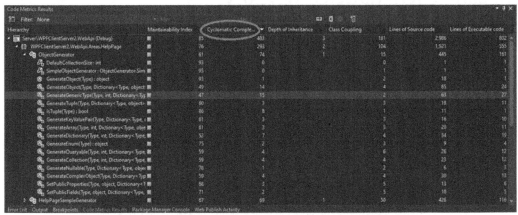

Figure 13.10 –Visual Studio's code analytics tool

Let's wrap up this chapter's content with a quick mention of yet another CodeMaid feature, its **Build Progress** window.

Build Progress

As a quick footnote, if you have large solutions with many projects then you may also want to check out CodeMaid's **Build Progress** feature. It provides a little additional information on the progress of a solution build and is illustrated in the following screenshot:

Figure 13.11 – CodeMaid's Build Progress window

This might not seem like a major feature, but it helps you decide if you have time for a quick coffee break.

Summary

This chapter brought to life an excellent example of a popular Visual Studio extension, CodeMaid. This tool emphasizes that your code should be as readable and maintainable as possible. Authors use things such as sections, chapters, and headings to organize writing to help the reader follow along. Similarly, developers should use clear and organized namespaces, variables, properties, and methods within class files.

You learned that the benefits of organized code include reductions of merge conflicts and code churn. Taken together, clean code has the main advantage of making it easier to read and modify during maintenance activities, which, over time, tends to outweigh time spent initially writing the code. And, of course, that not only makes it a more pleasant experience for developers that have to support the application, but can also save time and money.

We covered several of CodeMaid's capabilities and showed you how to configure options to control its behavior at a very granular level. Even though Visual Studio has grown to incorporate some of CodeMaid's functionality over time, it remains one of those must-have extensions. With dozens of contributors, CodeMaid also illustrates the kinds of things that can be done with community contributions. Its open source repository on GitHub serves as a good resource from which future extension developers, such as yourself, can learn.

In the next chapter, we are going to explore CodeGenHero™, a time-saving Visual Studio extension that generates source code instead of reorganizing it. This builds upon several of the concepts and skills learned throughout prior chapters in this book.

14
Be Your Team's Hero with CodeGenHero™

Too frequently, teams lack the headcount, senior talent, or software process methodology discipline necessary to succeed with enterprise projects. And by succeed, I mean managing a project so that it progresses sustainably and gets delivered in a reasonable – time period and on budget.

What if we could improve our chances of success by *leveraging code that outputs code itself*—in other words, take a small input, such as a database connection string, and use it to output a large number of coordinated class files that serve a targeted purpose? That is the general idea behind code generators, such as **CodeGenHero™**, the Visual Studio extension that we examine in this chapter. We will see how this tool can reverse-engineer information about the tables, fields, and data types in a database. It uses that schema metadata to automatically generate a fully functioning **REpresentational State Transfer application programming interface (REST API)**, along with a class that makes it easy to retrieve or update data from a client application.

You can visualize that, as the database schema changes in response to new requirements, keeping the Web API up to date is as simple as rerunning the code generator. This process is one way you, as a developer, can shorten the time it takes to iterate changes and improve the feedback loop that is critical to project success.

In this chapter, we will demonstrate how it is possible to deliver quality functionality using code generation techniques that adapt quickly to changing requirements. You will learn about the following topics:

- Understanding the core concepts of code generation

- Introducing CodeGenHero™

- The CodeGenHero™ solution

- Handling change with CodeGenHero™

Upon completion, you will have a better appreciation for what is possible with code generation techniques as well as Visual Studio extensions. Perhaps you will be inspired to explore other pre-packaged solution architectures that CodeGenHero™ offers, such as ASP.NET Core Blazor templates, or even consider the development of your own custom templates.

Technical requirements

The code examples in this chapter have been tested with Visual Studio 2019 and the full .NET Framework v4.7.2. Also, to follow along, make sure to clone the repository for this book. The code for this chapter may be cloned from GitHub using this repository location: https://github.com/PacktPublishing/Visual-Studio-2019-Tricks-and-Techniques.git.

The CodeGenHero™ Visual Studio extension used in this chapter is available for download at https://codegenhero.com/. Free trials are available with registration and email confirmation.

Please visit the following link to check the CiA videos: https://bit.ly/3oxE5QM.

> **Warning**
>
> Please read the following if you receive an error while cloning the repository. Starting in Git 2.28, `git init` will look to the value of `init.defaultBranch` when creating the first branch in a new repository. If that value is unset, `init.defaultBranch` defaults to `master`. Because this repository uses `main` as its default branch, you may have to run the following code from Command Prompt or Git Bash to avoid an error:
>
> `$ git config --global init.defaultBranch main`

Understanding the core concepts of code generation

The concepts of source code generation, generative programming, and metaprogramming have been around for a very long time. The central concept is to *develop programs* that use input parameters, metadata, or both to output code themselves.

Input parameters are self-explanatory to programmers, and metadata will be covered in the next section. Because this is a hands-on book, we will not include much theory behind these techniques. Instead, for context, we will cursorily consider that the Visual Studio project and item templates are basically code generators themselves. Likewise, if you are familiar with **T4 templates** (usually denoted by the file extension `.tt`, and **T4** stands for **Text Template Transformation Toolkit**), you know their entire purpose is to generate code. In fact, Visual Studio itself uses T4 templates behind the scenes to output code, as we will see shortly.

The important thing to understand here is that code generators such as these often work by accepting user-provided input. This input is then used to change their behavior and output code differently, depending on the values given. An example of this might be the project name and location values that you type when using the **Add | New Project** dialog. That information is used to tell the templates where to store the output files in the filesystem, as well as the default namespace to use.

Things get even more interesting when you have templates that combine the use of input parameters with metadata, which is described next.

Metadata and templates

Metadata is information that describes other data (data about data). There is a distinction between *input parameters* and *metadata* to make by example here. If you have ever developed an MVC 4 application, you may be familiar with the **Add View** modal dialog. This dialog appears with a right-click on an action method in a controller, and you then select the **Add View** context menu item, as shown in the following screenshot. The **View name** you provide and other selections, such as the **Model class** chosen, provide *input* that drives the T4 template behavior:

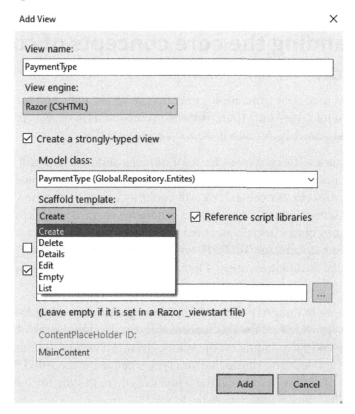

Figure 14.1 – MVC Add View

When you click the **Add** button, which template file is used behind the scenes depends upon what you select in the **Scaffold template** dropdown. The result is a new file being created under the `Views` folder. But how does the generated code know how to match up with properties in the chosen model class?

The answer is that each template has code that uses *reflection* to examine and extract information about the public properties within the chosen model class, as well as the data type of each property—that property and type information can be considered as *metadata*.

> **Location of MVC T4 templates**
>
> In case you are curious, it is possible to inspect and even customize the T4 templates used by Visual Studio. For example, if you have the *MVC 4* option installed, you can examine the `*.tt` T4 files located in the following directory: `C:\Program Files (x86)\Microsoft Visual Studio\2019\Enterprise\Common7\IDE\ItemTemplates\CSharp\Web\MVC 4\CodeTemplates\AddView\CSHTML\`. The location on your machine may be slightly different from **Enterprise**, depending on your version of Visual Studio 2019. For more information on T4 templates, see `https://docs.microsoft.com/en-us/visualstudio/modeling/code-generation-and-t4-text-templates?view=vs-2019`.

The following screenshot shows the T4 template files that you can expect to find if you have the **MVC 4** option installed:

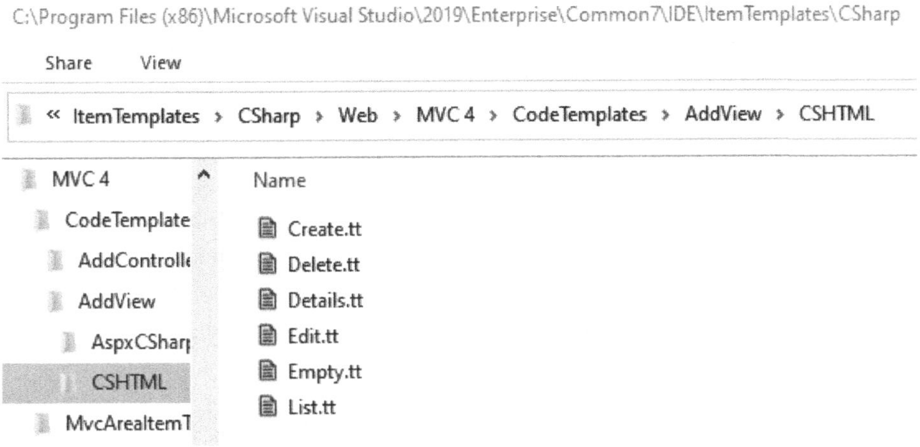

Figure 14.2 – Location of MVC 4 *.tt T4 files

As with those T4 templates, the CodeGenHero™ templates used in this chapter rely upon metadata. The metadata used by the CodeGenHero™ templates in this chapter focus on information about database tables, fields, and relationships between entities. We will look at this extension next.

Introducing CodeGenHero™

Ever noticed how users can better describe what they want after seeing what they don't want? Ever given a demo of a freshly completed functionality only to have someone verbalize a missed requirement that will require significant redesign? Does anyone on your development team resist creating maintainable, layered architectures because of the extra time and effort to change? Do you simply have too much to code and too little time? If any of these questions hit the mark and you are creating enterprise-grade applications, then CodeGenHero™ is something you want to investigate.

The CodeGenHero™ Visual Studio extension reverse-engineers your database schema and stores that metadata for use by code generation templates. Templates use this metadata to output any number of useful class files. In fact, while the templates demonstrated in this chapter output C# code, there is no reason why templates you use or write yourself cannot output F#, Blazor/Razor, **Extensible Application Markup Language** (**XAML**), Visual Basic, React, Angular, JavaScript, or **PHP: Hypertext Preprocessor** (**PHP**) syntax, or anything else.

Individual templates become exponentially more powerful when used in synergy with other templates to create coordinated **template bundles**. Coming up, we will use a .NET Full Framework bundle that moves data across a Web API boundary using generated repository classes, interfaces, mappers, controllers, and client-side data access code. Take just a moment to think about what this means and about the value offered. *Being able to automatically generate these classes in seconds saves developers a tremendous amount of time.* Not only does that time saving scale up in proportion with the number of tables and fields in our database, but the code produced is completely error-free. When was the last time you wrote dozens of classes and thousands of lines of code without any bugs?

Installing CodeGenHero™

Installation of the CodeGenHero™ Visual Studio extension, although recommended, is *not* required to view the exercises in this chapter. That said, to fully appreciate the tool and its capabilities, you are encouraged to register for a free trial. If you want to experiment on your own, register for a free trial at `https://codegenhero.com/`.

Once you have confirmed your email address, you may download the CodeGenHero™ Visual Studio for Windows 2019 extension from the **Subscriptions** tab of your profile, as illustrated in the following screenshot (or you could simply use this **Uniform Resource Locator (URL)**: https://codegenhero.com/Identity/Account/Manage/licenses):

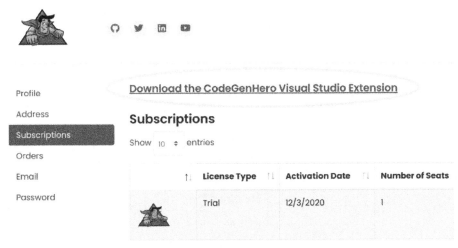

Figure 14.3 – Download CodeGenHero™ link

> **Open source contributors**
>
> CodeGenHero™ templates, NuGet packages, and sample projects are open source. If you do create your own templates or want to contribute to the many NuGet packages available at https://github.com/MSCTek/CodeGenHero, then pull requests are welcome!

The sample code that accompanies this chapter contains C# syntax output by CodeGenHero™. It simply compiles and runs as though you wrote it by hand. The obvious difference is that it was not written by hand. Rather, metadata about database tables, fields, and relationships between those entities was used to generate much of the code.

Example project overview

The sample project in this chapter should seem familiar as it is the same basic **City Selector Windows Presentation Foundation** (**WPF**) application used in prior chapters. When run, the user first selects a country, then a state, and finally a city. The selections available in the **State** dropdown depend upon the country selected. Similarly, selections available in the **City** dropdown depend upon the state selected. An extract from the application is shown in the following screenshot:

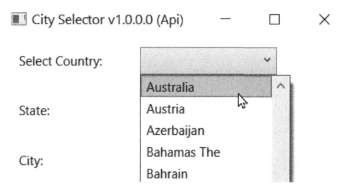

Figure 14.4 – City Selector WPF sample application

However, instead of using mock data, this time we are pulling data from an actual SQL Server Express LocalDB. The sample database provided contains three tables, Country, State, and City. Additionally, this data is serialized across a server-side Web API boundary, so the WPF client application does not have direct database access. Instead, we use a client-side data access client class that is designed to query our server-side Web API. This simulates a more realistic enterprise architecture.

Before we can run this sample application, we must first attach the provided database to the SQL Server Express instance that gets installed with Visual Studio. To do this, proceed as follows:

1. Assuming you have already cloned the repository, open the CGHClientServer1. sln solution located in this chapter's sample code folder.

2. Connect to LocalDB in **SQL Server Management Studio**, using the (localdb)\ MSSQLLocalDB server name. Alternatively, using **SQL Server Object Explorer** in Visual Studio, click the **Connect to Server** icon and expand the chevron next to **Local**, or input the (localdb)\MSSQLLocalDB server name.

> **What is (localdb)\ProjectsV13?**
>
> If you open **SQL Server Object Explorer** in Visual Studio for the first time, chances are that you will only see a `(localdb)\ProjectsV13` instance. It is not that you cannot use this instance, but it is considered a better practice to connect to the `(localdb)\MSSQLLocalDB` instance and use that for your own projects.

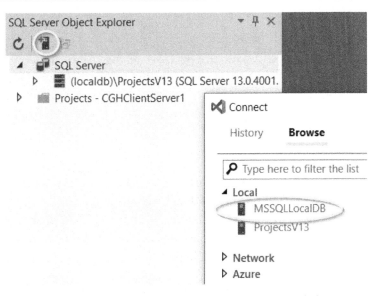

Figure 14.5 – Connecting to (localdb)\MSSQLLocalDb

3. Once you have a connection to `(localdb)\MSSQLLocalDB`, right-click on the instance's connection and select **New Query...** from the context menu.

4. Back in Visual Studio, locate the sample database provided in the `App_Data` folder of the `CGHClientServer1.WebApi` project, as illustrated in the following screenshot:

Figure 14.6 – Locating the sample database file

5.   Using file paths *adjusted for your own local directory paths*, attach the sample database using the following **Structured Query Language** (**SQL**) code. Run this script against your (localdb) \MSSQLLocalDB instance. You can do this using either **SQL Server Object Explorer** in Visual Studio or **SQL Server Management Studio** (**SSMS**):

```sql
USE [master]
GO
CREATE DATABASE [CountryStateCity] ON
( FILENAME = N'C:\Code\CH14\CGHClientServer1\Server\
CGHClientServer1.WebApi\App_Data\CountryStateCity.mdf' ),
( FILENAME = N'C:\Code\CH14\CGHClientServer1\Server\
CGHClientServer1.WebApi\App_Data\CountryStateCity.ldf' )
 FOR ATTACH
GO
```

6.   Verify that you receive a Command(s) completed successfully. message, as shown in the following screenshot. Once the command has successfully executed, click the **Refresh** icon located in the upper left of **SQL Server Object Explorer**. After drilling down a couple of levels, you should now see a new database, CountryStateCity, as illustrated here:

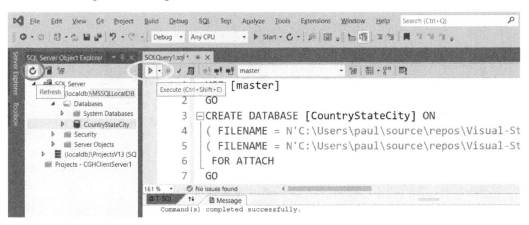

Figure 14.7 – SQL script successfully run in Object Explorer

7.   Once you have the database attached and have refreshed your view, take a moment to examine the tables and fields in the database, displayed here:

Figure 14.8 – Database tables and fields

8. Before running the application in Visual Studio, verify that multiple projects will start when you run by right-clicking on the solution in **Solution Explorer** and choosing the **Multiple startup projects** radio button. If they are not already configured, be sure that the CGHClientServer1.WebAPI and the CGHClientServer1.WPF applications are both set to **Start**. Then, click the **Apply** and/or **OK** buttons. *Both the server and client projects must be run simultaneously or the application will not work.* The projects are shown in the following screenshot:

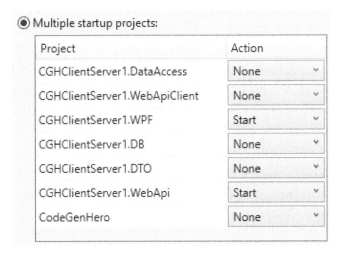

Figure 14.9 – Multiple startup projects

9. Run the application and be patient, as it may take some time for the SQL Express database to activate and for the Web API to make its connection. Note that in fresh installations of Visual Studio, it is not uncommon to receive a **Secure Sockets Layer (SSL)** warning due to **Internet Information Services Express (IIS Express)** not trusting its self-signed certificate, as illustrated in the following screenshot:

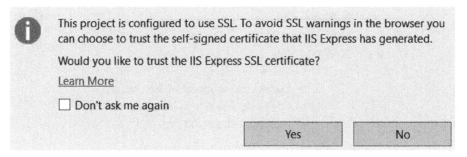

Figure 14.10 – Trusting the IIS Express SSL certificate

If you receive the preceding dialog, you may click the **Don't ask me again** checkbox, click the **Yes** button, and **confirm it's okay to install the certificate**. In many cases, that will be the end of it. However, do not be surprised if this dialog returns at some point down the road. Depending on how your instance of IIS Express was setup, you may receive a warning message:

```
This project is configured to use SSL. To avoid SSL
warnings in the browser you can choose to trust the self-
signed certificate that IIS Express has generated. Would
you like to trust the IIS Express SSL certificate?
```

If you get the above warning, you may want to check the Don't ask me again checkbox and click the Yes button. Then, confirm that you want to install the certificate on the next dialog that pops up. Alternatively, you should be able to run this command from a developer command prompt (two dashes before `trust`):

```
Dotnet dev-certs https --trust.
```

10. Once both the Web API and the WPF applications launch, make some drop-down selections and click the **OK** button. If for some reason the dropdowns do not load, and you are sure the LocalDB is attached as per the preceding *Step 3*, try clicking the **Refresh** icon, as illustrated in the following screenshot:

Figure 14.11 – City Selector running application

Remember that the result of this application is simply to copy your selections to the clipboard when the **OK** button is clicked. Close the application or stop debugging when you are finished. With multiple startup projects set, it is possible that you may receive the following error dialog:

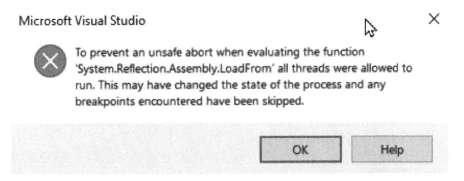

Figure 14.12 – Preventing unsafe abort error

If you do receive the error dialog shown in the preceding screenshot and it annoys you, stop debugging. Then, go to **Tools | Options | Debugging | General**. Once there, enable the **Use Managed Compatibility Mode** option and retry.

11. In Visual Studio, press *Shift + Ctrl + F* to bring up the **Find and Replace** dialog box. Be sure the **Look in** dropdown is set to **Entire solution** and change the **File types** being searched to *.cs. Next, type <auto-generated> as a search string and click the **Find All** button.

The files in the search result were generated using CodeGenHero™ templates, including Web API controllers and the `DataClient` class. Notice that *out of 54 files in the solution with a* `.cs` *extension, 21 (or almost 40%) of them were autogenerated.* Although this is significant, it is on the low end of what is possible because we are using a sample database schema with very few tables.

Take a moment to consider the possibility of using the skills gained in previous chapters on project items and project templates to create/scaffold your own application architectures. Those skills, when combined with the CodeGenHero™ workflow, make it possible to have a fully functional enterprise application in less than a day—not something architected as a **proof of concept (POC)** or a **minimum viable product (MVP)**, but the foundation of an architecture that can be adapted and maintained over the long term.

Soon, we will dive into the CodeGenHero™ extension itself. Before doing so, let's first take a quick detour to mention the .NET Core **command-line interface (CLI)** so that we are on the same page with respect to what it means to *scaffold* (that is, **code generate**) a project.

Scaffolding a solution – .NET Core CLI

If you are not already familiar with the .NET Core CLI, take a moment to open the **Developer Command Prompt for VS 2019** functionality. To list the available projects to the scaffold, type the following command:

```
dotnet new -l
```

There are many things you can do using the .NET Core CLI and, in fact, Visual Studio itself makes use of it. Scaffolding a project, such as we have previously done with the **Add Project** dialog in Visual Studio, can also be done using a command such as this (assuming you have the desktop workload installed):

```
dotnet new wpf
```

This will not be necessary, though, because we are going to begin with a pre-generated solution in this chapter. It is, however, worth noting that we could use the `dotnet new` command from the .NET Core CLI to create/scaffold a project that was preconfigured for use with CodeGenHero™. All we would then need to do is point it at our project's database to refresh the metadata and integrate the generated output files into our solution. You will be able to better understand the possibilities once we walk through how CodeGenHero™ works its magic, which is covered next.

The CodeGenHero™ solution

If you have not already done so, open the CGHClientServer1.sln solution located in this chapter's sample code folder using *Visual Studio 2019 for PC*. If you already installed the CodeGenHero™ extension using the instructions previously provided, now is the time to open the main window. You can do this by accessing the **Extensions |CodeGenHero | CodeGenHero Main Window** menu item, shown here:

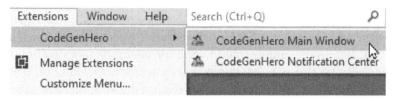

Figure 14.13 – Extensions | CodeGenHero™ Main Window

If you have already registered, enter your username and password credentials for your CodeGenHero™ account and click the **Login** button. If you have not registered, click the **Register** button, as illustrated in the following screenshot:

WELCOME	METADATA	BLUEPRINT	TEMPLATES

Already a Hero?
Username

Password

Login   Forgot Password

Want to be a Hero? ❓

Register

Figure 14.14 – CodeGenHero™ WELCOME tab

Once you have successfully authenticated, you should find yourself on the **WELCOME** tab with information about the Current CodeGenHero project to the right, shown in the following screenshot:

CodeGenHero Project: ❓

In Solution Explorer, highlight the CodeGenHero Project in your solution.

Set CodeGenHero Project

Current CodeGenHero project:
CodeGenHero\CodeGenHero.csproj

Figure 14.15 – Setting the CodeGenHero™ metadata project

> **Blank Current CodeGenHero project?**
>
> If the value of **Current CodeGenHero project** is blank, instead of
> CodeGenHero\CodeGenHero.csproj, and if this is your first
> successful login, simply close and reopen the solution. You should then be
> good to go.

At this point, it is good to understand that CodeGenHero™ stores metadata and template input values, aka *blueprints*, in a folder named CodeGenHero. This folder gets located in whatever project is set using the **Set CodeGenHero Project** button shown in the preceding screenshot. In the sample solution, *this metadata can be found in the dedicated project* named CodeGenHero. Leave things as they are for now, but know that a dedicated project is not required. If you want to change the location of this metadata, simply select another project in **Solution Explorer** and then click the **Set CodeGenHero Project** button.

The reason CodeGenHero™ stores information in files within the solution is to facilitate source control and enable the sharing of settings between developers. With the desired storage location to the CodeGenHero project already set, we can next learn about metadata and blueprint files.

Creating a metadata source

CodeGenHero™ templates consume database metadata that gets extracted from an existing database. The exercise toward the end of this chapter walks through the creation of a new metadata source. For now, the only *essential concept to grasp is that we could use any available relational database as our metadata source*. It does not have to be the sample database provided. The code that generates the RESTful Web API and client-side classes that invoke the Web API will adapt to whatever schema gets fed to it.

1. Either click the **METADATA** tab, as illustrated in the following screenshot, or click the **Next Step: Metadata** button:

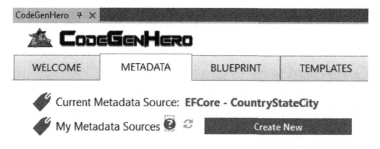

Figure 14.16 – CodeGenHero™ METADATA tab

2. If we were going to create a new metadata source based upon this database, we would click the **Create New** button on the **METADATA** tab, as shown in the preceding screenshot. That action brings up an empty **Create Metadata Source** dialog, as illustrated in the following screenshot:

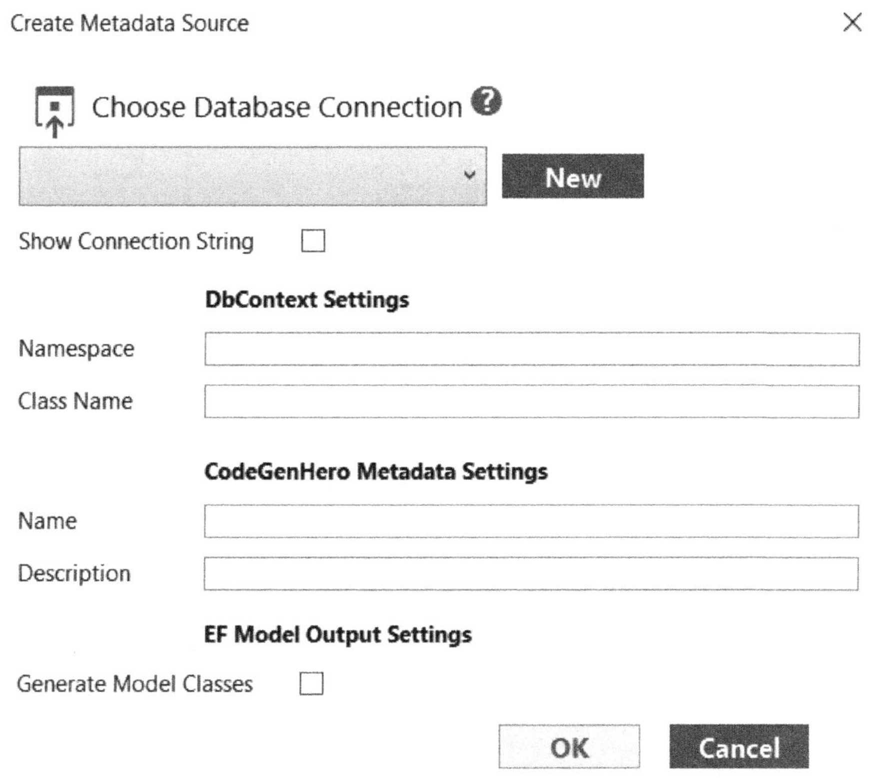

Create Metadata Source   ✕

    Choose Database Connection ❓

    [　　　　　　　　　　　　　 ⌄]   **New**

Show Connection String   ☐

DbContext Settings

Namespace   [　　　　　　　　　　　　　　　]

Class Name   [　　　　　　　　　　　　　　　]

CodeGenHero Metadata Settings

Name   [　　　　　　　　　　　　　　　]

Description   [　　　　　　　　　　　　　　　]

EF Model Output Settings

Generate Model Classes   ☐

             OK   **Cancel**

Figure 14.17 – Create new metadata source

Creating a new metadata source involves connecting to an existing database and setting the class name and namespace for your **Entity Framework** (**EF**) Core DbContext class. One very cool option is to have CodeGenHero™ also generate and output model classes for your EF DbContext (that is, **Plain Old CLR Objects** (**POCOs**) and DbContext itself). This option reverse-engineers the database, outputs Code-First model classes, and avoids the drudgery associated with manually writing all that code!

3. Click the **Cancel** button. As mentioned previously, our solution comes preloaded with a metadata file configured for the sample database. The output of the metadata source extraction process is files with a .cghm extension. Find the CountryStateCity.cghm file placed under the Metadata folder of the designated CodeGenHero™ project (previously shown/set in the **WELCOME** tab), as illustrated in the following screenshot:

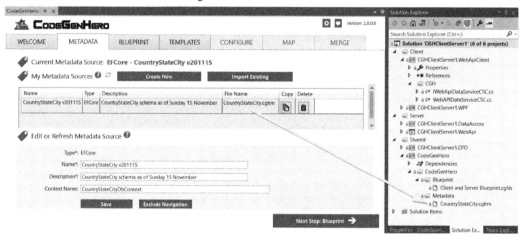

Figure 14.18 – CodeGenHero™ METADATA tab

Recall from the earlier section *Understanding core concepts of code generation* that our templates work using both *metadata* and *input parameters*. Having touched on metadata for now, we can next turn our attention to gathering input parameters. In CodeGenHero™, the equivalent of input parameters is something termed *blueprints*.

Configuring a blueprint

CodeGenHero™ *blueprints* capture and store input parameters using files with a .cghb extension. The upcoming *Choosing templates*, *Configuring template parameters*, and *Mapping target projects* steps collect different types of input parameters that are stored in blueprint files. As you may have guessed, it is the values of these parameters that drive template output.

Blueprint files, including the Client and Server Blueprint.cghb file shown in the lower right of the preceding screenshot, get placed under the Blueprint folder of the designated CodeGenHero™ project.

1. Click the **BLUEPRINT** tab or the **Next Step: Blueprint** button.

2. Our sample solution already has a blueprint file named Client and Server Blueprint, as shown in the next screenshot.

If the **My Blueprints** data grid in your instance does not immediately show this row, click the **Refresh** icon located just to the left of the **Import Blueprint File** button, as illustrated in the following screenshot:

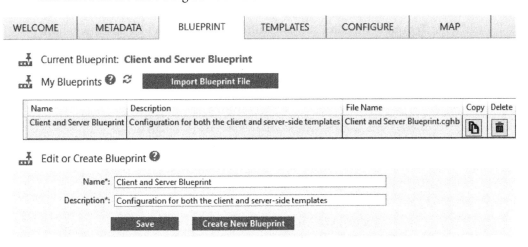

Figure 14.19 – BLUEPRINt tab

Because our sample solution comes with a blueprint file already created, we will not have to do anything in this **BLUEPRINT** tab. Rather, we will simply acknowledge that this is where you can create, import, copy, and delete blueprint files.

> **Multiple blueprint files**
>
> Note that it is possible to have multiple blueprint files and have each file contain different configuration settings. Thus, we could have made a second file to keep the configuration for client-side concerns separate from server-side concerns. This can be useful on teams where, say, mobile developers are separate from API developers.

3. Let's keep things moving and click the **TEMPLATES** tab or the **Next Step: Templates** button.

Input parameters for our code generation templates are gathered using the **TEMPLATES**, **CONFIGURE**, and **MAP** tabs in the **CodeGenHero Main Window** menu item. The values we enter in these tabs—coming up next—are stored in the currently selected blueprint file. These concepts may be clearer after we look at the available templates.

Choosing templates

The **TEMPLATES** tab in CodeGenHero™ is used to select which templates we want to use to generate output.

1. Click the **Template Bundles** sub-tab within the **TEMPLATES** tab. If you have not previously loaded templates, the tool will prompt you to import a template bundle:

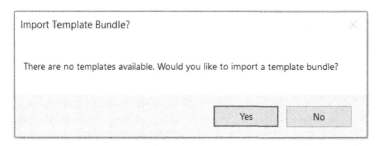

Figure 14.20 – Import Template Bundle Prompt

For now, click the **No** button and continue reading. In the steps that follow, we will first download templates and then manually import them. Because we have a fresh install of CodeGenHero™ and have not imported anything yet, the screen indicates that there are **0 Templates Currently Loaded**:

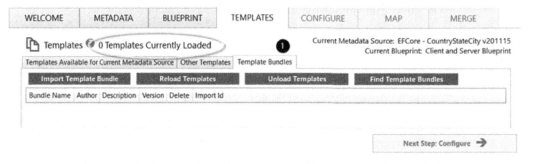

Figure 14.21 – Template Bundles sub-tab

This is no good—*what can a code generator do without any templates?* Let's see if we can fix this issue.

2. Using your favorite web browser, navigate to the **Downloads** menu on the `codegenhero.com` website. Or, more directly, use this URL: `https://codegenhero.com/docs/downloads`.

3. Find the link to download the `CodeGenHero.Template.WebAPI.FullFramework.cghpkg` template bundle.

The sample code in this solution was generated using version 2.0.0 of these templates. If you want the code you generate to exactly match the sample, be sure to use the download link for version 2.0.0, as indicated in the following screenshot:

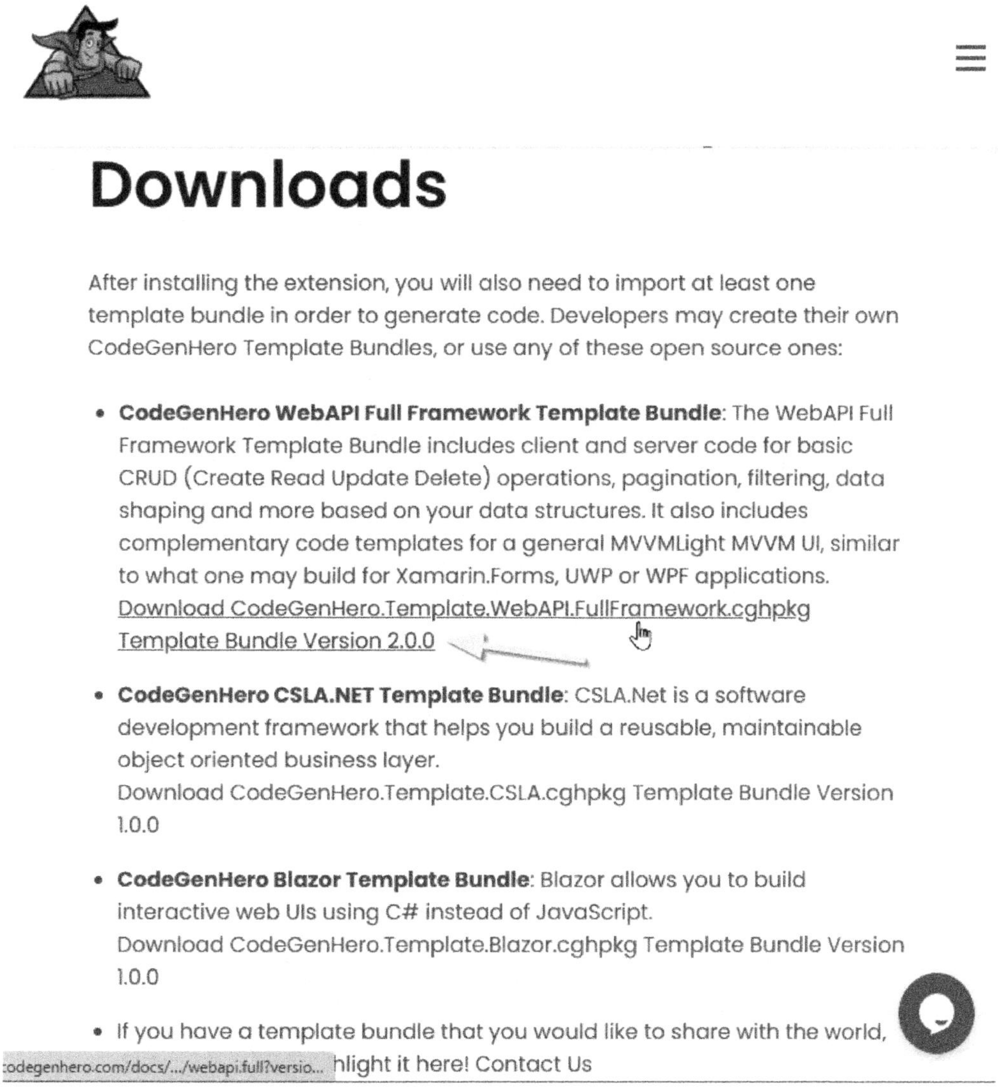

Downloads

After installing the extension, you will also need to import at least one template bundle in order to generate code. Developers may create their own CodeGenHero Template Bundles, or use any of these open source ones:

- **CodeGenHero WebAPI Full Framework Template Bundle**: The WebAPI Full Framework Template Bundle includes client and server code for basic CRUD (Create Read Update Delete) operations, pagination, filtering, data shaping and more based on your data structures. It also includes complementary code templates for a general MVVMLight MVVM UI, similar to what one may build for Xamarin.Forms, UWP or WPF applications. Download CodeGenHero.Template.WebAPI.FullFramework.cghpkg Template Bundle Version 2.0.0

- **CodeGenHero CSLA.NET Template Bundle**: CSLA.Net is a software development framework that helps you build a reusable, maintainable object oriented business layer. Download CodeGenHero.Template.CSLA.cghpkg Template Bundle Version 1.0.0

- **CodeGenHero Blazor Template Bundle**: Blazor allows you to build interactive web UIs using C# instead of JavaScript. Download CodeGenHero.Template.Blazor.cghpkg Template Bundle Version 1.0.0

- If you have a template bundle that you would like to share with the world,

:odegenhero.com/docs/.../webapi.full?versio... hlight it here! Contact Us

Figure 14.21 – Downloads area at codegenhero.com

The idea behind a template bundle is usually to provide a cohesive set of templates that, together, result in a solution that follows S.O.L.I.D. architecture principles (*search that if it is not familiar*). In other words, template bundles are generally aimed at providing developers with best-practice, proven solution structures that adhere to the **separation of concerns** (**SoC**) principle (*search SoC*). These are lofty goals that are sometimes difficult to achieve on typical time-crunched projects with limited senior talent.

> **Using Blazor or CSLA?**
>
> There are also template bundles available for the CSLA.NET architecture (see `https://cslanet.com/`), as well as a bundle designed for ASP. NET Core Blazor development that does not use **Component-based Scalable Logical Architecture** (**CSLA**). You are welcome to download and import these in the next step, but they will not be used in this exercise. The bundle we are using contains templates for doing a .NET Full Framework Web API and data client.

4. Once you have the template bundle downloaded, go back to Visual Studio and click the **Import Template Bundle** button located in the **Template Bundles** sub-tab of the **TEMPLATES** tab.

    An **Open File** dialog will appear. Navigate to the template bundle that you downloaded from `https://codegenhero.com/` (likely located in your `Downloads` folder) and click the **Open** button.

5. After a few moments, the **Template Bundles** grid should refresh and contain your newly imported bundle with a name of `CodeGenHero.Template.WebAPI.FullFramework` (and a *version of 2.0.0*), as illustrated in the following screenshot:

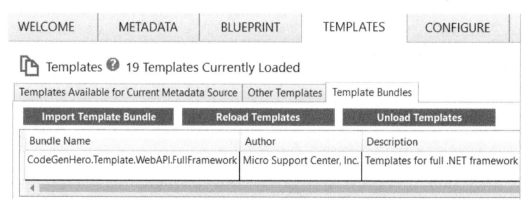

Figure 14.22 – Template Bundles grid

> **Just for the demo**
>
> I cringe every time a developer justifies taking illegitimate shortcuts with an application architecture, using justifications such as: "This is a POC" or: "It's just for the demo; I'll refactor that later, when we have more time." All too often, that POC finds its way into production and the time for design refactoring never materializes. The dangers of "demoware" typically emerge around the second or third major version of an application.

6. Once you see the `CodeGenHero.Template.WebAPI.FullFramework` row appear in the **Template Bundles** grid, click the **Templates Available for Current Metadata Source** sub-tab, as illustrated in the following screenshot:

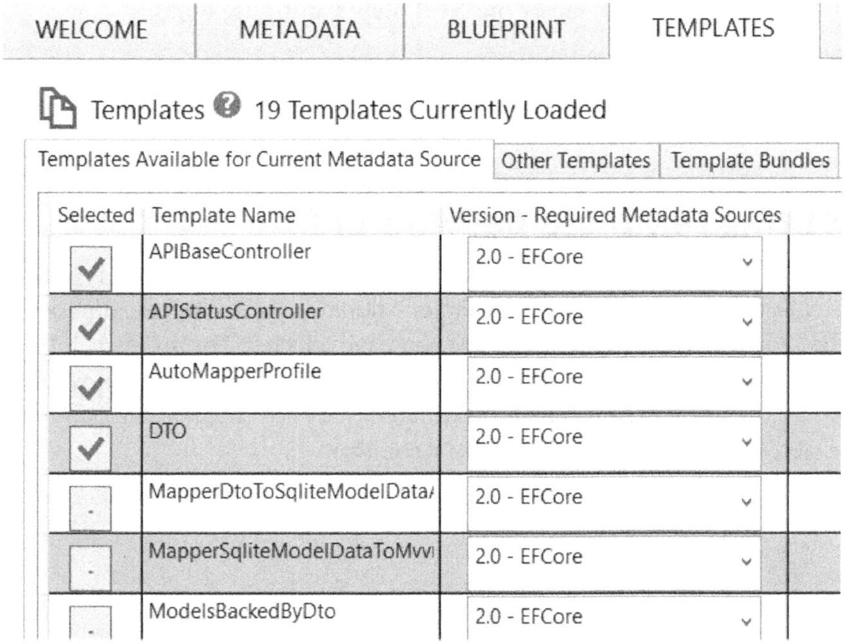

Figure 14.23 – Templates

In the preceding screenshot, we see some of the templates used by this solution displayed with selected checkboxes. Although there are 19 templates currently loaded that could be used to generate code, *only 13 are required by this particular solution architecture.*

> **Templates loaded, but none show as available**
>
> If by chance you successfully imported the template bundle but do not see templates available for the current metadata source, look in the upper right of the **TEMPLATES** tab. There, you should see the `EFCore - CountryStateCity v201221` metadata source displayed in the label. If not, go back to the **METADATA** tab and select that item in the grid.

Some of the other templates, such as `Mapper SQLite Model Data To MVVM Light Model Object`, are specialized for Xamarin mobile data synchronization across a Web API boundary. Because we do not need these for our basic WPF client project, we can simply continue.

7. Click the **CONFIGURE** tab or the **Next Step: Configure** button.

Now that we have selected which templates we want to use to generate code, the next step is to configure the variables that each template uses. This is done in the **CONFIGURE** tab, up next.

Configuring template parameters

When it comes to supplying values to template parameters, there are two types of variables: *global* and *template-specific* variables. Global variables represent parameters that are used by more than one of the templates you have selected. For instance, if two or more templates are using a DbContext within a given blueprint configuration, it would make little sense for the name of that class to be different between them. Some examples of global variables are shown in the following screenshot:

WELCOME	METADATA	BLUEPRINT	TEMPLATES	CONFIGURE

🔧 Global Variables ❓

Variable Name	Variable Value	
BaseNamespace	CGHClientServer1	
DbContextName	CountryStateCityDbContext	
DTONamespace	CGHClientServer1.DTO.{namespacePostfix}	
NamespacePostfix	CSC	
PrependSchemaNameIndicator	true	
RegexExclude		
RegexInclude		
RepositoryEntitiesNamespace	CGHClientServer1.DB.Entities	
RepositoryInterfaceNamespace	CGHClientServer1.Repository.Interface	
RepositoryNamespace	{baseNamespace}.Repository	
UseAuthorizedBaseController	False	
WebApiControllerNamespace	{baseNamespace}.API.Controllers.{namespacePostfix}	

Figure 14.24 – Global template variables

Template-specific variables represent parameters that are only used by a single template being generated. For example, in the screenshot that follows, we see a `UseIdentityBasicAuthenticationAttribute` variable. The value of this setting determines whether each controller that gets generated will authorize calls using an `IdentityBasicAuthentication` attribute or an `Authorize` attribute. This setting applies only to the base controller class generated by the `BaseApiController` template and is not used by other templates. Have a look at this example here:

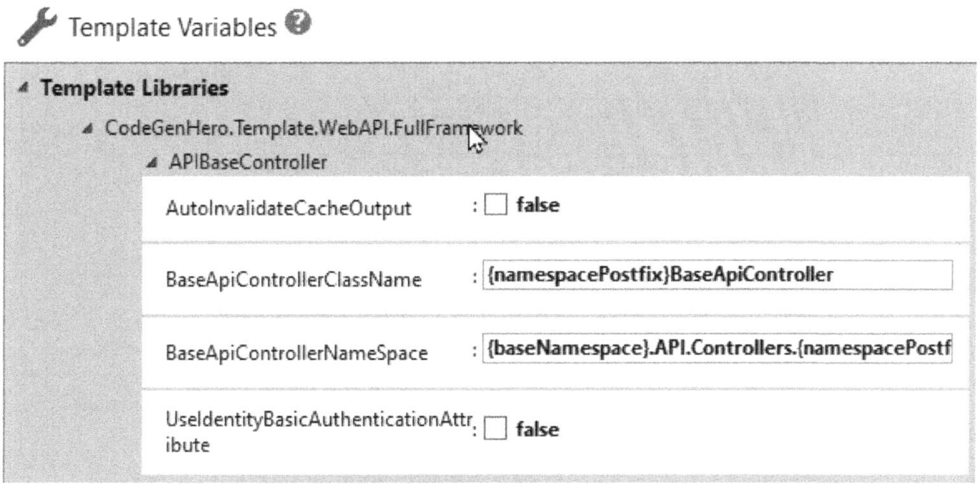

Figure 14.25 – Template-specific variables

Once again, we are lucky because the variables used by the selected templates in this sample solution are already configured for us. Soon, this exercise will be complete, and you are welcome to come back and change things to see the effects your changes have on the code that gets generated (seen in the final tab, **MERGE**). However, for now, there is no action we need to take on this tab.

Click the **MAP** tab or the **Next Step: Map** button. In the **MAP** tab, we will see how to configure where the output of each template should end up.

Mapping target projects

The **MAP** tab in CodeGenHero™ lists all the templates previously selected in the **TEMPLATES** tab. Next to each template, we use the dropdown to choose the desired output project, as well as a directory within that project to place the generated file(s). Templates can be designed to output more than one file. For example, a separate Web API controller or **data transfer object (DTO)** class might be generated for each table in the database. Imagine how long it might take you to perfectly code 100 Web API controllers compared to a code generator that can do it in seconds!

The map templates are shown in the following screenshot:

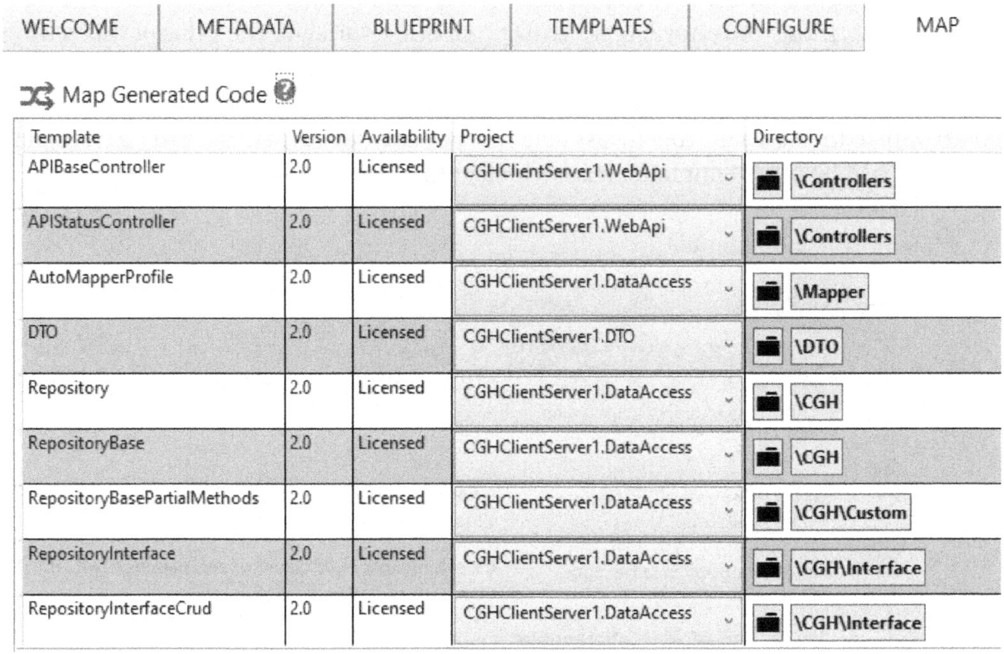

Figure 14.26 – Map templates

Click the **MERGE** tab or the **Next Step: Merge** button. Now that we have templates selected, configured, and mapped to the output directories, we are ready to integrate the code that gets generated into our solution.

Integrating generated code

When it comes to updating solution code, CodeGenHero™ leaves you, the developer, in charge. It does not simply replace code in your solution with the generated output. Rather, it compares the generated output to existing code and offers a recommended action. In the following screenshot, we see a boring result because everything has a recommended action of **Ignore**. *Surprise! When no variables change and no metadata changes, the tool ends up generating the exact same code as it did previously.* Thus, **Match** is the detected change for everything and **Ignore** is the recommended action, as illustrated here:

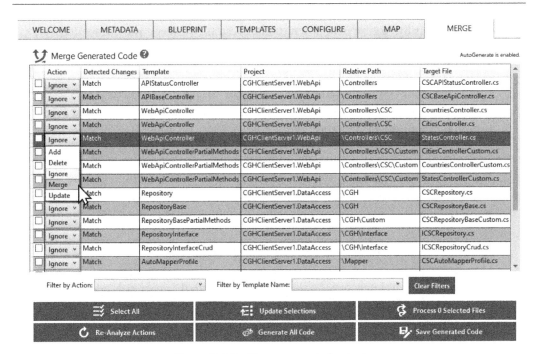

Figure 14.27 – Merge-generated output

To add a little excitement, let's see what would happen if the developer were to customize one of the generated files, as follows:

1. Open the `StatesController.cs` file located in the `CGHClientServer1.WebApi` project under the `Controllers\CSC` folder. Notice that this file begins with the `<auto-generated>` comment at the top. By now, you are probably already aware that this means the file was not hand-crafted.

2. Either add text to or remove some code from the `StatesCSCController` class. It does not matter what is added or removed, nor that the change even compiles.

3. Save the modified `StatesController.cs` file to persist whatever change you made.

4. Return to the main **CodeGenHero** tab and click the **Re-Analyze Actions** button located in the lower left of the **MERGE** tab. You will then see that a **Merge** action is recommended, as follows:

Figure 14.28 – Merge action recommended

5. Use the **Filter by Action** dropdown to filter results by **Merge**-recommended
    actions. You should see that the `StatesController.cs` file has now detected a
    `SourceChanged` condition. Also, the recommended action should now be **Merge**.

6. Check the checkbox to the left of the row in the data grid that corresponds to the
    modified `StatesController.cs` file. Then, click the **Process Selected Files**
    button located in the lower right of the screen. *Was your change correctly detected?*

In CodeGenHero™, performing a merge operation is pretty much the same as doing
a diff in source control. A side-by-side comparison window appears, highlighting the
differences between code that was generated and the project's existing code. This allows
a developer to inspect changes and decide what to do on a line-by-line basis.

> **Rapid change-processing tip**
>
> Rather than merging every file manually, for convenience, an **Update** action
> can be taken that simply replaces the solution code with the generated code.
> This can be useful in scenarios where the developer knows that metadata such
> as fields in a database table have been altered and changes are expected.

Adding generated files to the solution

1. Delete the `StatesController.cs` file from the `CGHClientServer1.`
    `WebApi` project. Click **OK** when prompted with a warning that this action will
    permanently delete the file.

2. Back in the **CodeGenHero** tab, again click the **Re-Analyze Actions** button located
    in the lower left of the **MERGE** tab.

3. Use the **Filter by Action** dropdown, located in the lower left, to filter results by **Add**
    recommended actions. You should now see that the `StatesController.cs` file
    has detected a **New** condition, as illustrated in the following screenshot:

Figure 14.29 – Add action recommended

4. Once more, check the checkbox to the left of the grid row corresponding to the
    `StatesController.cs` file. Then, click the **Process Selected Files** button
    located in the lower right of the screen.

Notice that the file you deleted has now been added back to the solution, using the generated output of the `WebApiController` template. Hopefully, this brief overview of the CodeGenHero™ Visual Studio extension gives you enough conceptually to grasp the implications of what is possible. In the next section, we will consider potential implications to the development workflow.

Handling change with CodeGenHero™

People find it easier to provide feedback and refine something close to what they need once they see it and, even better, can interact with it. Conversely, getting stakeholders to fully describe what is needed up front, along with detailed business rules, often proves difficult and time consuming. Moreover, not every team is blessed with the skills of a competent **business analyst (BA)** and a creative graphic designer. CodeGenHero™ was created to help developers overcome such issues.

CodeGenHero™ can enable small teams to perform as though they had not just more developers, but more *highly skilled* developers. By leveraging the power of code generation, developers can quickly place working applications in the hands of project stakeholders, get feedback, and rapidly incorporate requirement changes. Even better, shortcuts do not have to be taken when it comes to using best-practice layered application architectures that can make future enhancements and long-term maintenance work painless.

How does it work?

After the initial configuration, this tool enables super-fast iteration cycles that consist of four phases, including obtain new requirements, update the database schema, refresh the metadata, and generate/merge code changes. This process is illustrated in the following diagram:

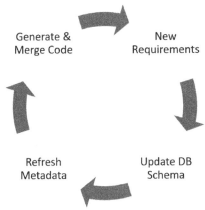

Figure 14.30 – Iterating changes with CodeGenHero™

As you may have experienced, handling new requirements often involves changes to the database schema. These changes typically have quite a ripple effect to the data-access layers of an application. The time and effort required to change all the layers is often a primary reason cited by developers who object to using a layered architecture. CodeGenHero™ virtually eliminates this objection.

Changing the database schema

There has been a lot to digest in this chapter already. If you feel that you have what you need for now, feel free to skip to the *Summary* content. For those of you that want to see how fast CodeGenHero can deal with change, please continue with this final exercise:

1. Using the sample `CountryStateCity` database, make some schema changes. Try adding or removing tables and/or fields. If you prefer, here is a sample SQL script you could run in **SQL Server Object Explorer** to add fields to multiple tables:

```
ALTER TABLE dbo.Country ADD
    Code nvarchar(20) NULL,
    PhoneCode nvarchar(20) NULL
GO
ALTER TABLE dbo.State ADD
    Abbreviation nvarchar(20) NULL
GO
```

    Of course, changing the database schema alone does not trigger anything to change in CodeGenHero™. For that to happen, we must refresh the metadata provided to the templates.

2. Open/click on the **METADATA** tab inside of the CodeGenHero™ window.

3. Click the **Create New** button on the **METADATA** tab to open the **Create Metadata Source** dialog.

    To see database changes reflected in the template output, we must create a new metadata source, ensure it is selected in the grid, and then return to the **MERGE** tab to see changes. Let's first get a connection to our database. We will use this connection to extract the schema metadata and store that information in a CodeGenHero™ metadata source file (.cghm extension).

4. Click the **New** button in the **Create Metadata Source** dialog to open the **Connection Properties** dialog. You should be able to use a **Server name** of `(localdb)\MSSQLLocalDB` and use `Windows Authentication` to then select the `CountryStateCity` database name, as shown in the following screenshot:

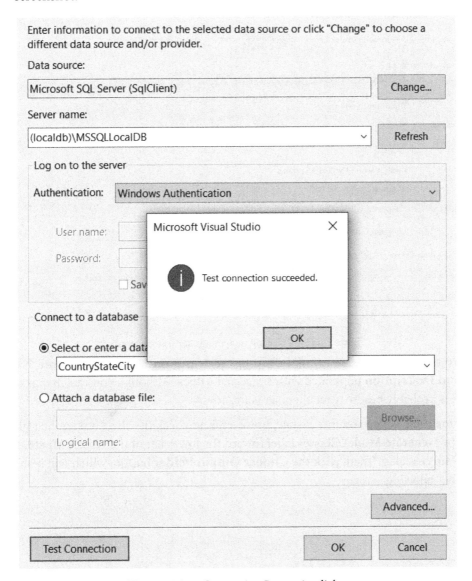

Figure 14.31 – Connection Properties dialog

5. Click the **Test Connection** button in the lower left of the **Connection Properties** dialog to verify that your settings are correct. If your test connection succeeded, click the **OK** button, as illustrated in the following screenshot:

Figure 14.32 – Creating new metadata source inputs

You should now see many of the settings such as **Namespace**, **Class Name**, **Name**, and **Description** populated with suggested values. Although you can change these, it is probably best to leave them as-is for now.

6. One thing we do want to change, however, is to check the checkbox to the right of the **Generate Model Classes** label toward the lower left of the **Create Metadata Source** dialog. Then, click the **Choose Output Folder** button, which will result in the following screen:

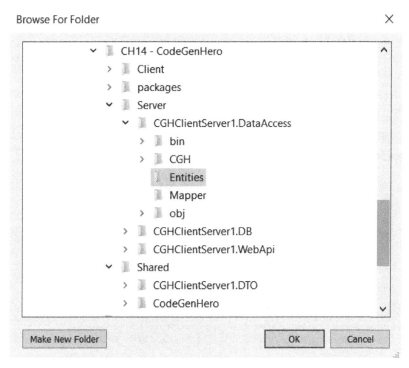

Figure 14.33 – Generate Model Classes/Choose Output Folder

7. *This step is kind of important, so pay careful attention.* The output folder you select should be the same folder that already contains the existing EF Core entities and DbContext. Use the folder named `Entities` that is located inside the `CGHClientServer1.DataAccess` project, found within the `Server` solution folder. Click the **OK** button once you have the correct output folder value.

8. About 15 seconds after clicking the **OK** button, the **My Metadata Sources** grid should refresh and show the newly created metadata file.

   If it does not show up automatically, you can try clicking the **Refresh** icon to the left of the **Create New** button. If it still does not appear, check the **Output** window in Visual Studio and choose **CodeGenHero** in the dropdown of the **Output** window. Any issues that need resolving should be captured as error messages in this window.

9. Next, *ensure the data grid row corresponding to the new metadata source is selected* as **Current Metadata Source** before proceeding (assuming success in the prior step).

10. Click the **MERGE** tab in the **CodeGenHero** window.

Merging changes

The process of merging changes following a change of metadata is the same as previously covered. This time, depending on the SQL changes you made, several **Merge**, **Add**, or **Delete** action recommendations should display (instead of just **Ignore** on all the generated files). If the schema changes you made were done using the provided SQL script in the *Changing the database schema* section, then your **MERGE** tab should look like this:

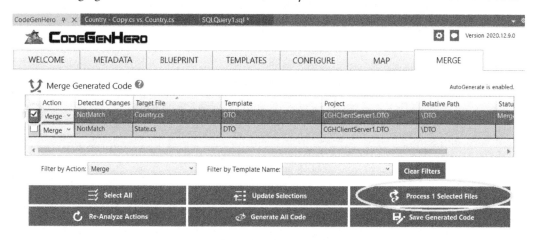

Figure 14.34 – MERGE tab after schema changes

The result shown in the preceding screenshot assumes you made schema changes to the database, made a new metadata source, and selected that new metadata source on the **METADATA** tab.

1.   Select the checkbox on the left of a row with a **Merge** recommended action.

2.   Click the **Process 1 Selected Files** button in the lower right. A difference-comparison window pops up for you to review changes and make manual adjustments, if needed. The proposed changes should mirror changes made earlier to the database schema.

Now, imagine having run a database script that added a dozen tables, each with a dozen or more fields. Being able to reflect those changes in multiple layers of code so quickly is incredibly powerful.

> **Your feedback is valuable**
>
> Please consider sending some of your valued feedback to the extension authors, good or bad. You can do this either by clicking the feedback icon in the upper right of the main CodeGenHero window, or directly via this URL: `https://codegenhero.com/feedback`.

Summary

When it comes to application development, there is no silver bullet for success. Each team must work within their own given constraints of time, skills, and available resources. The concepts of metadata and code generation were introduced as a way to help mitigate the impact of expected requirement changes, particularly with new developments. We began by calling out some of Visual Studio's own use of code generators to add new projects or scaffold **Model-View-Controller** (**MVC**) views. Some of CodeGenHero's™ objectives—such as to encourage use of a S.O.L.I.D. architecture and to rapidly adapt code to schema change, and how this allows the developer to remain in control of the process throughout—were discussed.

In this chapter, we walked through the configuration of metadata and input parameters that drive CodeGenHero's™ code generation. In doing so, we saw how CodeGenHero™ uses templates to generate various types of code files. These output files, when taken together, formed a comprehensive client-server architecture. This architecture included a WPF application leveraging a generated data client to call a Web API client that, in turn, calls repository classes for data access. Our final exercise demonstrated how quickly code can be adapted in response to a changing database schema. You now can consider the potential application of code generation concepts in your own work.

Yet, it is worth explicitly stating that *not every project is a good candidate for code generation*. If you are programming a simple application or a "brochureware" marketing website, or not using a relational database, then CodeGenHero™ may not be a good fit. Projects with lots of database tables, projects using EF, and solution architectures that use Web APIs tend to be better candidates. Likewise, there can be drawbacks to using anemic models that exactly mirror relational schemas. That, however, is a topic for another time. Keep in mind that the aim of code generators should never be to write 100% of an application. Nothing demonstrated in this chapter precludes evolving toward a more domain-driven model, particularly as requirements become more stable. Likewise, as much as developers like to code, a code generator cannot replace good business analysis or storyboard techniques.

What code generation can do is assist Agile and other iterative development processes to mitigate the risk of not having full and stable requirements up front. It does this by helping to shorten the development cycle, with more frequent deliveries of functionality. This, in turn, improves opportunities to gain feedback and adjust.

Perhaps you now have a better understanding of scenarios that can benefit from code generation, as well as an appreciation of just how powerful Visual Studio extensions such as CodeGenHero™ can be! In the next chapter, you will see another impressive extension, **PumaScan**, which can analyze code and identify potential security vulnerabilities.

15
Secure Code with Puma Scan

As developers, we are called on not only to implement business functionality but often to function as the first line of defense against attacks. The code that we write needs to be not only performant, flawless, and elegant, but also secure. Many developers have never been exposed to secure coding practices, let alone had the opportunity to develop any proficiency at implementing them.

One of the best ways to spot-check secure coding practices, especially for teams with little or no exposure to secure coding practices, is to use a tool, often called a static source code analyzer, or simply a static analyzer. Fortunately, we have one available for use right in Visual Studio 2019 for Windows and **Visual Studio Code** (**VS Code**), called Puma Scan.

In this chapter, we will discuss the following topics:

- Understanding common application security vulnerabilities
- Finding vulnerabilities for fun and profit
- Automating vulnerability detection with Puma Scan
- Extending Puma Scan with custom sinks
- Using Puma Scan in a DevSecOps pipeline

By the end of this chapter, you will have a basic understanding of some common application security vulnerabilities, and understand how to install and use Puma Scan to identify and fix many of those vulnerabilities.

Technical requirements

All of the vulnerabilities we will discuss are implemented in the project in the GitHub repository (https://github.com/PacktPublishing/Visual-Studio-2019-Tricks-and-Techniques/), in the Chapter15/WritingInstruments folder.

> **Port numbers in Visual Studio 2019 for Windows**
>
> By default, .NET Core projects in Visual Studio 2019 run under **IIS Express**. This will change the default port number of these projects from 5001 to 44300. As the examples in this chapter reference port 5001, you will need to either change the port number in the examples to the port your debugger is using, or select **WritingExample** instead of **IIS Express** at the top of the debugger.

You will also need to have the **.NET Core 3.1.402 SDK** installed to complete the exercises. You can get this SDK at https://dotnet.microsoft.com/download/dotnet-core/3.1.

Please visit the following link to check the CiA videos: https://bit.ly/3oxE5QM.

We will also require the Puma Scan Professional plugin (https://pumasecurity.io/) to get on with our exercises. To use the Puma Scan Professional plugin you will need either a full or trial license for Puma Scan. To get a trial license, navigate to https://pumasecurity.io/ and click the **Try It For Free** button.

Understanding common application security vulnerabilities

It seems like every day there is news about a company that lost millions of records in an attack by hackers. If you read the details of the attacks, they often stem from a small set of common vulnerabilities, many of which you have probably already heard of, such as **SQL injection** and **Cross-Site Scripting (XSS)**.

One organization that strives to educate developers, testers, and security professionals (to help them produce more secure applications) is the **Open Web Application Security Project (OWASP)**. This is a non-profit foundation that has produced a number of tools and projects over the years to this end, probably the most well known of these is the **OWASP Top 10 list**.

The **Top 10** list is a list compiled approximately every three years that enumerates the top 10 most prevalent application security vulnerabilities. The current list is located at `https://owasp.org/www-project-top-ten/2017/Top_10.html`. We will talk about a few of the most common issues from this list and how to exploit them, with a specific focus on the following:

- **A1:2017-Injection**
- **A6:2017-Security Misconfiguration**
- **A9:2017-Using Components with Known Vulnerabilities**
- **A7:2017-Cross-Site Scripting (XSS)**

Let's talk about how to discover these types of issues, and what they really are. First, let's talk about injection.

A1:2017-Injection

There are a few types of injection that we need to focus on as developers, the most common of which are SQL injection, command injection, XML injection, HTML injection, and LDAP injection. This may seem like a lot of different vulnerabilities, but they all stem from the same issue. Each of these injection vulnerabilities arises from trusting **unvalidated user input** and sending it to a backend text parser.

What do we mean by **unvalidated user input**? This is anything that the user (also known as the **attacker**) controls, such as form fields, URL parameters, request headers, cookies, database fields, web services, and just about anything else you can think of. You might be thinking that the request headers, cookies, and other things are controlled by the browser, and you would be technically right. The browser does manage these things for us, but the HTTP request is merely a text request that is sent to the web server and parsed, and as an attacker, I can control every piece of that text by either constructing it manually and sending it with something like `curl` or `wget`, or installing an interception proxy like Fiddler or BurpSuite.

The takeaway here is that we can't trust anything that comes from the browser, or the database (users and other systems put things in the database), or web services (who controls those services?), or, well, you get the picture. We need to validate and properly prepare data that is passed to the backend parsers to ensure that the values we pass are safe for that parser.

In the case of command injection, the text parser is CMD, PowerShell, or something like `/bin/bash`. If the untrusted input contains command control characters (such as `;`, `&`, `&&`, or `|`), the attacker can control the executing command (think `Process.Start`) and control the command line.

We'll talk more about HTML injection when we talk about XSS, but the text parser in this case is the browser, and we are controlling the page.

The most well-known of the injection techniques is SQL injection. In this attack, the unvalidated user input is generally concatenated into a SQL string and executed at the database. The database server has no idea what part of the string to trust so it blindly executes the query. Most people mitigate this issue by using parameterized queries, stored procedures, or an **Object Relational Mapper (ORM)** like **Entity Framework (EF)**. While these are all good strategies (as long as they are implemented correctly), they all have potential issues. Stored procedures with concatenated SQL can expose SQL injection vulnerabilities, and while EF uses parameterized queries in the queries it creates, functions such as `ExecuteQuery` and `FromSqlRaw` allow unsafe queries to be passed directly to the database server.

Take a look at the `Controllers/WritingInstrumentController.cs` file's *line 53*:

```
var instrument = await context.Crayons.FromSqlRaw("SELECT
    * FROM Crayons WHERE HTMLColor = '" + Color + "'").
    FirstOrDefaultAsync();
```

This is a very common concatenated query, and we see it often when the need arises to create a complex query or search.

When the user enters an HTML color value such as `#15df7b`, the query is constructed and the desired result is rendered:

```
SELECT * FROM Crayons WHERE HTMLColor = '#15df7b'
```

You will see in the following screenshot the desired result from the query:

Figure 15.1 – Normal search

What happens when the user enters something a little more creative, like `' or 1=1--`? Let's find out:

```
SELECT * FROM Crayons WHERE HTMLColor = '' or 1=1--'
```

Looking at the following screenshot, we can see that the user was able to alter the query:

Figure 15.2 – SQL injected search

Wait, what happened? We didn't put in #df1515. We changed the query, we told it to search for Crayons where HTMLColor was empty, **OR** 1=1 (**true**). The **OR true** statement in this case matches all the records in the table, and our query takes FirstOrDefaultAsync(), so we get the first record in the table. Imagine if this were the AspNetUsers table. I don't know about you, but I always add an administrator as the first user so I can create other users, products, settings, and so on. There are a few tools such as **sqlmap** (http://sqlmap.org) that can be used to extract data, execute SQL commands, execute server commands (such as CMD, PowerShell, or /bin/bash), and many other things.

Injection issues can be found in numerous places and used to attack a large number of text parsers. Luckily, they are fairly easy to find just by looking for places where unvalidated user input is passed to a text parser. Now let's talk about another common vulnerability that's pretty easy to find: security misconfiguration.

A6:2017-Security Misconfiguration

Security misconfiguration vulnerabilities often stem from configuration decisions that were made to either aid in debugging or from a lack of understanding of security best practices.

One common issue is *custom error pages*. These usually appear either in the web.config file or in the Startup.cs file, but can appear in other places also. We always want to use a custom error page so the attacker gets a consistent response no matter what error occurs. We also need to make sure that no debugging information, such as the framework version, source code, or other information, is returned.

In the web.config file the customErrors block usually looks like the following:

```
<customErrors mode="Off" defaultRedirect="/home/error"/>
```

The most common errors in the `Startup.cs` file are as follows:

```
app.UseDeveloperExceptionPage();
app.UseDatabaseErrorPage();
```

Look at *lines 79* and *80* of `Startup.cs` and you will notice that `if (env.IsDevelopment())` has been removed by the developer, and the application always returns the developer exception and database error pages. This will return detailed debugging information to the attacker to help them formulate an attack.

Another common misconfiguration deals with user passwords. If you look at *lines 37-55* of `Startup.cs`, you will see the following code:

```
services.Configure<IdentityOptions>(options =>
{
    // Password settings.
    options.Password.RequireDigit = false;
    options.Password.RequireLowercase = false;
    options.Password.RequireNonAlphanumeric = false;
    options.Password.RequireUppercase = false;
    options.Password.RequiredLength = 6;
    options.Password.RequiredUniqueChars = 1;


    // Lockout settings.
    options.Lockout.DefaultLockoutTimeSpan = TimeSpan.
        FromMinutes(10);
    options.Lockout.MaxFailedAccessAttempts = 25;
    options.Lockout.AllowedForNewUsers = true;


    // User settings.
    options.User.AllowedUserNameCharacters =
        "abcdefghijklmnopqrstuvwxyzABCDEFGHIJKLMNOPQRSTUVWXYZ
        0123456789-._@+";
    options.User.RequireUniqueEmail = false;
});
```

Do you see any issues here? Some would say that we aren't requiring numbers, symbols, and lowercase and uppercase characters; however, current best practices are now recommending using passphrases in place of traditional passwords, so to ensure we can support this we need to turn off these requirements. The primary issues here are the `Minimum Length (6)` setting and the number of `Unique Characters (1)`. Our users could enter `aaaaaa` for a password and it would be accepted by our policy.

To fix these issues, we need to increase the minimum length to a reasonable length, such as 15 characters, with at least 10 unique characters, and we need to check the submitted passwords against a breached password list, such as the *Have I Been Pwned* service (https://haveibeenpwned.com/).

Additional concerns in this code are the lockout time period (10 minutes) and the number of failed attempts we allow (25). If accounts are automatically unlocked, a time period such as 24 hours should be sufficient to block brute force attempts. We should also ensure that accounts are locked out after a minimal number of attempts, such as 3-5. Additionally, we should present the user with a challenge such as a CAPTCHA or email validation to ensure that it is actually the user attempting to login, and not an attacker.

Now that we have a better understanding of configuration issues, let's move on to one that we have all heard of but that most of us don't understand: XSS.

A7:2017-Cross-Site Scripting (XSS)

Remember when we mentioned HTML injection? HTML injection vulnerabilities show up when we are able to insert HTML into a page, using something like URL or form parameters that are written to the response. XSS is a subclass of HTML injection where we are able to write a script instead of just HTML. This can be with a simple `<script>`... `</script>` tag, or a `<script src="...">`/`</script>` tag, or even an `<img src= "X" onerror="..."/>` tag. In each of these examples, the page doesn't properly encode special characters and we are able to control the response. Depending on the application we can even control scripts on the page, CSS blocks, and anything else that contains user input.

Let take a look at a common XSS issue in some code. Open `Views/ WritingInstrument/Crayon.cshtml` and look at *line 7*:

```
<h1 style="color: @Html.Raw(Model.Color)">Crayons!!</h1>
```

`@HTML.Raw` is a useful, but very dangerous function if not used carefully. If the user saved the color as `#18e713`, the output would render in a nice green color:

Figure 15.3 – Normal output

What if we put in something more malicious? Let's put `"><script>alert('Visual Studio Rules');</script>` into the box and click **Save**. You should notice two things happening. First, there is an `alert` box with **Visual Studio Rules** in it:

Figure 15.4 – Visual Studio Rules popup

After you click **OK**, you will notice that there are some stray characters before **Crayons!!**:

Figure 15.5 – XSS output with stray characters

What caused this to happen? Remember our original code:

```
<h1 style="color: @Html.Raw(Model.Color)">Crayons!!</h1>
```

What happens when we replace `@Html.Raw(Model.Color)` with the malicious code we sent?

```
<h1 style="color: "><script>alert('Visual Studio Rules');
</script>">Crayons!!</h1>
```

This closes off the style tag with the `">` we inserted, then adds the `<script>` tag with the `alert` tag inside. Remember the stray characters? The `">` was left over from the original code, and might alert our victim to the fact that something strange is going on. Let's construct a better XSS string that makes things a little subtler.

Now let's put `"><script src="https://localhost:5001/js/evilscript.js"></script></h1><h1 style="color: #11c2e2` into the input box and click **Save**. What happens now?

As you can see in the following screenshot, the `evilscript.js` script we included didn't alter the page, nor did it show an alert box, but instead just wrote a message to the console:

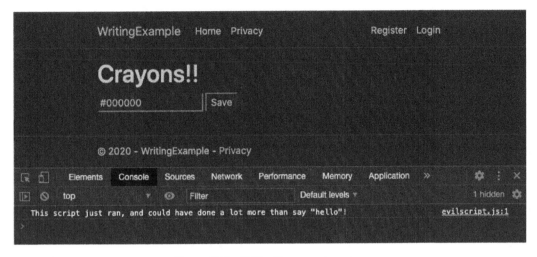

Figure 15.6 – XSS with a remote source

Our updated attack code renders to the page like this:

```
<h1 style="color: "><script src="https://localhost:5001/
js/evilscript.js"></script></h1><h1 style="color:
#11c2e2">Crayons!!</h1>
```

This time, we have included a script (which, for simplicity, comes from our application, but could come from anywhere on the internet) instead of writing one to inject. We also closed off the " > characters with an additional style tag to make the stray characters disappear.

To fix these types of issues, we need to find where unencoded characters are being written in our application and apply the proper encoding.

A9:2017-Using Components with Known Vulnerabilities

One of the more common vulnerabilities occurs not in our code, but in the code written by others that we include in our own work. Many packages that we find in NuGet or other places have known vulnerabilities.

Common places to find these issues are in the `.csproj` file and other locations where references are included. In the following code, we can see a vulnerable version of Bootstrap that has multiple reported vulnerabilities:

```
<package id="bootstrap" version="3.0.0"
    targetFramework="net462" />
```

The following code shows the same reference in a .NET Core project:

```
<PackageReference Include="bootstrap" Version="3.0.0"/>
```

If you look in the `WritingExample.csproj` file, you will see that we are including `bootstrap` version 3.0.0. This component has a number of known XSS vulnerabilities. One of these vulnerabilities is CVE-2019-8331 (`https://cve.mitre.org/cgi-bin/cvename.cgi?name=CVE-2019-8331`). This vulnerability description reads as follows:

In Bootstrap before 3.4.1 and 4.3.x before 4.3.1, XSS is possible in the tooltip or popover data-template attribute.

There are several tooltip-related vulnerabilities in this version of Bootstrap, as well as jQuery issues. We should update our application to use a newer version of this package that doesn't have these vulnerabilities.

A10:2017-Insufficient Logging and Monitoring

Insufficient logging and monitoring issues plague nearly every application, and don't usually come to light until after an attack or data breach has already occurred, at which point the forensics professionals come in to figure out what happened.

Minimally, we need to log all authentication attempts (both successful and failed), any authorization failures (that is, trying to go to `/Admin` when you're not an admin), and session management issues (that is, `Invalid Session Tokens or Session Tokens` from multiple IP addresses).

Any attempts to access high-risk data such as PII, PCI, HIPAA, and other sensitive data should be recorded.

We need to log any errors the application generates, especially in high-risk code dealing with functionality such as authentication or data access. User creation and deletion, permission changes, and configuration changes should be high on the list. Also, input validation and output encoding failures should be audited, as should any application startup and shutdown events.

These issues should trigger alerts in a centralized, monitored logging solution such as a **Security Operations Center** (**SOC**).

Finding vulnerabilities for fun and profit

There are several online sources available to learn about vulnerabilities, and a lot of applications available to help detect them. As your familiarity with the various vulnerabilities grows, along with your skills in detecting them, you will be able to quickly identify and correct them, or preferably fix them at the point of writing the code.

One great way to build your skills is to participate in *bug bounty programs*. There are a number of them available, and a quick online search will reveal a number of programs. Essentially, a company will give you authorization to test one of their online assets, and will potentially pay you for disclosing vulnerabilities that you find. This is a great way to not only build skills against actual websites, but potentially to make a few dollars also!

There are also a number of intentionally vulnerable web applications available on the internet, such as WebGoat, Juice Shop, **Damn Vulnerable Web Application** (**DVWA**), and Mutillidae. These applications are readily available for download and provide a nice training ground to play in.

Let's discuss automating vulnerability discovery in our applications.

Automating vulnerability detection with Puma Scan

One of the best ways to find vulnerabilities in code is to use a **Static Application Security Testing** (**SAST**) scanning tool. One of the best tools for Visual Studio users is Puma Scan Professional. Puma Scan provides real-time feedback to developers on security vulnerabilities as the code is written, in a format the developer is used to seeing (making use of errors, warnings, and squiggly underlines in the code). This helps catch most of the security errors before they ever make it into the code repository.

Installing Puma Scan in Visual Studio 2019

Puma Scan Professional is available from the marketplace and installed just like any other extension. Let's install Puma Scan:

1. Open the **Extensions** menu and then select **Manage Extensions**.

2. Search for Puma Scan Professional and click the **Download** button:

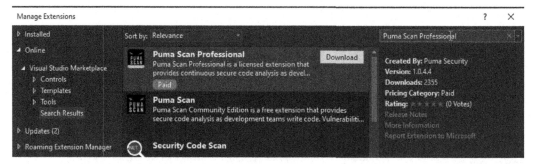

Figure 15.7 – Find and download the extension

3. You will see a message that the extension will be installed once all Visual Studio windows are closed. When you see this message, close Visual Studio:

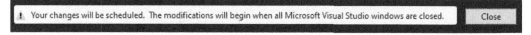

Figure 15.8 – Changes scheduled

4. When the **VSIX Installer** pops up, click the **Modify** button. Once the installer completes, reopen Visual Studio 2019:

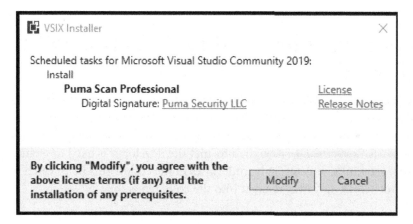

Figure 15.9 – VSIX Installer

5. Click the **Extensions** menu, then select **Puma Scan**, then **Activate Puma Scan**. In the **Activate License** dialog, enter your email and password for pumasecurity. io and click **Sign In**.

6. Visual Studio will present an **Activate License** window. Click **Select** under the **Activate** column next to your active license:

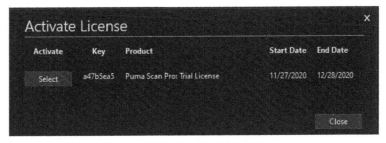

Figure 15.10 – Select your license

7. Click **Close** to close the **Activate License** window.

8. We need to allow Puma Scan to analyze the entire solution, instead of just the currently open documents. Click the **Tools | Options** menu and scroll down to **Text Editor**. Open the C# item and select **Advanced**, then select **Entire solution** under **Background analysis scope**:

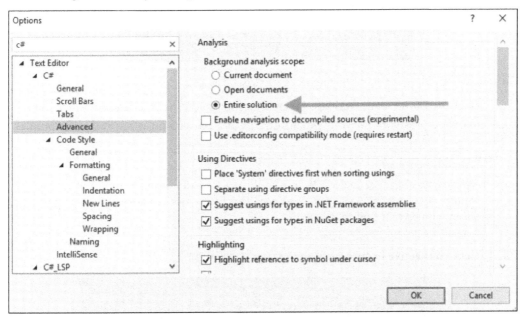

Figure 15.11 – Enable entire solution analysis

Installing Puma Scan in VS Code

Installing Puma Scan in VS Code is just like installing any other extension. Let's install it:

1. From the **Extensions** window, search for `Puma Scan Professional`. Install the **Puma Scan Professional** extension for VS Code by clicking on the **Install** button:

Figure 15.12 – Puma Scan Professional extension

2. Once the extension is installed, press *Ctrl + Shift + P* (*Shift + Command + P on the Mac*) and type `PumaScan` to see all the Puma Scan actions:

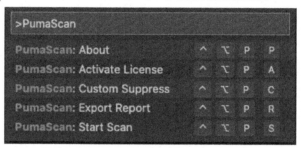

Figure 15.13 – Extension actions

3. Select the **PumaScan: Activate License** action to add the trial license. Enter the email and password for your `pumasecurity.io` account when you are prompted.

> **Already activated?**
> If you have already activated a license on the machine (for example, in Visual Studio 2019 for Windows), you won't need to activate your license as the license is tied to the machine.

4. Select your active license from the options presented:

Figure 15.14 – Selecting the active license

5. VS Code will present a message letting you know your activation was successful:

Figure 15.15 – VS Code activation message

> **Puma Scan for Visual Studio 2019 for Mac**
>
> Unfortunately, at this time, there is no Puma Scan plugin for Visual Studio 2019 for Mac. Hopefully, something will become available soon as the user base for this product continues to grow.

Running Puma Scan and viewing the results

Once we have Puma Scan installed, the hard part is done! All we have to do now is sit back and let it work. Open the **Writing Instruments** project in `Chapter15\WritingInstruments`.

In VS Code, by default each save causes the tool to run and update the **Problems** tab with findings. You can cause it to execute on demand by pressing *Ctrl + Shift + P* (*Shift + Command + P on the Mac*) and selecting **PumaScan**: **Start Scan**

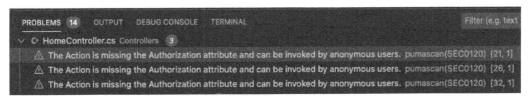

Figure 15.16 – VS Code Problems tab

In Visual Studio 2019 for Windows, the results are updated dynamically as you type, when you save, or any other time the compiler runs. To force it to run, select **Build** then **Rebuild Solution**. The results are returned to the **Error List**. Ensure you have **Warnings** enabled, and that your **Show issues generated** dropdown is set to **Build + IntelliSense**, as shown in the following screenshot:

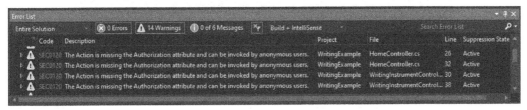

Figure 15.17 – Visual Studio 2019 for Windows Error List

We should update a few of these items, as they don't quite represent our environment. Look at the returned issues, and find the result from **pumascan(SEC0120)** on line 21 of the `/Controllers/HomeController.cs` file. This issue says that **The Action is missing the Authorization attribute and can be invoked by anonymous users**. While it is technically correct, this is the home page for our application, and it should be publicly available. Let's tell Puma Scan to ignore this finding:

1. Click on the issue to take us to the code. You will see that there is a squiggly underline on line 21.

2. In VS Code, click on the squiggles and click the lightbulb to show the **Quick Actions and Refactoring** menu, then click **Suppress this issue**. VS Code will prompt with an input box to enter a reason for the suppression. Enter a reason such as `This method should be publicly accessible as it is the home page`. You will see a notification that the issue was suppressed:

Figure 15.18 – VS Code suppression successful notification

3. In Visual Studio 2019, right-click on the issue in the Error List, and select **Suppress** then **In .pumafile**. Set the **Reason** to `This method should be publicly accessible as it is the home page.` and then select **Save & Analyze**:

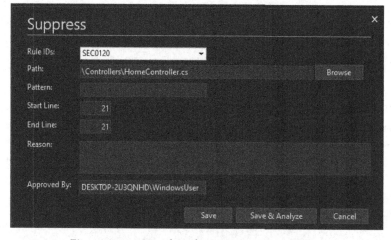

Figure 15.19 – Visual Studio 2019 issue suppression

4. Run Puma Scan Pro by either pressing *Ctrl + Shift + P* (*Shift + Command + P on the Mac*) and selecting **PumaScan**: **Start Scan** in VS Code, or by rebuilding the application in Visual Studio 2019 for Windows. You will notice that the issue goes away.

5. Repeat this process for the `Privacy()` and `Error()` actions.

6. Take a quick look at `../../.pumafile` and you will see new exceptions in the `Exceptions` block for our `/Controllers/HomeController.cs` file.

Now that we have an understanding of the `.pumafile` file, let's look at how we can extend it using custom sinks.

Extending Puma Scan with custom sinks

Puma Scan traces data as it flows through the code, from its source (the origin of the data in the system, for example, an HTTP request) to the sink (the output or endpoint for the data, such as to an HTTP response or a database).

Let's modify our code to use a custom extension method, and then add a sink to the SQL injection rule so Puma Scan knows about it:

1. Open the `Controllers/WritingInstrumentController.cs` file and comment out the line with `FromSqlRaw` in it. Also, uncomment the `FromSqlWriting` method. This method is a simple extension method that just calls `FromSqlWriting`. When you are done it should look like this:

    ```
    //var instrument = await context.Crayons.
        FromSqlRaw("SELECT * FROM Crayons WHERE HTMLColor
        = '" + Color + "'").FirstOrDefaultAsync();
    var instrument = await context.Crayons.
        FromSqlWriting("SELECT * FROM Crayons WHERE HTMLColor
        = '" + Color + "'").FirstOrDefaultAsync();
    ```

2. Now we need to tell Puma Scan about our extension method. When Puma Scan runs it creates a file in the root of the repository called `.pumafile`. Open that file and find the line that contains `CustomSinks`:

    ```
    "CustomSinks": [],
    ```

3. We need to add a new sink to this section to tell Puma Scan about our new extension method. Replace the `CustomSinks` section with a new section:

    ```
    "CustomSinks": [
      {
    ```

```
    "RuleIds": [],
    "Flag": "",
    "Syntax": "",
    "Namespace": "",
    "Type": "",
    "Property": "",
    "Method": "",
    "Arguments": []
  }
]
```

4. Set `RuleIds` to `SEC0108` – this is the SQL injection rule for dynamic EF queries.

5. Set `Flag` to `Database`, and `Syntax` to `InvocationExpressionSyntax`. This tells Puma Scan to look for this object when it's invoked.

6. Set `Namespace` to our method namespace, `WritingExample.Data`, and `Type` to `RelationalQueryExtensions`.

7. Set `Method` to `FromSqlWriting`, and `Arguments` to `0`, since the SQL query is the first parameter that gets passed in.

8. When we are done, the section should look like this:

```
"CustomSinks": [
  {
    "RuleIds": [
      "SEC0108"
    ],
    "Flag": "Database",
    "Syntax": "InvocationExpressionSyntax",
    "Namespace": "WritingExample.Data",
    "Type": "RelationalQueryExtensions",
    "Property": "",
    "Method": "FromSqlWriting",
    "Arguments": [0]
  }
]
```

9. Now when we run Puma Scan again, it will flag our new method as a vulnerable SQL injection.

> **Reloading .pumafile**
>
> If you are using Visual Studio 2019 for Windows, you may need to pause and resume Puma Scan, or restart Visual Studio to pick up any changes you've made to the `.pumafile` file. Pause the scanner from the **Extensions | PumaScan | Pause Scanner** menu option, and resume it with the **Resume Scanner** option.

Next, let's talk about adding this type of scan to a DevOps pipeline.

Using Puma Scan in a DevSecOps pipeline

Puma Scan can also be integrated into DevSecOps pipelines, such as Azure DevOps, using the Azure DevOps Standard Edition. Why DevSecOps, you ask? Well, we should be integrating security into everything we do!

While a separate license is required for this product, it is possible to include static scanning directly in the build pipeline, ensuring that code quality is maintained throughout each and every build.

To add the functionality to our pipeline, all we need to do is go to the Visual Studio marketplace in Azure and add the **Puma Scan Professional Azure DevOps** extension:

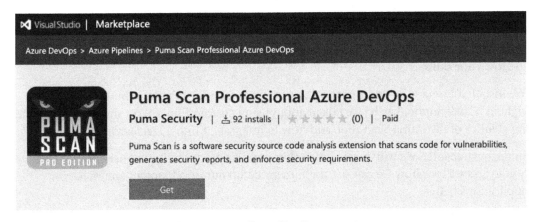

Figure 15.20 – Puma DevOps extension

Confirm with the dropdown the organization for which you want to install the extension, and select **Install**:

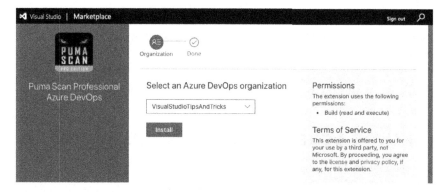

Figure 15.21 – Puma DevOps installation

Once we activate the license, we just need to integrate the extension into our pipeline and our scans will run every time the pipeline runs! More information is available on the Puma Scan site at `https://pumascan.com/installation/`.

Summary

In this chapter, we discussed some common application security vulnerabilities including SQL injection, XSS, and security misconfigurations. We also talked about how to find these types of vulnerabilities in your code, along with some places where you can practice to grow your skills.

We installed Puma Scan and saw the power of finding security vulnerabilities as we type right in Visual Studio. Lastly, we talked about using custom Puma Scan sinks to extend the capabilities of the Puma Scan tool, and how to integrate it into a DecSecOps pipeline.

In the next chapter, we will cover some other popular productivity extensions for Visual Studio and will see how we can use them to speed up our development and make our applications better.

Appendix
Other Popular
Productivity
Extensions

By now you should have a pretty good understanding of the fact that extensions are add-ons that enhance your experience in Visual Studio. Visual Studio's plug-in architecture allows the community and third-party developers to provide you with new features that boost your productivity and enrich your workflow.

In the previous chapters, we introduced you to a few extensions to help you in your development, including CodeMaid, CodeGenHero™, and Puma Scan. If you love extensions as much as we do, then this chapter is where you will find information about some of our favorite plugins for all flavors of Visual Studio.

In this chapter, we'll discuss the following topics:

- Presenting some great Visual Studio 2019 for Windows extensions
- Sharing our favorite Visual Studio Code extensions
- Choosing useful Visual Studio 2019 for Mac extensions

By the end of this chapter, you will have a good overview of several commonly used extensions, along with some tips for their configuration and use. Let's start with extensions for Visual Studio 2019 for Windows.

It's okay to pay

Open source software has many benefits, and we all enjoy the countless hours that we as developers spend developing it. It also makes sense that extension authors should be reimbursed somehow for their time, in the same way that as developers, we expect to be paid for our work. There are countless stories of open source developers becoming cynical and burnt out over time. Consumers of software, even free software, can be quite demanding. It is good to keep a healthy respect for the toll it takes on developers who spend many hours slinging code, supporting users, and evangelizing a product, often for little or no monetary benefit at all.

For evidence of this struggle, see `https://github.com/PrismLibrary/Prism/issues/1755`. In the discussion content you can see the open source maintainers, Dan and Brian, face a genuine community need while trying to balance their own need to make a living. Rising frustration on both sides, IP theft, and appreciative praise is all bundled together in one issue!

Many extensions are written by just a couple, or even one, developer. So, if you like an extension, think about donating to the OSS team that maintains it. This can often be done directly by purchasing a license or through something like the GitHub Sponsors program. Consider the improved experience it provides or how much time it saves you. Additionally, if there is a feature you want to see, consider adding it and making a pull request to make the product better!

Presenting some great Visual Studio 2019 for Windows extensions

With such a long history, it is no wonder that literally thousands of extensions are available for this flavor of Visual Studio. As a disclaimer, some of the extensions featured here are free, some have free trials, and others require payment.

Conveyor by Keyoti

If you are a web developer, this free extension may be of interest. It allows you to share a web application running on your local machine over the internet without having to deploy it to a public-facing web server. In other words, the Conveyor extension allows you or others to see it as though it was published online, when, in fact, the application is just running on your local machine.

It works by creating a tunnel through the firewall (once you open the inbound port) and establishes a proxy connection through a remote URL. By default, you can open your localhost (IIS Express) to the private network. If you want to use an internet-addressable URL, then you are required to register for a Conveyor website account. Once you register, it becomes possible to log in to the extension. Logging in has the benefit of providing a custom remote URL that looks something like `https://yourappname.conveyor.cloud/default.html`. Once you have such a URL, it is easy to test your web application from, say, a mobile phone running iOS or Android. Of course, tablets, desktop computers, and basically any device with internet access will also work.

This is certainly one of the easiest ways to provide a form of remote access to your machine for testing and debugging purposes. You can find Conveyor at `https://marketplace.visualstudio.com/items?itemName=vs-publisher-1448185.ConveyorbyKeyoti`.

Ozcode – Magical C# debugging

How much of your development time is spent debugging? Have you ever taken a screen capture of a **Quick Watch** window just so you don't forget the state of the variables prior to stepping through the code? If you want a Visual Studio extension that reduces the time it takes to isolate bugs, then check out the Ozcode Visual Studio extension. There are so many neat features that it would be impossible to cover them all here, but we'll cover the ones we like the most.

In short, this extension makes it easier to understand the execution paths taken by the code, based on the input data. If you have a set of data objects and something in there is triggering a problem, then Ozcode provides advanced search and filtering capabilities to isolate the problem object. Even better, once you do isolate the object, Ozcode provides a mechanism to quickly export the object as a C# class file, XML, or JSON. As shown in the following screenshot, this can be very useful for creating a unit test:

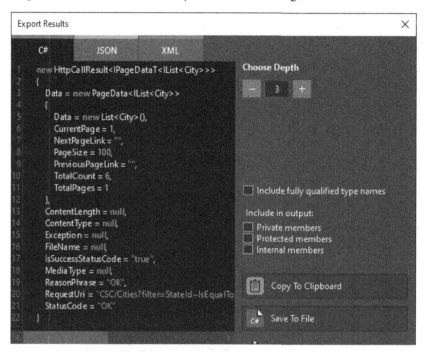

Figure 16.1 – Ozcode Export Results

The enhancements this extension makes to the debugging UI are really cool. Words cannot adequately describe a feature Ozcode calls a *time-travel debugging experience*. As you step through code, the paths of execution are predicted. This enables the tool to examine Boolean expressions further down in the code. It highlights items that will return true in green and those that will return false in red. In other words, Ozcode figures out how upcoming code further down in the file, or in a loop, will execute before your current line of execution in the debugger ever gets there. This insight allows it to gray out blocks of code that will not execute, as shown here:

```
if (!callResult.IsSuccessStatusCode)   5 1ms elapsed
{
    Log.LogWarning(exception: callResult.Exception, message: "Failure occurred
    {RequestUri}", callResult.StatusCode, callResult.RequestUri);
}
```

Figure 16.2 – Ozcode time travel

In case you are wondering, yes, using the predicted paths of execution does mean that code in those paths is actually executed and that any side effects, such as database calls, are actually happening.

Ozcode provides its own version of a **Quick Watch** window. When using this to examine a collection of objects, it is possible to *star* properties of interest. This reveal capability has the effect of displaying the selected values instead of the standard `ToString()` result. This handy feature allows you to quickly glance through the enumerated collection without having to click the down chevron and drill down into every item in the collection to see values. The following screenshot shows the before-and-after results of selecting the `Name` property of the `items` collection that is being assigned to the `CountryList` property:

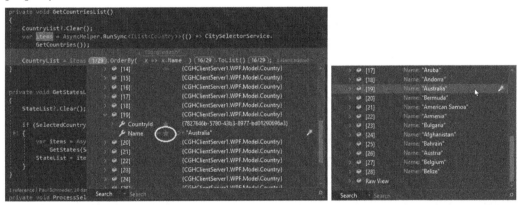

Figure 16.3 – Ozcode reveal functionality

Notice how the actual Name property value corresponding to each country is now displayed instead of the useless CGHClientServer1.WPF.Model.Country class name being repeated. Even more crazy is that you can add a **custom expression** to the object as though you were appending a new property on the fly.

If you are using LINQ, there is a built-in remarkable query analysis feature that dissects the results for examination. Another feature allows you to compare objects and collections in memory (think of performing a *diff* in the debugger). There is more to this tool than we can cover here.

If this extension excites you, there is a free 14-day trial for you to give it a spin. Personal licenses sell for $99.95 annually and team licenses start at $175 per year. See https://oz-code.com/debugging-redefined for more information.

> **One free feature: Object Exporter**
>
> If you want the handy export object values capability while debugging, but do not want to use Ozcode, check out the **Object Exporter** extension in the Visual Studio Marketplace. This extension is also able to export live object values into C#, XML, and JSON while live-debugging code.

Open Command Line

This simple but useful extension by Mads Kristensen comes in handy for those that prefer to use the command line. It features syntax highlighting, IntelliSense, and can even handle the execution of .cmd and .bat files. In **Solution Explorer**, when you right-click on a command or batch file, a context menu pops up that allows you to open the default **Command Prompt**, the **Developer Command Prompt**, or **PowerShell**:

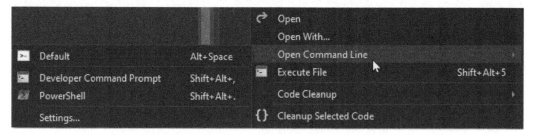

Figure 16.4 – The Open Command Line right-click context menu

If you enjoy the Git command-line experience, then you need to know that this extension also supports several more consoles including **Git Bash**. To configure this as the default, simply access the **Settings…** context menu item (shown at the bottom of the prior screenshot) or use the **Tools | Options | Command Line** menu, as shown here:

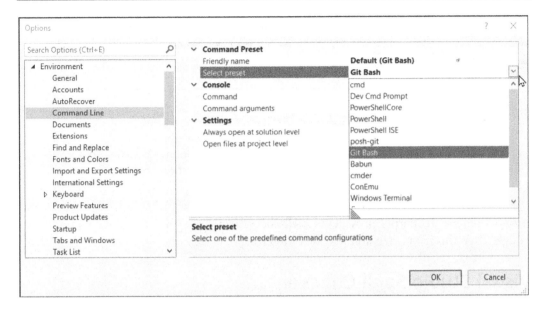

Figure 16.5 – Open Command Line configurable options

One of the coolest features of this extension is the *Alt + spacebar* shortcut that opens whatever console you set as the default using a keyboard shortcut. Even better, the path of the console window is already set to the root of your Visual Studio solution! When not editing a code file, use the *Shift + Alt + .* shortcut to open **PowerShell** and use *Shift + Alt + ,* to open the **Developer Command Prompt**.

You can find this extension in the Marketplace at https://marketplace.visualstudio.com/items?itemName=MadsKristensen.OpenCommandLine.

ReSharper

Published by JetBrains, this was considered a must-have productivity extension by serious developers for a long time. ReSharper performs code analysis in the background and then offers quick fixes (via light bulbs) to improve your code. These suggestions include helpful refactoring tips and the identification/removal of unused code. Like CodeMaid, ReSharper helps with code formatting and cleanup. However, this is not quite the advantage it once was, because Visual Studio's own capabilities have increased significantly in this area. ReSharper also offers enhanced navigation and search features, light code generation capabilities, and even assistance with unit tests. In my experience, JetBrains has been rather generous in providing free one year licenses to user groups as a giveaway.

If you are not lucky enough to win a free copy, an individual license runs at $129 per year and a corporate license at $299 per year. See https://www.jetbrains.com/resharper/ for more info.

> **Second place goes to… Roslynator**
>
> If you want some of the functionality ReSharper provides, but without shelling out for a license, check out the free **Roslynator extension**. Think of it as a middle ground that is better than the refactoring suggestions Visual Studio 2019 provides, but not quite as good as ReSharper's suggestions that help you write better code.

Another feature ReSharper provides is spell-checking. Once again, if you're on a tight budget, then this next extension may be of interest.

Visual Studio Spell Checker

If you've ever published an app only to find a misspelled word in a pop-up box or a menu, then you'll really appreciate this extension. This extension checks your spelling in plain text, comments, and strings, either as you type or in a tool window. It has support for replacing all occurrences of a misspelling and can check any combination of a solution, project, or individual items.

If your primary platform isn't Visual Studio 2019 for Windows, or you switch between Visual Studio 2019 and **Visual Studio Code** (**VS Code**), there are a number of extensions that can help make your VS Code experience more productive. Let's talk about a few of the VS Code extensions.

Sharing our favorite Visual Studio Code extensions

With the popularity of VS Code as an IDE, it should come as no surprise that there are also thousands of extensions available for this flavor of Visual Studio. Once again, some of the extensions featured here are free, some have free trials, and others require payment.

Increment selection

Previously, we discussed the multiple cursors feature in VS Code. This extension makes quick work of a task that I surprisingly end up doing fairly often. When creating sample data, seed data, or just updating a list, I often need to increment a number of some sort. I used to jump over to another tool, but with this handy extension, there is no need.

Once you make your multiple selections, activate the extension with *Ctrl + Alt + I* (Option + *Command + option + I* on a Mac):

```
static void Main(string[] args)          static void Main(string[] args)
{                                        {
    Console.WriteLine("1. Hello Visual       Console.WriteLine("1. Hello Visual
    Console.WriteLine("1. Hello Visual       Console.WriteLine("2. Hello Visual
    Console.WriteLine("1. Hello Visual       Console.WriteLine("3. Hello Visual
    Console.WriteLine("1. Hello Visual       Console.WriteLine("4. Hello Visual
    Console.WriteLine("1. Hello Visual       Console.WriteLine("5. Hello Visual
    Console.WriteLine("1. Hello Visual       Console.WriteLine("6. Hello Visual
    Console.WriteLine("1. Hello Visual       Console.WriteLine("7. Hello Visual
    Console.WriteLine("1. Hello Visual       Console.WriteLine("8. Hello Visual
    Console.WriteLine("1. Hello Visual       Console.WriteLine("9. Hello Visual
    Console.WriteLine("1. Hello Visual       Console.WriteLine("10. Hello Visual
    Console.WriteLine("1. Hello Visual       Console.WriteLine("11. Hello Visual
}                                        }
```

Figure 16.6 – Incrementing a list of numbers

CamelCase

Not just a clever name, this little utility is a quick way to camel case strings. Select the string and press *Ctrl + Alt + C* (*Ctrl + Command + C* on a Mac) and it will eliminate the spacing and special characters. It will also change the capitalization to camel case. It uses the **Lodash** CamelCase function, so any functionality that works in the library also works in the extension. You'll notice in the following screenshot that you can select a string and activate the extension, and it replaces the selection with a camel case string:

```
static void Main(string[] args)          static void Main(string[] args)
{                                        {
    Console.WriteLine("Hello Visual Studio Code!");       Console.WriteLine("helloVisualStudioCode");
}                                        }
```

Figure 16.7 – Apply camel case to a string

This extension is available in the Marketplace. While it doesn't provide a ton of functionality, the functionality it provides is solid and easy to use.

C# extensions

Creating C# applications in VS Code isn't terrible, but I look for any shortcut I can find to save time. One of the best features of this extension is the ability to add interfaces and classes directly from the IDE by right-clicking on a location in the **File Explorer** and selecting **New C# Class** or **New C# Interface**:

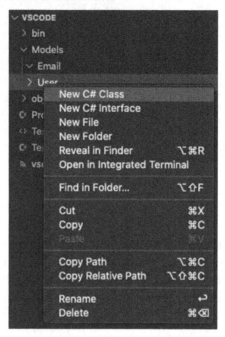

Figure 16.8 – Create a new class

Another interesting feature allows you to add a constructor from the properties in the class. Add any properties you want to the class, click on one of the properties and select the light bulb icon, then select **Initialize ctor from properties...**, and it will create the constructor for you, including variables and setting all of the properties:

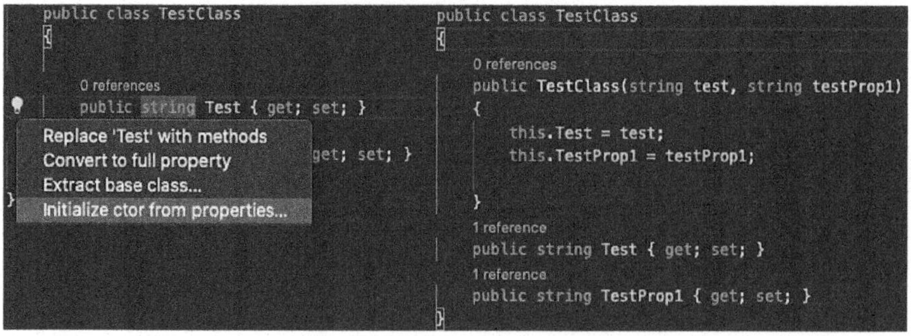

Figure 16.9 – Create a constructor from class properties

This is the only extension that I use every time I work in VS Code. It's cheap at twice the price (did I mention that it was free?).

The vscode-icons and vscode-icons-mac extensions

I read somewhere that if you like the way your IDE looks, you will enjoy writing code in it. I have to say that the more visually appealing VS Code is, the more time I spend using it.

One extension that helps us to that end is `vscode-icons`. This is an icon set that replaces the default VS Code icons with some that are more visually appealing, with actual **folders** instead of just a > icon.

The `vscode-icons-mac` extension is another icon set with the classic Mac folder icons that make it feel a little more like true development on the Mac. Whichever you install (or install both, they work fine with both installed), your eyes will thank you:

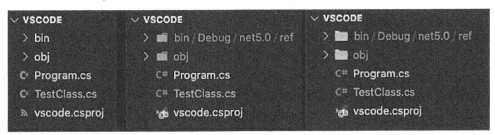

Figure 16.10 – The original, vscode-icons, and vscode-icons-mac icons

You might say that changing icons doesn't really make a difference in your day-to-day programming. If you think this is true, pull up a copy of Visual Basic 3 and try to write code in it, and you'll agree with me that every little thing we can do to make the process more pleasant helps us be more productive.

Beautify

While VS Code uses `js-beautify` internally, you can't make any changes to the `.jsbeautifyrc` file, making it difficult to change any of the settings. With this extension, you have all the original settings, plus any customizations you've made that are available and stored as part of the project.

Activate the extension with *F1* or *Ctrl + Shift + P* (*Command+ Shift + P* on a Mac) and type `Beautify`. If it's a native type (`.js`, `.html`, and so on), Beautify will take over and clean up the file. Otherwise, if the Beautify extension cannot work out the file type based on the filename, it will ask you. I use this extension for `.cshtml` files and tell Beautify to treat these files as `.html` files when it cleans them.

In the following screenshot, you can see some simple HTML content before and after running the Beautify extension:

```
<> Test.html > ...                            <> Test.html > ...
 1   !DOCTYPE html                         1   !DOCTYPE html
 2   <html>                                2   <html>
 3   <head>                                3
 4   <title>Visual Studio Tips and Tricks</title>  4   <head>
 5   </head>                               5     <title>Visual Studio Tips and Tricks</title>
 6   <body>                                6   </head>
 7   <h1>Visual Studio</h1>                7
 8   <h1>Tips and Tricks</h1>              8   <body>
 9   <p>Other Extensions</p>               9     <h1>Visual Studio</h1>
10   </body>                              10     <h1>Tips and Tricks</h1>
11   </html>                              11     <p>Other Extensions</p>
                                          12   </body>
                                          13
                                          14   </html>
```

Figure 16.11 – Beautify cleaning up HTML

This is one of my personal favorites because it does a nice job cleaning up files with an unobtrusive workflow, and it's another one of those extensions that just works.

The vscode-spotify extension

If you're like me, you need to have some music going while you code. While not strictly a productivity extension, we would be remiss if we didn't mention the `vscode-spotify` extension for VS Code. This extension lets you control Spotify without ever leaving the VS Code IDE. There are controls to select the previous track, play/pause, and play the next song, as well as a mute/unmute button. To the right of the mute button, there is a lyrics button that brings up the lyrics of the current song (displayed next to the button) in a new tab:

Figure 16.12 – The vscode-spotify extension

Now that we have VS Code tuned and pretty, let's take a look at some extensions for Visual Studio 2019 for Mac.

Choosing useful Visual Studio 2019 for Mac extensions

Unlike VS Code and Visual Studio 2019 for Windows, Visual Studio 2019 for Mac is a newer offering and hasn't really had time to build the following that the other two flavors have. As such, the number of extensions available pale in comparison. That isn't to say that there aren't any available, and there are a number of them that you should definitely install, but they tend to fill a very specific purpose. Here are a few of our favorites.

LiveXAML for Xamarin.Forms

Developing Xamarin apps and constantly editing, pushing to the emulator, loading the app, looking at the rendered output, stopping the app, changing the XAML, and repeating the process can get very tedious quickly. LiveXAML activates when you start the debugger and automatically updates the view in the app as you make changes to the XAML in Visual Studio:

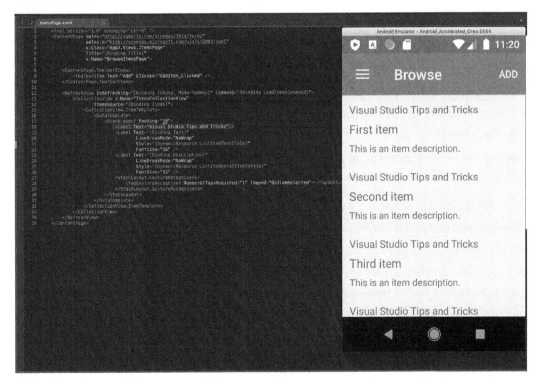

Figure 16.13 – Editing XAML with live results in the debugger

LiveXAML is available at `http://www.livexaml.com/` and runs at about $240 for a permanent license, or $24 per month otherwise.

What if LiveXAML is too expensive?

The functionality of LiveXAML is great, but if you're on a budget, you can try one of these free options: **XAML Hot Reload for Xamarin.Forms** (`https://docs.microsoft.com/en-us/xamarin/xamarin-forms/xaml/hot-reload`), **HotReload** (`https://github.com/AndreiMisiukevich/HotReload`), or **HotReloading** (`https://github.com/pranshu-aggarwal/HotReloading`). The first one in particular has had a couple of false starts, but, after several releases, has come a long way and is worth a try.

MFractor

This is a great extension for anyone who is doing development on a Mac (it's also available on Windows), especially if you are doing Xamarin development. It has Android Resource IntelliSense, and it can help with resource lookup in navigation and replace functions. There are XAML helpers and a XAML editor for Xamarin.Forms. It has lots of refactorings to help fix the more than 90 XAML issues that it can spot.

It also has built-in MVVM ViewModel detection to make the XAML and ViewModel creation process easier. The additional data-binding IntelliSense feature makes data binding a breeze!

Possibly the biggest time-saving features of the extension concern managing images and fonts. Between the **Image Import Wizard**, which automates the entire process of importing, resizing, naming, and adding images to your projects, and the **Image Manager** that lets you optimize, delete, and run other common image management tasks, there are a lot of useful productivity features here.

I really like the Scaffold feature, which is basically the **Add New Class** functionality on steroids. You can control all the functions of the **New Class**, plus select a template based on the context of where you are generating it. Select a type of class to generate and let it handle the extras for you:

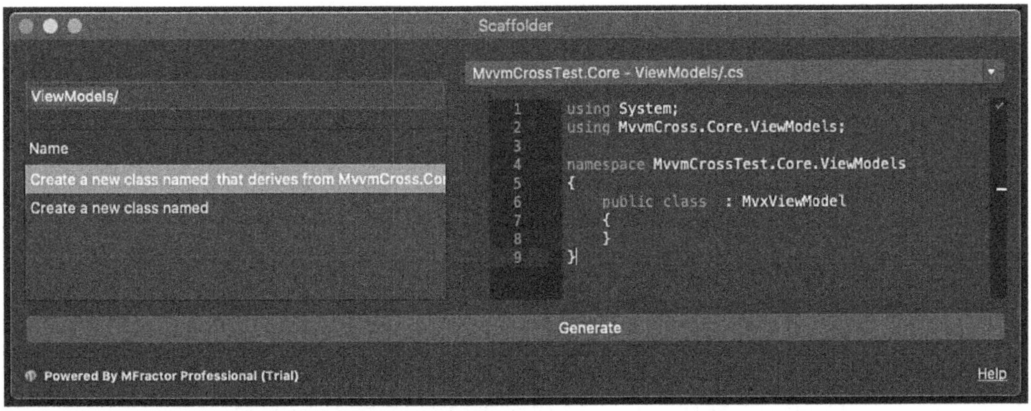

Figure 16.14 – MFractor Scaffolder

The MFractor extension, along with more information, is available in the Visual Studio Marketplace. For more info, see `https://www.mfractor.com/`.

NuGet package management extensions

This little gem is often overlooked (in fact, I didn't find it until recently), but it is a great little productivity extension. It adds the ability to list **Portable Class Libraries** (**PCLs**) that are available on the local machine. It also lets you add, update, and remove NuGet packages from multiple projects in a single step. You also get a PowerShell window that uses PowerShell Core under the covers.

My favorite feature of this extension, however, is the ability to add NuGet packages to the project from the **Unified Search** window. As you can see in the following screenshots, when I search for `AutoMapper` it gives me the option to search for packages, but with the extension I also have to option to add the package directly to my project. To put it simply, clicks saved equals dollars earned:

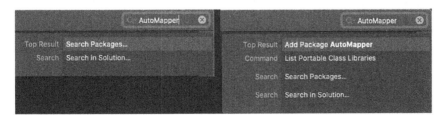

Figure 16.15 – Add a NuGet package from the Unified Search window

With all of these features, this free extension is a must-install.

MvvmCross Template Pack

If you are doing MVVM using MvvmCross, this extension has templates for both native and Xamarin.Forms targets on both iOS and Android. It creates solutions with a Core PCL with a ViewModel, an iOS project, and an Android project ready for you to get started! Take a look at the following screenshot of the template projects generated using the extension, and you'll see it's a complete project ready to customize:

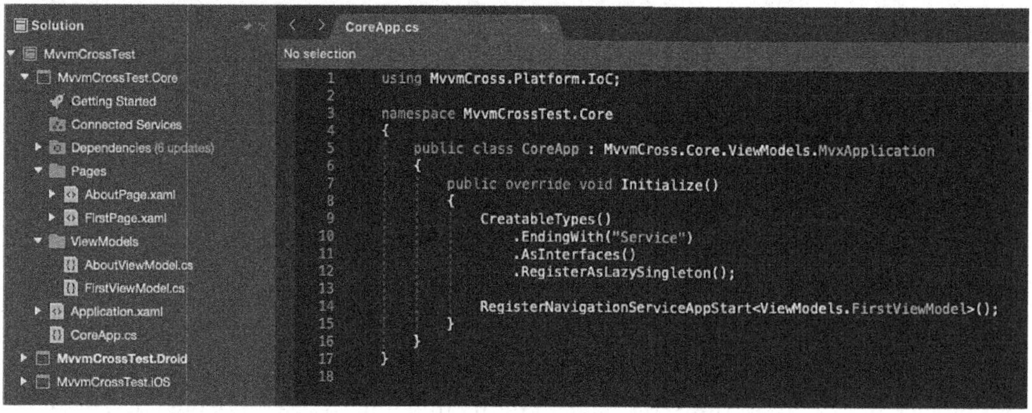

Figure 16.16 – MvvmCross generated project

> **Alternative Model-View-Update pattern**
>
> At the time of this writing, the **Model-View-Update** (**MVU**) pattern is gaining in popularity. So, if you are not already locked into MVVM, you may want to investigate MVU. This is especially true if you are planning to build .NET **Multi-Platform App UI** (**MAUI**) apps.
>
> If you prefer MVVM, however, we want to specifically state that you may want to consider other options for new development. Many developers prefer to use either Prism or FreshMvvm instead of MvvmCross.

So, with all these great extensions, are you are ready to turbo-charge your development and crank out some awesome code?

Summary

In this chapter, we discussed a number of extensions. We talked about extensions for Visual Studio 2019 for Windows, VS Code, and Visual Studio 2019 for Mac, some for productivity and some just for fun. We found extensions for Xamarin, refactoring, debugging, image generation, package management, and a whole host of other things. Between the extensions covered in detail in prior chapters and those outlined here, we hope you are at least inspired to explore more. Better yet, you can apply the skills gained to create your own extension! Some extensions just make our lives a little easier, some a little prettier, and some are just fun. No matter which kind you choose to use, we hope they make your overall development experience more pleasant and productive!

Whether you are just getting started as a developer or are a seasoned vet, the nuggets that you have picked up in this book will help you create better apps faster. Certainly, the advanced techniques we shared provide insight into how Visual Studio works its magic behind the scenes. And, hopefully, all of this expands your perspective and encourages you to unleash the full power of Visual Studio.

This is it, the last chapter – you made it! We hope you had as much fun reading it as we did writing it. Throughout this process, we learned so much about each of the Visual Studio flavors, both their similarities and their differences. We have done our best to pass that knowledge on to you so that you, too, can be a more productive and happier developer.

We wish you good luck and may your future be filled with better architected and more secure applications made in record time! Goodbye, dear readers – if you would like to send some feedback on this book, or keep in touch with the authors, you can find Paul and Aaron on Twitter at `@PaulBSchroeder` and `@curea`.

Other Books You May Enjoy

If you enjoyed this book, you may be interested in these other books by Packt:

Developing Multi-Platform Apps with Visual Studio Code

Ovais Mehboob Ahmed Khan, Khusro Habib

ISBN: 978-1-83882-293-4

- Explore various editing, formatting, and navigational features of VS Code
- Understand how to add, delete, and configure extensions in VS Code
- Develop web APIs using Node.js, Java, and Python in VS Code
- Develop background service in .NET Core and explore Dapr
- Delve into debugging techniques such as breakpoints, log points, and data inspection
- Use Git with Azure DevOps to share and synchronize code with VS Code
- Create custom extensions in VS Code to increase developer productivity
- Understand the concepts of remote development using VS Code

Adopting .NET 5 Create Create

Hammad Arif, Habib Qureshi

ISBN: 978-1-80056-056-7

- Explore the key performance improvement areas when migrating to modern architectures

- Understand app design and development using .NET 5

- Discover how to shift from legacy to modern application design using microservices and cloud-native architecture

- Explore common migration pitfalls and make the right decisions in situations where multiple options are available

- Understand the process of deploying .NET 5 code on serverless and containerized hosts, along with its benefits

- Find out what ML.NET has to offer and build .NET apps that use machine learning services

Leave a review - let other readers know what you think

Please share your thoughts on this book with others by leaving a review on the site that you bought it from. If you purchased the book from Amazon, please leave us an honest review on this book's Amazon page. This is vital so that other potential readers can see and use your unbiased opinion to make purchasing decisions, we can understand what our customers think about our products, and our authors can see your feedback on the title that they have worked with Packt to create. It will only take a few minutes of your time, but is valuable to other potential customers, our authors, and Packt. Thank you!

Index

Symbols

.NET Core
  versioning 159, 160
  versus .NET Framework v4.7.2 193
.NET Framework v4.7.2
  versus .NET Core 193

A

advanced debugging
  breakpoint 141-143
  Immediate window 143
  investigating 141
  remote debugging 145
  viewers 144, 145
analyzers 241
application programming
    interface (API) 173
application security vulnerabilities
  about 310
  components, using with known
    vulnerabilities 317
  Cross-Site Scripting (XSS) 315-317
  injection 311-313

  insufficient logging and monitoring 318
  security misconfiguration 313-315
attacker 311
Azure Blueprints
  reference link 170
Azure Data Studio 120
Azure DevOps (ADO) 7
Azure Resource Manager
    (ARM) templates 170

B

basic VS Code extensions
  generating 251-253
Beautify 339, 340
Blazor app 97
branch
  about 88
  creating 89
  creating, for Mac 91
  creating, for VS Code 90, 91
  creating, for Windows 89
breakpoint 141-143
business analyst (BA) 301

C

Made in the USA
Las Vegas, NV
30 June 2021